THE BIG BOOK OF GIRL STUFF

THE BIG BOOK OF GIRL STUFF

Bart King
and His Five Sisters

Illustrations by Jennifer Kalis

GIBBS SMITH
TO ENRICH AND INSPIRE HUMANKIND

Manufactured in Dongguan, China in August 2014 by Crash Paper Co.

Revised Edition
18 17 16 15 14   5 4 3 2

Text © 2006, 2014 Bart King
Illustrations © 2006, 2014 Jennifer Kalis, except page 3 © 2014 n8w
Cover illustration © 2014 n8w

This book makes mention of some activities that could theoretically carry an element of risk. Readers naturally assume all legal responsibility for their actions.

We have relied on our own experiences as well as many different sources for this book and we have done our best to fact-check and to give credit where it is due. In the event that any material is incorrect or has been used without proper permission, please contact us care of the publisher so that it can be properly amended.

Published by
Gibbs Smith
P.O. Box 667
Layton, Utah 84041

1.800.835.4993 orders
www.gibbs-smith.com

Cover designed by n8w
Interior designed by Renee Bond
Gibbs Smith books are printed on either recycled, 100% post-consumer waste, FSC-certified papers or on paper produced from sustainable PEFC-certified forest/controlled wood source. Learn more at www.pefc.org.

Library of Congress Cataloging-in-Publication Data

King, Bart, 1962-
  Big book of girls' stuff / Bart King ; illustrations by Jennifer Kalis.— 1st ed.
     p. cm.
  Includes bibliographical references.
  ISBN 13: 978-1-58685-819-3 (first edition)
  ISBN 13: 978-1-4236-3762-2 (Revised edition)
  1. Teenage girls—Life skills guides—Juvenile literature. 2. Teenage girls—Conduct of life—Juvenile literature. I. Title.
  HQ798.K515 2006
  646.700835'2—dc22
                    2006004975

For Lynn, the best girl of all

Contents

GIRL INTRODUCTION

Hello! Take your time with this book. It may be the best book you'll ever read. (Of course, the odds against that are pretty high, but you never know!)

We hope you enjoy it. Now, let's skip the other boring intro below and get started!

ADULT INTRODUCTION

"First things first, second things never."

~Shirley Conran

The collaborators on this book include dozens of girls, young women, teachers, and mothers.* It's our hope that a preteen, 'tween, or teen girl can find some good laughs, empowerment, and maybe even inspiration in the following pages.

We've kept a light tone throughout most of the book, partly because that's more fun but also because there is already plenty of high drama in the literature for and about girls in this age group. Although the voyage from girlhood to the teen years can be a tough one, we strongly believe that being a girl today is exciting and enjoyable. And while this book includes many nontraditional female activities, it also features (for lack of a better term) plenty of classic "girl stuff." Why did we do this? Because girls asked us to!

Although ostensibly written for eight- to fourteen-year-old girls, *The Big Book of Girl Stuff* also may appeal to immature adults. And, as a special bonus, we have included a few deliberate and outrageous "mistakes" in this book to keep you, the adult, vigilant in your reading. If you can find them, write to us (care of the publisher), and you may be eligible for an Amazing Reward.†

Finally, there are several gratuitous references to loofahs in this book. We just think it's a funny word.

---

* For the full list of contributors, please see page 306.

† We assume that you will find the satisfaction in being a perfectionist to be Amazingly Rewarding.

BABYSITTING
Tips and Tricks

"We spend the first 12 months of our children's lives teaching them to walk and talk, and the next 12 months telling them to sit down and be quiet."

~Phyllis Diller

Babysitting is fantastic! You get paid to hang out with younger kids, and if you do a good job, you'll be their hero. You get *paid* to be some kid's hero?! This is an especially good job for a girl. Although boys can also babysit, we can all agree that girls make better role models. ☺ Plus, almost every culture in the world trusts girl babysitters more than boy babysitters. That's because girls are responsible (of course!), and they know the secrets of being a good babysitter. These secrets have been recorded in *The Ancient Book of Babysitting Wisdom** as follows:

Babysitting Wisdom

1. You really *should* take a babysitting or first-aid class before you accept responsibility for other people's kids. (The Red Cross or your local parks department probably offers these in your area.) Besides, you get a cool-looking "official" card!

2. Do not call the children you babysit any of the following names:

orcs	*munchkins*
rug rats	*droolers*
house-apes	*li'l monsters*
hobgoblins	*smurfs*
ankle-biters	

3. Pay *attention* to the kids you're babysitting and *play* with them. (Stay off the phone!)

4. Even if the parents have weird rules, like "Junior should wear his safety helmet and body armor if he goes outside," it's best to follow them. This keeps the kids in their routine. Once you break one rule, they'll want to break all the other ones.

---

* This selection from *The Ancient Book of Babysitting Wisdom* is reprinted with permission of the publisher.

5. Clean up any messes that get made. (Better yet, have the kids clean up!) And if you *really* want to impress the parents, straighten up messes that were there before you arrived.

6. Don't invite any friends (*especially* boys) over! That is a big no-no.

7. When the parents come home, tell them some funny stories about what the kids did while they were gone. Parents love to hear stuff like this.

Experienced babysitters know that all children are legally required to say, "But my mom *always* lets me do [fill in the blank] when she's here." This is often a lie. What the child is asking to do might be really kooky, like feeding a goldfish to his little sister or washing his hands with soap *and* water.

Don't let yourself be tricked! Instead, use the amazing comeback to the right. It is so clever, no child has ever come up with a response to it.

Ta-dah! Problem solved.

But YouR Mom isn't heRe Right now, iS She?

Money: The Hardest Question

So you've made a "babysitting connection." *Yes!* You have a job! Then comes the hard part. The parents ask how much money you charge to babysit. Uh-oh! How much money *should* you charge for babysitting?

You can always babysit for free, but don't get into the habit of it, because people will take advantage of your good nature. We think you should get paid at least $10 an hour for taking care of one child. Add another kid, add another $2 to that rate. At the *very* least, you should get the federal minimum wage, which was $7.15 an hour in 2014. And did you know that states have their *own* minimum wages? Over 40 states have minimum wages greater than (or equal to) the federal minimum. *Sweet!*

But not all things are equal. Are you a beginning babysitter who's taking care of one child? Or are you an experienced, in-demand, Red Cross–certified babysitter in charge of four kids? We can agree that these two girls shouldn't make the same! After all, that second girl might be making over $22 an hour. (And she's worth a lot more than that!)

You can always ask your friends what they charge and use that for a comparison. If you're still really not sure, ask the parents what they think is fair. Try to be honest if it's not what you had in mind.

 A **mother's helper** is a girl who helps take care of children while the mother is actually there. Because this isn't as much responsibility as babysitting, she's usually paid from 60 to 75 percent of what a babysitter makes.

Okay, to *earn* that money, you'll end up having to do this sooner or later, so let's get to the ugly truth of:

Changing Diapers

If baby went poopy, remember to breathe through your mouth.

You will need: A strong stomach, a baby, a dirty diaper, a clean diaper, a warm, wet washcloth or wipes, and a changing area covered with a towel. *Optional:* A toy (to distract the baby with), diaper rash ointment, an assistant.

First of all, when changing a boy's diapers, know that the boy may decide to pee as soon as you get his diapers off, and the pee will go UP . . . toward you! We suggest putting a clean diaper over his private parts as soon as you get his diaper off. (That, or just steer clear of boy babies.)

It's a good idea to get your supplies ready *before* laying the baby down for a change. That's because as soon as you try to change a baby's diapers, she will usually fight against it. We don't know if the smell of their own poop makes them mad or if they think the diapers you picked out for them are ugly and unfashionable, but babies never make this process easy.

Make sure the baby can't escape your changing area. You don't want to have to explain to the parents why their new couch got **poopified**.

After getting your supplies ready and washing your hands, put the baby on her back. Open up the diaper. Breathe through your mouth and sing to the baby as you remove the toxic waste. Give her a toy to distract her.

With one hand, hold the baby's ankles gently together and lift up. With the other hand, pull out the dirty diaper. Once the dirty diaper is off, move it off to the side (and don't step in it later!).

Take your baby wipes and start wiping off little baby's hindquarters. Wipe from back to front with boys, and from front to back with girls. Then stick the dirty wipes into the poopy diaper and wrap the whole mess up tightly. (This is what adults call *hazardous material*.)

Whew! Now baby's clean. As far as getting a clean diaper on, just make sure the front is laid down on the towel closest to you. Raise the baby's legs like before, slide the clean diaper under her, rest her down on the diaper, and lift it up between her legs. Fasten the diaper tightly, and you're done.

If the baby's wearing cloth diapers, make sure to get them on snug and pull those little plastic pants over them. You don't want anything sneaking out of the diapers and going down Junior's leg!

The baby will show her appreciation for your hard work by going poop right away. This is a baby's way of saying, "I recognize your talent. Another demonstration, please!"

Do Babies Need Diapers? In China, India, and over 70 other countries, most kids are diaper-free. They either go bottomless or have "split-tail" pants. Their parents are good at spotting when the little one has to go and then just holds the baby over a toilet or other good spot. No more diaper rash or yucky stuff sticking to the kid's bottom! And no more landfills of baby diapers—those are really gross and a huge source of pollution.

Tricks

A good trick is to have little prizes or treats with you when you babysit. Depending on the age of the kids, these can come in pretty handy. For example, if you had some M&M's, Life Savers, or Tic Tacs, you could put them in a container or small bag and call them "Proton Pills." If the kids do something good, like pick up their toys or foil a bank robbery, give them a Proton Pill! (Naturally, these give them superpowers.) Or you can use the treats as "Sweet Dream" candies for when it's bedtime (but before the kids brush their teeth!). But first be sure it's okay with their parents to give them a little candy.

Silly tricks like these are priceless in babysitting. Let's say the kids don't want to go to bed. You could threaten them with a wet noodle until they flee in terror, but why not make it a game? Turn going to bed into a bus ride. You're the school bus driver, and you pull up in the bus. *All aboard!* The kids need to line up behind you as the passengers. Then you start driving (with the kids following behind you). Stop anywhere you need to for them to get ready for bed. Once they're in their pajamas and have brushed their teeth, drive them right to their bed and tuck them in.

> *Cool Word!* **pajamafy (pa-JAM-uh-fie):** The act of getting the kids into their pajamas. It can make going to bed a fun adventure.
>
> **Babysitter:** Who wants to be pajamafied?
>
> **Little Timmy:** I do! It's pajamafication time!

But no matter how skilled a babysitter you are, the time will come when you can't keep the kids from screaming and running around. Since parents don't want their children to disappear or be hauled away in an ambulance before they return (*picky, picky, picky!*), here's some important safety advice.

DO: Let the baby sit in your lap.

DON'T: Sit on the baby.

DO: Make sure the child eats his dinner and goes to bed.

DON'T: Eat his dinner and go to bed.

DO: Let the kids play in the sandbox.

DON'T: Let the kids play in the *quicksand* box (right).

More Tricks

One of the best ways to keep the kids from going nuts is to have some good tricks up your sleeve. The following tricks and activities in this chapter will work with any person, kids included. We have listed them from the easiest to the most challenging. If the kid you're

babysitting is really young, all of these will be a little too advanced. (But this would be a boring chapter if all we had were tips on baby talk and snuggling!)

 The **best trick** a babysitter can bring is patience and a smile.

Kung Fu Grip

Try this trick yourself once, to see how simple it is.

Ask Junior to clench his hands together so that his fingers are all interlocking. Have him squeeze tightly for about 20 seconds in a good *kung fu grip.* Then, while his hands are still gripping each other, have him stick his forefingers (the ones closest to the thumbs) straight out so that they don't touch.

Quickly wave your hands over his hands and say a magic word, such as "googly-moogly." The fingers will "magically" start moving toward each other! (They would have even if you hadn't said the magic word, but still.)

Why Is Baby Talk Baby Talk?

The first sounds out of a little baby's mouth (besides crying) are usually long vowel sounds that are easy to make, *"Aaaa!"* being the most frequent, followed by *"Ooooo!"* Some of the easiest consonants to put in front of these vowels are "G," "M," "D," and "P." Put it all together and you get *Googoo, Mama, Dada,* and lots and lots of *Poopoo!*

Belly Button Question

If you push your belly button, will your legs fall off?*

You will need: Belly buttons, some pets in the house.

Ask Junior to show you his belly button. Once you've established that he has one, tell him that *all* people have them. (As you know, before a person is born, an umbilical cord leads into this spot and gives the baby all of its food and oxygen.)

Ask Junior how many total belly buttons there are in the house. We're not sure how smart your kid will be, but the correct answer will be however many *mammals* there are in the

---

* Okay, just checking to see if you're awake.

house. Almost all mammals have belly buttons, including any humans, dogs, cats, guinea pigs, mice, ferrets, or woolly mammoths that are around.

Note: Anything born in an *egg* won't have a belly button, so don't count fish, frogs, insects, reptiles, or the strange neighbor kid who's hanging out in your family room.

The Impossible Tippy-Toes

Challenge your challenging child to flex his tootsies!

You will need: Any person, an open door.

Kids love hearing a challenge like "I bet you can't [insert challenge here]."

Start your kid off with some easy challenges. Try, "I bet you can't wink!" or "I bet you can't inhale oxygen and exhale carbon dioxide!" Once the little troll has met these challenges, try this one:

"I bet you can't stand on your tippy-toes!" Naturally, the child will be able to do it. Then say, "No, that's the easy way to do it. Try it like this."

Open up a door and have the child stand up against the outside edge of the door, so that his feet are on either side and his nose and stomach touch the door.

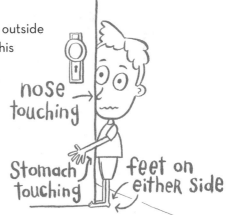

nose → touching

Stomach touching

feet on either side

Now, without using his hands, have him try to stand on tiptoe! He won't be able to because it's *impossible*. (Try it yourself!) But that won't stop him from trying.

Easy Candy Trick

Kids love candy! Use this to your advantage.

You will need: Candy, a rug that's more than a few feet across (not wall-to-wall carpeting).

Put a piece of candy in the middle of a good-sized rug. (Unlike a carpet, a rug isn't wall-to-wall.) Tell the kids that if they can pick up the candy without their feet touching the rug, they can have it. The key is that the first thing to touch the candy must be one of their *hands*.

Let them brainstorm on that for a while. If you feel nice, let them use tools to reach out to it, even though these won't be that useful for this challenge. (The easiest solution is just to roll or push the rug up until you are close enough to pick up the candy. Be sure to give them hints as they try to figure it out so they don't give up and so they can earn the candy.)

Mysterious Crayons

Don't let crayons color your opinion of this trick!

You will need: Some crayons. Duh!

Get from four to 20 crayons and spread them out on a table. Tell Junior that you will magically be able to identify a crayon that he picks without looking.

Turn your back on Junior and put your hands behind your back. Tell him to take a "mystery" crayon and to put it in one of your hands. Then have him come around to where you can see him in front.

While he's coming around, take the hand that's not holding the crayon and scratch the crayon slightly with your fingernail. When Junior comes around, look him in the eyes and tell him you're going to read his mind!

Place the hand *not* holding the crayon on Junior's shoulder or head as you begin "reading" him. At some point, glance at your fingernail to see what color crayon you scratched. Make a big deal out of getting a "color signal" from him, and amaze him with the correct answer!

What to Do If a Baby Won't Stop Crying!

Step 1: Secure the Area! Make sure there is nothing painful or uncomfortable afflicting the poor child. Is he stepping on a Lego? Remove the Lego. Are his diapers dirty? Good luck with that! Is he lying on a sledgehammer? What the heck is a sledgehammer doing in his crib?

Step 2: TLC! The little sweetie might just need some tender loving care and attention. Pick her up and give her some. In case there is any gas in her system, you might want to put her in burping position. Make sure to get a towel or cloth over your shoulder, so that when baby burps she doesn't ruin your evening gown.

Step 3: Is He Hungry? Offer him a bottle. Not just any bottle, but one of his baby bottles with a rubber nipple at the end. (And make sure there's some formula in it, too.)

Step 4: Bored or Tired? Assuming that her teeth aren't coming in and there's no diaper rash, our best guess now is that she is either bored (play with her) or really tired and grumpy (quietly soothe her with lullabies or maybe a loofah).

Step 5: Last Resort! If Junior is really getting hysterical and nothing you can do is working, you might want to consider texting or calling his folks. They might have an idea for you.

Free Tip! The wrong time for horseplay and games is right *after* a baby or young kid has eaten (unless you really want your clothes covered with Gerber baby barf) or right *before* bedtime (unless you want them to be too hyper to go to bed).

Babysitting Emergencies

A good babysitter keeps cool in the face of emergencies. Here are some things that might happen to you, and some solutions to keep the situation under control.

Junior Freaks Out When His Parents Leave

It's a conniption fit!

Do you remember how on the first day of kindergarten some kids would completely spazz out as their moms dropped them off for school? Wow. (Maybe *you* were one of those kids!)

A little kid can really hit the wall when his trusted parents leave him with a total stranger. If this happens (or before it *can* happen), you need to imagine being the kindergarten teacher who is trying to calm down a child and make him feel welcome and safe. One advantage you have over a teacher is you can ask the child to show you his room. "Wow! Are all these toys yours? Which one is your favorite? I like this one." Try to engage him by giving him attention; read a book together, go outside to play, or ask for a home tour. Steer the conversation away from his parents. Anything to distract him—even tickling can work! If all else fails, you can try this amazing Jumping Stuffed Animal trick.

The Jumping Stuffed Animal

If you have rhythm, this one will amaze younger kids.

You will need: Some coordination, a small stuffed animal (or any light object that isn't bouncy), and something you can sit or stand behind, like a table or sofa, for example.

This trick is easy, but you'll want to practice it a few times before doing it for Junior.

1. Sit at a table. (Your audience will be on the other side of it.) Take a small stuffed animal (or any small, nonbouncy item) and hold it out to your shoulder height. Have the toes of one of your feet raised up.

2. Say something like "Hey, watch this! Your tiger can jump!" Then bring your hand down below the edge of the table, as if you were throwing it on the floor.

3. The next steps happen quickly. As you're bringing your hand down below the table's edge, turn your wrist so that the animal is facing up. Tap your toe down, to make a noise, as if the animal hit the floor. And then, with a flick of your wrist (not your arm!) toss the animal straight up. You should practice your timing at home beforehand, so that this looks right.

4. As the animal "bounces" upwards, look at it, amazed! Junior will have fun trying to figure out how you did it.

Teresa Crane: Now before I go, do you have any questions for me?
Adrian Monk: Yes, yes, I have a couple of questions. What does [a two-year-old] eat?
Teresa Crane: He . . . eats food. He eats whatever you eat, only in smaller portions.
Adrian Monk: Oh. So he's like a person.

~*From* Monk

Junior Is Making Too Much Noise or a Big Mess

Fun contests to stop you from losing your mind!

For some reason, little kids are REALLY good at making a lot of noise and a lot of messes. Since their parents probably don't want them to do too much of either one of these things, here's a way to deal with that problem.

You will need: The ability to get kids excited about a game. *Optional:* Silly prizes at the end for all those who enter the contests.

Contest 1. If the kids are really screaming and spazzing out, tell them it's time for a Very Important Contest. Tell them that wise women invented this contest many years ago to see who the best child in a village was. It's called the *Silent Contest.* The contestants must sit at a table and see who can be quiet for the longest amount of time.

Get everyone seated and then officially start the time. Don't expect the kids to stay quiet for too long—these contests tend to turn into giggle fests! But anything is better than screaming.

Contest 2. Sheesh, there are toys everywhere! The easiest way to get them picked up is to have a *See Who Can Pick Up the Most Toys Contest.* As before, you may want to give the kids some background about how, in the olden days, the Child Who Could Pick Up the Most Toys was destined to be a great leader. Plus, the kid who wins gets candy! (Make sure you have candy before saying this.)

If you can "sell" this contest to them, any mess the kids have made can be cleaned up in no time. (It's amazing how fast kids can move when they want to!) Singing a song while you do it will help. "Clean up, clean up, everyone do their share. Clean up, clean up, the babysitter's very unfair."

Contest 3. Believe it or not, there may be times when the kids you're in charge of are really shy and quiet. Maybe they're naturally quiet and shy. Or maybe they're afraid of you! Anyway, you're worried that this visit will be boring for them and you.

To pump these kids up and get some energy in the house, put on some music. Then say, "I want any *bad* kids in this room to be really quiet." At this, the kids should start screaming and going nuts (okay, or at least start talking). If not, it's time for a *Dance Contest.* Anyone can be a judge for a Dance Contest. There might be categories for Slickest Moves, Coolest Outfit, or Most Likely to Hurt Himself When Dancing.

Junior Got Stuck Playing with Super Glue

Why do kids do things like this?

You will need: Nail polish remover or hot water.

At least once in a kid's life, he will goof around with Super Glue, and get stuck to something . . . like himself. And for whatever reason, he will do it on your watch.

The solution is pretty simple. If there is any nail polish remover around, soak some tissues or cotton balls in it and wedge them between the kid and whatever he is glued to. The acetone in the nail polish quickly dissolves the glue.

If you don't have any nail polish remover, soak the stuck parts in hot water. (**Note:** Don't do this if he stuck his lips, eyes, or nostrils together.) This is much slower than using nail polish, but it's better than listening to him yell. (**Note:** If he stuck his lips together, the bright side is he won't be yelling!)

Those Kids Are Just SO Cute!

Kids are so goofy and funny, and they don't even realize it! Here are some of the cutest things that the kids you babysit might do.

1. Playing hide-and-seek, you find your three-year-old in the middle of the room with her eyes covered, "hiding" from you. She figures that if she can't see you, then you can't see her! How precious is that?

2. You ask your two-year-old if she has a sister. She says, "Yes." Then you ask her if her sister has a sister. She looks at you like you're nuts and shakes her head. Cute!

3. You tell Junior that you will give him five shiny dimes for his dollar bill. He thinks he's getting a good deal, and trades with you. Darling!

Junior Is Bored

Here are a couple fun tricks to keep your kids entertained.

Magic Bucket

Round and round it goes, but it doesn't get you wet.

You will need: A rubber bucket, some water. Optional: a long rope, gloves.

Do this one outside and at a safe distance from the kids. Fill the bucket halfway up with water. Then announce that you are going to turn the bucket upside down—but no water will spill. (The children will gasp!)

Grab the bucket by the handle and start swinging it around your body. Once you have it going pretty fast, start swinging it at more of an angle so that it goes over your head.

If you are swinging it fast enough, no water will come out. That's because the force of the swinging pushes the water toward the bottom of the bucket. (This is called centrifugal force.)

If you want, you can tie some rope to the handle so that the bucket can swing farther, making the whole scene more dramatic.

WARNING: Do not ever "kick the bucket"! This is instantly fatal, and results in death, too.

Those Kids Are Not Cute at All!

Two of the least cute things Junior can do:

1. Get his head stuck in the railings.

2. Clog the toilet.

If he has either of the above two accidents, be sure to consult the "Emergencies!" chapter of *The Big Book of Boy Stuff*. You really should have a copy of that book around in case of trouble. The great thing about it is that you can give it to Junior to read after he gets his head out of the railings. (As a matter of fact, it might be the only thing that keeps him from crying!)

Upside-Down Wa-Wa: The Encore

It doesn't seem like this would work. It does!

You will need: A cardboard square (between 3 and 5 inches), a full glass of water.

Do this trick over the sink, just in case. Slip the piece of cardboard over the glass of water. Hold it in place and flip the glass upside down. Let go of the cardboard. Ta-dah! It stays put! Don't tell the kids you're babysitting that it's just air pressure holding it there—say it's magic.

What to Do If You Really Don't Want to Babysit *Those* Kids

Okay, you babysat for a certain family once or twice, and it was a pretty bad experience. Let's be honest: those kids are brats! If you really feel this way, you shouldn't work for the family anymore. It gets tricky, though, because they are going to keep asking for you because you are so great. What to do?

Sure, if you have the guts you can just tell the parents that you might not be the best person for their kids. The problem is that they will know what this means. And saying "Your kids are brats!" doesn't sound like such a good idea. (Honesty may not be the best policy here.)

We think this is a good problem to get your parents' help with. If that family calls, have your own family excuse, like "Tonight is family night" or "I need to study tonight" or something. Brainstorm with your mom and dad. They may have some great ideas. After you say "no" one or two times, the family will get the idea and find another babysitter.

GIRL POWER

"Have the courage and the daring to think that you can make a difference. That's what being young is all about."

~Ruby Dee

The United States has slightly more women than men. *Yes!* And compared to the men, a higher percentage of those women vote. *Yes, yes!* So, since the United States is a democracy and elects most of its politicians, about half of its politicians must be women, right? **WRONG!**

In the United States, there are 100 senators. Yet as of 2014, we've never had more than 20 female senators at any one time. There are 50 governors. But there have never been more than *six* female governors at any one time. There are 435 U.S. representatives. But there have never been more than *81* female representatives. So what's going on?

The United Nations rates Sweden as the only country where women really are equal to men. About half of their politicians (including the cabinet and parliament) are female. Sweden is also usually rated as having the highest standard of living in the world. **Coincidence? We think not!**

It gets worse. The odds that a boy will grow up to be the president of the United States are about 10 million to 1. But the odds for a girl to become president are much lower than that. Up until 2016, the highest office in the United States a woman has held is Secretary of State. Sure, that's a super-important job. But why do women always have to be secretaries? ☺

If we look around, we see that women have served as president (or in a job with similar responsibilities) in countries on every continent of the world, except Antarctica. (Those sexist penguins!)

France has a law called *loi sur la parité*, which means *law of equality*. This law says that political parties must have as many female candidates running for office as male candidates. This helps make sure that there are enough leaders in the country who are women.

Since TV was invented, if you wanted to bet on which candidate would be elected president of the United States, it has almost always been the one with the most hair. So when a woman runs for president, she should always win!

How is all this possible? For starters, this is still a sexist world, but it used to be a lot more sexist. Heck, before 1920, women weren't even legally allowed to vote in the United States in national elections!

Back in 1878, an amendment to the U.S. Constitution allowing women to vote was introduced in Congress. And this amendment failed to pass every year for the next 40 years. You see, the amendment was really controversial. It basically said, "The right of female citizens to vote shall not be denied." Want to know why it took so long to pass this amendment? Because all the politicians and voters were men!

Times may have changed a lot since then, but most of our politicians are STILL men. Why should they get a majority voice? Is it because we trust men to always do the right thing? No! About 93 percent of all the criminals locked up in U.S. prisons are men, so they're not exactly showing us good leadership qualities.

 "That Dress Is So Cute, It's a Crime I Don't Have It!" About 70 percent of women who get arrested are taken in for shoplifting. It's probably better just to wait for a sale. ☺

Women have had to fight hard to get rights in this country. The time will come in your life when someone thinks you can't do something just because you are female. Don't wait for that to happen to start getting involved in how our country is run.

 Sexism, Part I Until about 1900, girls in the United States didn't usually go to school. And even when girls were allowed to go to high school, college was considered to be a bad influence for

them. Men didn't believe that the female brain could learn math or science, and there were worries that the smarter a woman got, the more health problems she might have. Really!

 Sexism, Part II Right up until 1963, if a job was listed in the classified ads, it could have two different pay scales—one for men and one for women. The women's pay scale would be lower, even though the job was the same.

School

"For every one of us that succeeds, it's because there's somebody there to show you the way out. The light doesn't always necessarily have to be in your family; for me it was teachers and school."

~*Oprah Winfrey*

To be all you can be you'll need a good education. You don't want a lecture on this, so here's just ONE thing to think about: A girl might grow up and choose to have kids. Guess who usually raises the kids and teaches them about the world? Women! So what a girl learns in her life is what she is going to pass along to her children. In other words, a girl has to get an education for herself *and* her future family.

Do you think that the school year is too long? Please! You have it easy. The odds are that you go to school 185 days a year. Look at the number of school days in each year of these countries:

Switzerland, 207	South Korea, 220
Russia and Germany, 210	Japan, 243
Israel, 215	China, 251

Start Improving the World Today

"If you have a bit of knowledge, a piece of information, or some love to give, you ought to give it up."

~*Lauryn Hill*

Hey, if we can't count on girls, we can't count on anybody! We know that girls like you are interested in helping others. More than half of girls your age think of themselves as leaders, so go show the world what you're made of.

If you're not sure where to find out about opportunities for helping out, there are many places to turn. Check with your local Girl Scouts troop, YWCA, zoo, or contact one of the organizations below. See what you can do to make this world a better place. We need your help!

American Red Cross: *www.redcross.org*

Guide Dogs for the Blind (western United States): *www.guidedogs.com*

Guiding Eyes for the Blind (eastern United States): *www.guiding-eyes.org*

The Humane Society of the United States: *www.hsus.org/home.html*

Pets 911: *www.pets911.com/index.php*

Sierra Student Coalition: *http://ssc.org/about*

Special Olympics, Inc.: *www.specialolympics.org*

BOYS

"Of all the animals, the boy is the most troublesome and the most fascinating."

~Apricot Plum

If boys are the "opposite sex," does that mean that they really are completely different from girls? Let's find out!

Look at the cross section of a boy's brain. It looks pretty different!

As you go through school, at some point it will seem like all your friends are always talking about boys and couples. And you'll think, "Everyone's boy crazy! How did things change so fast? We used to dislike boys."

And it's true! If you ask little girls in kindergarten how much they like boys, the girls will rate boys as being "okay." After that, the boys will get steadily worse ratings from the girls every year, all the way through fourth grade. Why do little girls dislike little boys? One theory is that it's because little boys are brats! (What's with all this "cooties" stuff, anyway?)

If ever you find yourself annoyed by a bratty little boy, try using this mystical chant to solve your problem. It was written by wise girls many years ago:

> Boys go to Jupiter to get more stupider,
> Girls go to college to get more knowledge.
> Crisscross, applesauce,
> I hate boys!

That just might help you.

Annoying Boy Problems

Here are some other annoying problems that younger boys sometimes have.

Annoying Problem: He picks his nose.
Is This Normal? Yes.

Annoying Problem: He likes to give wedgies.
Why Does He Do This? Scientists have been studying Boys and the Mystery of the Wedgie for years, and still have no idea why boys do this. It may be a way primitive people communicate with each other. No one knows for sure. What *is* certain is that you should keep an eye on any boy who likes to give wedgies.

Annoying Problem: He winked at you.
Is This Normal? The technical term for winking is *nictitating*. Does that sound normal to you?

Annoying Problem: He wrote you this note:

> Hi!
> I'm guessing that you're from Tennessee, because you're the only "ten," I see! I know you're good at science. Are you going to be a female astronaut? Because you are really out of this world! If I could rewrite the alphabet, I would put U and I together! What do you say?
> ♡ Timmy ♡

Is This Normal? Not unless you think it's funny.

As you can see, most boys' problems have to do with maturity. The fact is that most boys mature more slowly than girls. That's mentally *and* physically!

This is why girls and boys sometimes don't have a lot in common in sixth through eighth grade. (Of course, this is also when many girls get interested in boys.) But boys are sooo immature. It makes sense that in many cultures throughout history, girls got married in their early teens, while boys weren't allowed to get married until they were in their 20s or older. This may also explain why so many women end up marrying men who are a few years older than they are.

If you're trying to understand boys, one important thing to know is that a boy never wants to look like a sissy to the *other* boys. That's why even little boys will act macho, like they weigh 300 pounds and are covered in tattoos. It's silly, but a boy starts pretending he's a man when he's just a kid. (And then he never stops pretending for the rest of his life.)

Because of this, as boys get older, many boys often won't show much emotion. These older boys are like poker players, but instead of hiding their *cards*, they hide their *feelings*. Your average boy is not going to want to tell you any of his feelings because for him these are his "secrets."

It's not their fault, though. Boys are often told if they show their feelings that they are "acting like a girl." A boy playing with dolls (or doing any other "girl" activity) is teased much more than a girl playing football (or any other "boy" activity). So life can be tough for boys in ways that girls don't have to worry about.

 Did you know that **"MACHO"** actually stands for "**M**ales **A**cting **C**hildish, **H**orrible, and **O**bnoxious"?

 "Father, May I Grow?" A tribe of people named the Malagasy live in Madagascar. One of their customs is that a boy cannot grow taller than his father without permission. If he wants permission, he must buy the right to grow taller by giving his dad an ox.

Communication

"Boys frustrate me. I hate all their indirect messages . . . Do you like me or don't you? Just tell me so I can get over you."
~**Kirsten Dunst**

Girls like to talk. That's because it's fun to do something you're good at! There is a scientific reason for this. A girl has shorter vocal cords than a boy, so it actually takes less effort for her to talk. As for boys, their vocal cords double in length during puberty. This can make it a lot of work for them to spit something out! Guys are four times more likely than girls to have a stuttering problem. So, because many boys aren't as good at talking as girls, they do less of it.

 Studies show the *number one thing guys find annoying* about girls is that they "talk too much."

Boys and their talking problems may not get better anytime soon. Every year, boys spend more and more time playing video games, which isn't very good for their social skills. In Japan, a "love simulation" game is a bestseller. In it, a boy tries to get a girl to go on a date with him . . . in the *game*. One young man wrote that he liked this because he was "not interested in real girls." Scary, huh?

Because many boys aren't the greatest communicators, they often don't understand basic girl language. For example, if you say, "I don't have anything to wear," you *mean* that you're frustrated with all your clothes and none of them look good on you at the moment.

But when a boy hears you say, "I don't have anything to wear," he thinks you're insane because you have a closet full of clothes. ☺

Often boys don't use words to show their feelings. Instead, they let their facial expressions communicate for them. See if you can guess which feeling matches up with the boy's expression.

LOVE   JEALOUSY   ANGER

Guy Fashion

You might be able to tell a little something about a boy from the way he dresses. Many boys just wear whatever specific T-shirt/shorts/jeans/cap/jacket combo is the guy uniform of the year. Sometimes a boy will even be wearing new clothes, but you'll think they are the same ones from the day before because they look identical. But other guys will branch out more and express themselves with their clothes, shoes, and even hair.

If a boy dresses with style (good or bad), you have to give him points for trying. Let's see what some of the more unusual fashion choices for boys might mean.

Shoes

none *Your school allows this?*

Birkenstocks *He cares about the environment!*

sandals with socks *He's either a real rebel or a real nerd . . . or both!*

penny loafers *Look at the sentence right above this one.*

tube socks with short shorts *He just got out of a time machine.*

Pants

jeans *Pretty basic.*

khakis *A little more style.*

white pants *He's probably friendly and he might have ice cream!*

leather pants *He probably isn't friendly. He probably doesn't have ice cream.*

Shirts

tie-dyed T-shirts *Mean people never wear tie-dye, so he must be nice.*

T-shirts with odd or funny sayings *How funny is it?*

muscle shirts or tank tops *Not a good sign.*

satin or silk shirts *Fancy! He might be a better dresser than most girls.*

velvet shirts *That's REALLY fancy.*

Velveeta shirts *Yech!*

Hair

mullet *If he plays hockey or is Canadian, it's okay.*

shaved head *Fine, as long as his scalp doesn't look like oatmeal.*

long hair or ponytail *If he plays guitar, okay. If he is the Dungeon Master of the D&D club, not so okay.*

dreadlocks *Cool!*

crew cut *Retro!*

greasy or with dandruff *Ick! He's shampoo challenged!*

frosted/highlighted hair *He spends more time on his hair than you do.*

lots of mousse or hair products *If the fire alarm goes off, avoid him—he could be a fire hazard!*

Other

suspenders *His grandfather helps him dress!*

suspenders with a belt *How hard IS it to keep up his pants?*

bolo tie *Rodeo star!*

bow tie *Do you live in North America?*

kilt *Now THIS guy's an individual!*

lots of rings, chains, or other jewelry *Not a good sign.*

a chain attached to his wallet *Smart! This stops all those pickpockets at your school.*

pierced ear *Fine, but more than one per ear is a little fishy.*

pierced face *Smile politely and walk away.*

pierced internal organs *Smile politely, then RUN away!*

tattoos *How old is this kid?*

Friendship

So far in this chapter, we've done a fair amount of trash-talking about boys. But it's all in good fun! The truth is that boys can be great friends. We're not talking about *boyfriends,* we're talking about *guy* friends. There's a difference.

Guy friends can be easier to hang out with than girls. Even though boys may not be better listeners, you don't have to worry as much about what you say around them. That's partly because the odds are that boys are not necessarily big gossipers. Plus, you probably won't be competing with guy friends, so there's less friction. Finally, guys have their own perspective on life, which means they have interesting ideas you might never have thought about.

Don't let a guy friend assume that being your friend means more than it does, though. A guy might fall madly in love with a girl if he believes the girl is friends with him because she *likes* him. If he goes from *friend*ship to *love*ship, there may be no cure!

Crushes

"You see an awful lot of smart guys with dumb women, but you hardly ever see a smart woman with a dumb guy."

~*Erica Jong*

Do You LIKE ME?
Mark the correct box:
☐ Yes!
☐ Yes, with all my heart!
☐ Yes, yes, a thousand times yes!
☐ No. I do not like you. I LOVE YOU!

Look, this isn't a romance book, but you'll probably have crushes on different people during your life. Crushes are normal, but girls often confuse having a crush with falling in love. You have to be careful. Some girls *fall* in love easily, and others just *step in it*. (That's a joke.)

Sometimes a crush can be so powerful that a girl gets completely obsessed with a boy. She can't stop thinking about how great he is and hoping that he feels the same way about her. She gets butterflies in her stomach just thinking about him! Maybe the longest-lasting crushes are the ones we have with celebrities. That's because we (almost) never meet the actual celebrity to find out he's not perfect.

If you ever have a killer crush and want to come back down to Earth, think about this: Almost all women wash their hands after using the restroom. But only 75 percent of men (celebrities included!) do, and the percentage is even lower for boys. Do you really want to hold hands with someone who might not use soap?

If you do have a crush on someone, you might want to keep it to yourself. That's because when other girls find out you like someone, a magical spell is cast and they realize that he's fantastic too! Then they might try to be tricky.

You: That Timmy sure is great!

Your "friend": Oh, let me tell you, he is SUCH a creep! Let me steer you in the right direction . . . You should be interested in Brandon. He is a great guy!

You: Really?

Your "friend": You bet! (*To herself*: Now Timmy is mine! All mine! Ha ha ha!)

Another classic is when you share that you have a crush on a boy you don't really know. When you find out that your friend likes him too, you feel jealous and possessive, even though he's a stranger!

Finally, this can happen when you tell your friend who you have a crush on:

You: That Timmy is sure great!

Your friends (all together): Ew! He is SO nerdy!

You: Just kidding, heh heh.

Your Magic Song

If there's a special someone you like (whether he's famous or at your school), have a magic song that the two of you share. To find it, get a picture of your someone. (The beauty of this spell is that the other person doesn't have to know about it!)

Hold the picture and look into your love's dreamy eyes. Murmur his name five times. Then hit "shuffle" on your iPod, or turn on your radio. Whatever song comes on is *your* song together! You must

now learn all the words to it, and anytime you hear this song in the future, it will remind you of your special someone.

Are You a Good Match?

Are you wondering if you would get along with the boy you like? Lesley Ann Dunking has a system called Love Letters that can help answer this question. (Keep in mind that this is just a game, okay?)

First, write down your first and last name. Below them, write the first and last name of the boy you like. (This has to do with the letters in your name, which you can learn more about on pages 124–127.) Here's an example:

Summer Wheatly
Pedro Sanchez

Now go letter by letter through your name. Look at each letter in your name to see if the same letter is in the boy's name. If the letter IS also in his name, you cross off that letter in both your name and the boy's name. Keep a running total of the letters you have in common. If a letter isn't in his name, just keep going with no score.

S̶ummer Wheatly
Pedro S̶anchez

In the example above, the "S" in "Summer" would be crossed off, because "Sanchez" also has an "S."

S̶umme̶r Wheatly
Pe̶dr̶o S̶anchez

Although the next three letters in "Summer" have no match with "Pedro Sanchez," the last two letters ("e" and "r") do. As you can see in the example above, the tally is three after finishing with Summer's first name.

Now do the last name. Here's what the names would look like when you're done, using this example:

~~Summer~~ Wheatly
Pe~~dro~~ ~~Sanch~~ez

SCORING: There are a total of five matched letters between the two people in our example. Let's see how you score your names.

2 or less: There is no hope of a relationship between you.

3 to 4: You might have something, but it probably won't last long.

5 to 6: The prospects are good!

7 or more: True love! ♡

Common Questions Girls Ask about Boys

Q. *How do I get a boy's attention?*

A. An easy way to get a boy's attention is to ask for his advice or opinion about something. Boys love to give girls advice on stuff. Compliments work, but don't overdo it.

Q. *Do boys pay more attention to pretty girls?*

A. What is "pretty" anyway? Haven't you read the "Beauty" chapter in this book? But still, for most boys, the answer to this question is probably "yes." But guess what? The girl who's prettiest in seventh grade may not be the prettiest in high school, or college, or real life after that. *Anyone* could be the prettiest girl then!

Q. *I know a boy who only pays attention to blonde girls (or girls who play sports, or . . .) Why does he do that?*

A. Boys are just as insecure about peer pressure as girls are. A guy may feel he should like a certain type of girl. The boy might avoid a girl he *actually* likes, because there is another girl he is *supposed* to like. (BTW, girls are just as bad about this!)

Q. *How does flirting work?*

A. The simplest and least embarrassing way to flirt is just to make eye contact with that special someone. Then *hold the look* for around two seconds. (That's an eternity in flirt time!)

Going too much longer turns it into a staring contest, which is sort of weird and NOT flirting anymore. While you're making eye contact, smile. Then look away. That's flirting!

Q. *How can I tell if a boy has a crush on me?*

A. If someone has a crush on you, it's like having your own *fan club*. Somebody out there loves to hear news about you and thinks you're great! We divide boy crushes into two types:

* **The Shy Crush:** This boy gets embarrassed if you even look at him. If you talk to him, he will stammer. But you notice that he stares at you a lot. He's either really shy or he just can't believe (or won't admit!) that he has a crush on you. And yet he will defend you to other people.

* **Outgoing Crush:** This is a much easier crush to see coming. This boy seeks you out and always has an excuse to talk to you. In short, he couldn't be more obvious!

Q. *I know this is off the topic, but do boys ever walk down the hallway judging each other's hairdos?*

A. No. Boys are so different from girls. For example, boys see male fashion models all the time, but most boys don't want to *be* male fashion models. What's wrong with them?

Q. *How do I tell a boy I like him?*

A. Don't play mind games. Try being friendly to a boy you like when you see him WITHOUT paying *too much* attention to him. Don't call or text him constantly. Resist the impulse to hang out together ALL THE TIME. Hold something back. That's because if he *knows* that you have a crush on him, then he is in the driver's seat. And he's probably a bad driver!

Q. *I'm smart and I get good grades. There's a guy who I think likes me, but he also seems to avoid me. What does that mean?*

A. He might be scared of you. Evidence suggests that some boys (and men) avoid smart, successful girls. This is because guys are competitive, so they think they have to be the smart ones. If a girl is smart, a guy might think he is "losing."

Believe it or not, research seems to show that the higher an adult woman's IQ, the more some men will be afraid of her. But as the world changes, smart girls are being seen as leaders and role models more and more each year. So PLEASE don't act dumb so a guy will like you. If a boy can't accept that a girl can be intelligent, you really don't want to be around him anyway.

Q. *So that's it? He's afraid of me?*

A. He might be naturally shy. Or maybe he actually doesn't like you. (Wait, that's impossible! You're adorable!)

Q. *When should I give up on a guy?*

A. You can't talk someone into liking you. Nobody can explain these things; we just have to learn to live with them. So give a boy a couple of chances to get to know you. If he's not interested, move on. You will just seem needy if you keep trying after that.

Q. *He rejected me! I am so hurt and mad. Can I destroy him?*

A. Getting rejected can make anyone angry, disappointed, embarrassed, or all three. You want him to explain *why* he doesn't like you, or to just give you *one* more chance, or maybe you want sweet revenge on that jerk! Who does he think he is?

You may have these reactions, but remember: he's not your *enemy*. He's just a guy who doesn't want to go out with you. You're going to have to do the same exact thing to other boys in your life, and that won't make you a bad person either. It's just the way it is!

Relationships

"I don't understand it when people say, 'We're going out.' What does that mean? You're not going anywhere."

~*Tori Allen*

Hey, you're too *young* to have a boyfriend! (If you're over the age of 30, ignore that statement.) So if you don't have a boyfriend—good for you. Who needs 'em?!

Things a Guy Will Never Say!

"Do I look good in this?"   "Do these pants make me look fat?"
"Everybody dance!"   "Why didn't you get me a present?"
"Am I your best friend?"

But if you *do* have a boyfriend, don't talk about him too much to your girlfriends, *especially* if they don't have boyfriends. It might seem like bragging, and then you'll have relationship problems with the people who really matter: *your girlfriends*! You might only go out with a boy for a day, so if you burn your bridges with your girlfriends, you had better be a good bridge builder when the day is over. ☺

As for boys, remember that they are as sensitive or *more* sensitive than you and your girlfriends. Although they may *act* like they have no emotions, it is just an act. They can (and do) get their feelings hurt, but most boys will never admit it.

If you and a boy like each other, keep it private. That way you don't have to talk to *everyone* about it! If the two of you can make it past the initial news flash of being an "item," you move into *hanging out together*. Even though this is usually more public, you should avoid PDAs (public displays of affection). Good couples don't show off!

Although it sounds cheesy, it's possible that at some point he'll ask you a question that is some version of "Will you be my girlfriend?" We don't know what kind of rules your family has about this kind of thing, so use your common sense. If you do decide to officially become someone's girlfriend, at this point a lot of younger boys will enter the *protective/jealous* stage. You know you've reached that stage if he wants to hang out with you constantly and is jealous of everyone you talk to. Try to stay in groups as much as possible so that it doesn't get weird, and hope he grows out of it.

BTW, don't go out with the boyfriend (or former boyfriend) of one of your girlfriends. This is almost always a disaster. If something goes wrong (and it will!), you are ruining *six* relationships by doing this!

YOU

HER
BOYFRIEND

YOUR
FRIEND

Kissing

"Why ruin a good friendship with a kiss?"

~Paige Lundy

In a perfect world, people who share a kiss are sharing a feeling and showing how much they trust and like the other person. The average woman will spend about two weeks of her life kissing people. As for you, you're still a *girl,* so stick with holding hands!

Kissing Around the World!

Not everyone kisses. In Japan, people do not usually kiss in public. And the Chinese were supposedly horrified when they first saw Europeans kissing! It also appears possible that some Native Americans didn't even know what kissing was until sailors brought the practice from Europe during the 1500s.

Types of Kisses

The following information is amazing, insightful, and informative. (But remember, you're too young to be kissing anyone!)

The Eskimo Kiss

The *Eskimo kiss* is practiced by the Inuit people of the Pacific Northwest. Two people who like each other gently rub noses as a sign of affection. Some people think they do this because their lips would freeze together if they lip-kissed. (And this may not be as silly as it sounds!)

The Cheek Kiss

Cheek kissing is common in North and Central America and the Middle East as a greeting to a friend or relative. Usually it's one kiss to the cheek (sometimes with a hug), and you're done. In countries like Colombia and Bolivia, a person *always* kisses *everyone* present when arriving or leaving a party or dinner. When you go to a party, you kiss everyone. It doesn't matter if you know them or not, nobody's cheek is a stranger to your lips!

In Italy, Spain, and Holland, there may be two (or three) kisses to the cheeks to greet a person. But the French win for most total kisses: as a gesture of respect, leaders in France sometimes get *four* kisses to the cheeks!

 The Kiss of Death! In the 1500s, it was a crime to be caught kissing in Naples, Italy. The punishment? *Death!*

The Air Kiss

The *air kiss* is a fake cheek kiss. This is where you get within an inch or so of the person and then "kiss the air" instead of their cheek. This is done as a joke with friends and as an emergency kiss with someone that has dirty cheeks.

Mistletoe! For a poisonous plant whose name means *"dung twig,"* the mistletoe has a pretty romantic reputation.

French Kissing

You may have heard of *French kissing*. It is also known as *snogging, soul kissing,* and *tonsil hockey.* The term "French kiss" was invented in 1923, and is not used in France. One reason the French are linked with kissing has to do with a ritual they had 1,500 years ago, where a dance between partners would end with a kiss.

Kissing Facts

Most people turn their heads somewhat to the side when moving in for a kiss. They do this because knocking noggins or banging teeth together does not set the mood correctly.

> **Research shows that 66 percent of kissers turn their head to the right.**

People with braces have to be careful not to hurt each other when kissing. There are horror stories of brace-faces locking into place and having to dial 911 to be separated.

Ever wonder how "X" came to mean a kiss? (Pretend that you have wondered this.) Well, back in the days before most people could read or write, if a girl had to sign a legal document, she would put down a big "X" for her name. Then to make it more official, she would *kiss* her signature. And even though most people can write now, the tradition of kisses and "X"s just sort of stuck around.

If you're not sure yet about your future career, think about becoming a Kiss Mixer. That's the person at Hershey's who puts together the ingredients for their candy Kisses. Then if someone ever asks you for a hug, you can tell him that that's not your department!

> **FUN WORD! nigglywiggly:** *The little paper tag that comes out of the top of Hershey's Kisses.*

Hugs

GULP

So what about hugs? Well, at some point in every middle school, girl groups go through a "hug phase." This usually continues well into high school. It is when girls, or groups of girls, get the *hug bug.* Girls are suddenly hugging each other in the hallway all the time, to greet each other, or provide support. While girls in other countries have long been affectionate with hugs, this is still pretty new to U.S. schools.

Hugs rock! In the words of one girl, "hugs are jolly and mood boosting." Two-armed hugs with the heads side by side are the most affectionate hugs. The one-armed hug is the least personal. This is when a girl is next to her "huggee" and puts one arm around his shoulders and pulls in. The most personal hug is the Oreo hug, where two people hug a person in between them.

Fights!

There's no avoiding arguments. Sooner or later, every couple has them. Who knows what it will be about? Maybe he thinks that vanilla is better than chocolate (the fool!), or maybe he is trying to get you to do *his* homework. Whatever.

You'll have to work through these things yourself. We think that most fights are really about communication problems, and guys just aren't the best communicators. Remember that just because a boy *likes* you doesn't mean he *understands* you! And remember, these fights are not the end of the world. Both of you will get over it.

If you are in the right, the good part about a fight is that he will apologize and maybe even get a gift to make up with you. Happy endings with presents are good! If you are in the wrong (hard to imagine, but still), you will apologize and maybe even give him a gift to make up with you. (Don't give him a gift of makeup, though. He won't think it's funny.)

Breaking Up

"Only time can heal your broken heart, just as only time can heal his broken arms and legs."

~ *Miss Piggy*

Hey, unless you're getting married, breaking up has to happen eventually. According to our statistics, 100 percent of breakups happen after a couple has already been going out. There are times when the two people decide together that breaking up is the best idea and they are both happy with the decision. (Of course, we've never actually *seen* this happen . . .)

But if *you* need to break up with *him*, there's almost never a good way to do it. There are **BAD** ways to break up, though.

The Bottom Four Worst Ways to Break Up:

4. By text message.

3. With a voice mail.

2. Having a friend tell him.

1. Just ignoring him and hoping he gets the hint.

You really need to tell him in person and in private. School is a bad place for this, but it will do in a pinch. Try to keep a time limit on the conversation so that you can say your part, he can respond, and you can leave him alone to process it.

Breaking up always sucks, but it's even worse if *he* breaks up with *you*. Many girls get a bad case of *breakup-rexia* after breaking up, especially if it's the first time it's happened. Girls suffering from this illness lose their appetites and don't want to talk much. If you ever get breakup-rexia, you will notice that every sad song you hear seems to have been written just for you. Fun things don't seem so fun anymore. Friends and family can't seem to help. But guess what? There is a cure for breakup-rexia! The one surefire cure for it is *time*. (Chocolate also helps.) Yep, if you give anything enough time, it will get better. It always does.

Marriage

Marriage?! Hey, slow down there! You should stay single and independent for another decade—or even forever. But still, a girl can't help but think what it would be like if she were married to her special someone . . . even if he is only eleven!

Here's an amazing marriage fact: adult men and women are usually attracted to people who are like *they* are. Have you ever noticed married couples who look like each other? Believe it or not, the odds are that married couples will have the same kind of nose and the same distance between their eyes. (If you haven't noticed this before, start taking a look.)

> **A woman's odds** of marrying a millionaire are 215 to 1. And a woman's odds of *becoming* a millionaire are about 215 to 1. (So go for the second option. That way, the money will be all yours!)

Research also shows that married couples are usually alike with their education, race, religion, politics, and attitudes towards life. Think about your parents. Does this apply to them?

Speaking of your parents, until about two hundred years ago, most girls married someone who her parents picked out for her. Even today, this sort of "arranged marriage" is common in some parts of the world, like India. An arranged marriage is not the same thing as a *forced* marriage. Either the young man or woman can call off an arranged marriage if they want.

Do arranged marriages work? Well, the United States has a divorce rate of about 50 percent; in other words, about half of all marriages end in divorce. (Among the states with the lowest divorce rates are Massachusetts, New York, and New Jersey. States with the highest rates include Nevada, Maine, and Kentucky.) In India, the divorce rate is currently less than 2 percent. *Interesting!*

Our Favorite Proposal Story!

An Illinois man named Bob decided to propose to his girlfriend, Teri, by renting a billboard. He had his marriage proposal printed on it: **Teri, Please Marry Me! Love, Bob.** Then he waited for Teri to drive past it.

Good news: Teri saw the message and said "yes."

Bad news: Ten other women named Teri who were also dating men named Bob saw the same billboard! This led to eleven relationship problems. (That's because one of those women was dating *TWO* men named Bob!)

FRIENDS, CLIQUES, SECRETS, AND GOSSIP

"Many friends will walk in and out of your life. But only true friends will leave footprints in your heart."

~ Eleanor Roosevelt

A good friend is one of the best things that life has to offer . . . just think, without one, you'd have to walk everywhere alone! To have somebody you can be yourself around is a great gift. You can both say what you really think, because you're comfortable with each other. Also, a recent study suggests that having close friends leads to a longer life. That's simply perfect. This means that "lifelong friendships" just got longer!

The Compliment Kit

"Always accept all compliments. Ignore any other remarks."

~Kay Oss

Different friends talk and communicate in different ways. Some girls like to talk so much, they would make good talk show hosts (as long as there were no guests to interrupt them). Other girls use so few words, you might think they are giving you the "silent treatment." But there is one category of words that ALL friends like to hear. *Compliments!*

The cool thing about compliments is that they are *free.* It doesn't cost you anything to make a friend feel good about herself. So if you have a friend who seems down, try cheering her up with the amazing Compliment Kit! To use it, just combine two of the adjectives from columns ONE and TWO with a noun from column THREE to create a compliment that will make your friend feel great!

One	Two	Three
gorgeous	witty	queen
smart	fabulous	genius
elegant	friendly	cutie
creative	sweet	duchess
adorable	confident	empress
thoughtful	sparkly	optimist
generous	loving	goddess
striking	responsible	trendsetter
capable	ingenious	princess
fashionable	amazing	diva*
wonderful	fantastic	original
magnificent	adorabubble	countess
shiny	happy	person
fascinating	graceful	lady
svelte	stunning	monarch
saucy	lovely	leader
intelligent	insightful	highness
funny	honest	sister (SIS-tah)
open-minded	positive	chica
interesting	pretty	woman
dependable	breathtaking	viscountess
humorous	foxy	pioneer
caring	artistic	czarina (zar-EEN-uh)

* One meaning of "diva" is "a glamorous, admired woman." (Another meaning is "a horribly spoiled woman," but that's not the one we mean!)

Complimentary Information! Girls give way more compliments than boys. Also, girls make their compliments personal; for example, **"I love your hair."** Boys tend to be more generic: "Nice shot." Over 60 percent of all compliments have to do with a person's appearance. And according to the *Oxford Dictionary of English* there are only about forty one-word compliments in the English language.

"Shared joy is double joy. Shared sorrow is half sorrow."

~Swedish proverb

Friend Test

Answer the following multiple-choice questions about one of your friends.

1. Your friend says she will be ready in a minute. This means:

    A. She will be ready in sixty seconds.

    B. She will be ready in five minutes.

    C. She will be ready in about an hour. Go get a bite to eat and come back.

    D. You will never see her again.

2. You suggest to your friend that you go to the mall. Your friend wants to:

    A. Do some volunteer community service instead.

    B. Go to the mall to see the latest fashions at the clothing stores.

    C. Look at guys in the mall's food court.

    D. Visit the most expensive store in the mall, because they have the best stuff to shoplift.

3. Your friend has a rip in her jeans that you point out to her. Your friend:

    A. Laughs and either sews up the rip herself, or ignores it.

    B. Is surprised and then a little sad as she donates the jeans to charity.

    C. Immediately throws the jeans out and goes shopping for a new pair.

    D. Says, "I know. I put it there." Then she shows you the switchblade that she cut the jeans with.

4. You had a *really* bad day, and as you're talking to your friend about it on the phone, you start to cry. Your friend:

    A. Tells you she's coming over with ice cream.

    B. Tells you that everything will be okay, and that you're wonderful.

    C. Says, "Hang on *one* second, I have another call coming through."

    D. Says, "Get over it!" and then starts eating potato chips really loudly.

5. You're at a movie theater and your friend needs to use the restroom before the film starts. What does your friend do?

   A. She goes to the restroom.

   B. She asks you to come with her to the restroom.

   C. She holds it for the whole movie because she doesn't use public restrooms.

   D. She asks all 12 girls in the group to come with her.

6. You ask your friend what the most important part of being a friend is. She says:

   A. "Loyalty and support."

   B. "Enjoying good laughs together."

   C. "Forgiving my friends when they let me down."

   D. "Sorry, I wasn't listening. Hey, can I borrow ten dollars?"

7. A shy girl walks by. You've noticed she always sits by herself at the cafeteria and doesn't have anyone to hang out with on field trips. You think that it might be cool to go talk to her and get to know her a little better, and you suggest this to your friend. Your friend says:

   A. "Oh my gosh, you read my mind. Let's go!"

   B. "Her? Really? Okay, if you think it's a good idea."

   C. "Funny joke. She is SUCH a freak."

   D. "I see your plan. We'll pretend to be her friends and then take her lunch money!"

Scoring

A = 1 point   B = 2 points   C = 3 points   D = 4 points

Score Totals:

1–8: She may be *your* friend, but she is *our* hero! She's either a great role model for you or it's impossible to live up to her standards. Or both!

9–16: Your friend sounds like an easygoing, good-hearted person. Stick with her.

17–24: Your friend really needs you. (She needs you to teach her to be less selfish.)

25–28: Put down this book and call the police.

Secret Friend Greetings

You see your friend or maybe someone who's on your soccer team walking toward you in the hallway at school. You both smile, exchange your secret handshake, and keep on walking. How cool is that?

Handshakes and greetings vary from place to place. In Central and South America and southern Europe, a handshake can last a long time, and while people shake, they often use their other hand to touch their friend's shoulder or arm. In many Asian countries, handshakes are gentle and there is no eye contact.

Get a secret handshake to share with your crowd or group of friends. Whatever combination of finger wiggles and hand jive you come up with is up to you. We're sure you already know classics like the Soul Shake, the Pinky-Swear Shake, and the Moldavian Friendship Grip. Here are a few other ideas to get you started.

Salaam Greeting: In many Arab countries, people touch their right hand to their chest, lips, and forehead. This ends with the hand raised (palm out) and a head bow. Extra credit for saying "Salaam" (which is a pledge of devoted friendship).

Salaam Greeting

CHEST — LIPS — forehead — bow — Salaam

Tiger Claw Handshake: Hold your hand out at eye level with the fingers outstretched like claws. Your friend does the same, and you come together and clasp hands up high.

The Heart Pump Handshake: Shake hands however you want to, but don't release! Give a slow squeeze, *relax,* give a slow squeeze, *relax.*

Apache Handshake: Reach for your friend's hand like a regular handshake and then keep going and grab them just behind the wrist, while she does the same to you. (This handshake was also a favorite with Roman gladiators.)

Namaste Greeting: In India and Thailand, a friend is greeted by putting the hands together (like you're praying) and following that with a slight bow.

Handshaking experts agree that the perfect way to end a secret handshake is with a quick hug. How sweet!

Friendship Bracelets

These are a great way to make the ties of friendship stronger.

You will need: Scissors, tape, ruler or measuring tape. For the bracelet threads, you can use twine, hemp, embroidery thread, or floss. *Optional:* beads (with big holes).

First, this doesn't *have* to be a wrist bracelet. It can be for an ankle, or it can be attached to a key chain or used as a choker. For our example, we'll assume you're using hemp or some nice colored twine.

Measure out your twine according to what you want to make. We suggest that you cut two pieces that are 2 feet long and two pieces that are 1 foot long.

We are going to describe a pattern using four strings. Tie a regular plain knot about an inch from the ends of all four of your pieces. Then tape down the ends of all of them.

So the ends of these pieces are now taped to each other on a worktable. Have the two *short* strands in the middle, with the two *longer* strands on the outsides.

Throughout the process, you will keep the middle strands tight and straight. Only the outside ones will be moving around. To begin, cross your long left strand over the middle strands and under the right strand. Then take the right strand and pass it under the middle strands and over and through the first (far left) strand. Tighten it! If you tighten the same tightness each time, the bracelet will come out better.

Then repeat the process for the left strand (over the middle and under the far right strand) but this time after you go under the right strand, form a loop. That way, when the right strand comes back under the middle strands, it can just go *through* the loop that you created.

Tighten it!

If you have any beads, just slide them up the middle strands (which is why the beads need big holes) and keep working around them. When the piece is long enough, you can braid or knot the ends together. Or you can make a loop at the end, stick a bead on it, and tie it off. Or you can tie the ends into a knot right onto your friend's wrist or ankle, which would be the best friendship bracelet of all!

Do not give in to the dark side and make someone an "enemy bracelet." ☺

Girl Types

Helen: *Everyone's* special, Dash.
Dash: *That's just another way of saying no one is.*

~*from* **The Incredibles**

Everyone IS special, just like everyone else! Oh well. No matter how unique we are, sometimes we fall into the same categories as other people. The following categories are *just for fun;* check out the girl types below and see if you recognize anyone you know! (And remember, nobody is as clear cut as a "type" when you get to know them. People are more complicated than that!)

The Nurturing Friend

The superhero of friends! The Nurturing Friend is always prepared to help.

Attitude: Terrific! She's there to help, and she makes the world a better place. If you need someone to walk you to the bathroom because you're crying, she's there. Need some advice? Candy? Clothes? Help with homework? She's got you covered.

Accessories: A heart of gold. (Wait, you can't see that!) A big purse or backpack that contains snacks, gum, makeup, pens with cool colors, safety pins, change . . . whatever you need to borrow.

Nicknames: Old Faithful, Best Pal, the Helper.

Trademark Lines: "Call anytime!" "It'll be okay!" "Can I do anything to help?"

Interesting Fact: Because she is always taking care of others, the Nurturing Friend may ignore her own needs. Don't take advantage of her good nature, and help her out when you can.

The Frienemy

The Frienemy is the opposite of the Nurturing Friend.

Attitude: The Frienemy is not there *for* you, but she is there to take advantage *of* you! She might pretend to like you as long as *other people* in your group like you.

Nickname: The Double Agent, the User, Me-Me.

Warning: The Frienemy is probably friends with one of your *real* friends, so you just have to tolerate her. She will know some of your secrets, which makes her a possible "mean note writer."

Clothing: Whatever you have in your closet seems to look good on her . . . She loves to borrow stuff and hates to return it!

Trademark Line: "If my mom calls for me at your house, tell her I'm there and that I'll call her right back. Then text me and let me know."

So WHERE is my sweater?

After you loaned it to me, I let Debbie borrow it. Maybe she'll let you borrow it!

Let's Celebrate! March 9 is National Backstabbers' Day.

The Athlete

A tomboy is a **girl.** *Go figure!*

Attitude: One of the coolest things about the Athlete is that her self-esteem isn't wrapped up in how she looks or what other people think about her. She has her own interests and friends. She usually has good energy and encourages others. The Athlete is disciplined, but because she is used to doing things *her* way, she can be stubborn.

Clothing: The Athlete will come to school in a soccer or lacrosse outfit, and if someone doesn't like it, it's just tough luck. Nongirly clothes are more practical!

Trademark Line: "Think fast!"

Fun Fact: The term "tomboy" dates all the way back to 1562. It could mean a rude boy (apparently a kid named Tom was sort of a jerk back then) or "a girl who enjoys rough, noisy activities, like a boy." Shakespeare refers to tomboys in one of his plays.

Supergirl

Some girls are genuinely nice, beautiful people. Supergirls have such high self-esteem, they don't worry about what others think of them.

Attitude: Supergirl will sit with pretty much anyone at lunch. She is friendly and smiles easily. She wants everyone to feel as good about themselves as she feels about herself.

Nicknames: Prom Queen, Miss Congeniality.

Likes: Being a good listener to other people, including everybody in her group.

Surprising Fact: Even though everyone loves Supergirl, she may be really hard on herself in private.

Girlie Girl

This is the girl who was born wearing a pink outfit and a princess crown.

Attitude: She is the sweetest! Girlie Girls don't walk; they float and bounce. Things that can distract them include flowers, little animals, rainbows, candy, and babies.

Aliases: Little Fluffy Froufrou, HRH (Her Royal Highness).

Clothing: She likes summer dresses; T-shirts with puppy dogs, rainbows, and unicorns on them; blouses and skirts with flowers on them. She may have a tiara hidden in her locker.

Likes: Speaking in a high-pitched, singsong style.

Dislikes: No profanity EVER.

Heroes: Little Bo-Peep, the Little Mermaid.

Fun Fact: Girlie Girl may be a Creative Genius in hiding. See if you can borrow a unicorn sticker or a fuzzy pen and really get to know her.

Creative Girl

She's the queen of art, poetry, and fashion!

Attitude: Creative Girl can express herself in so many ways. Maybe she makes her own earrings or clothes, or styles her own hair (which, last you looked, was dyed green), or has a black belt in karate, or does needlework.

Clothing: Creative Girl can come to school with a far-out look and pull it off! That's because she has *style*.

Trademark Line: "My hair is chartreuse today. Do you like it?"

Beware! If you stand next to Creative Girl and don't move, she will either paint you a different color or cover you in papier-mâché. Also, look out if she's holding pipe cleaners, fabric swatches, or glitter.

Goth Girl

Gothic fashion got started in the early 1980s by musicians who wanted to be seen as sad, wistful, and gloomy.

Attitude: Goth Girl will be sarcastic, especially about things she really likes. It's fun for her to pretend to be a romantic, misunderstood loner. *Optional version:* Theatrical and dramatic!

Fashion: Black clothing, black hair, and white face makeup. Big boots. Some black eyeliner and as many piercings as her parents will allow. Overcoats are good; capes are better.

Extra Credit: Rebel Goths wear white lipstick and T-shirts that say "Choose Life."

Nicknames: Night Angel, Raven, Princess Darkness, you get the idea.

If You Want to Scare Her, Say: "I took your black lipstick."

Likes: Candles. Tim Burton movies. Keanu Reeves in *The Matrix*. Anne Rice.

Dislikes: Bright colors, pink candy hearts, khakis, and daylight. And no sports, ever!

Interesting Fact: Goths get their name from an ancient tribe of German barbarians who actually did not wear much black. They preferred animal furs and turtleneck sweaters.

Funny Girl

Anytime you need the mood lightened, she's the one to have around.

Attitude: She can make fun of almost anything!

Nicknames: The Class Clown.

Trademark Line: "Hahahahahaha. Oh, HA!"

Likes: Funny Girl is never too shy or embarrassed to make silly faces or dance in front of the class. She laughs at herself if she is the butt of a joke, or even if she is in a bit of trouble with the teacher.

Dislikes: People who don't laugh at her Funny Girl jokes.

Interesting Fact: Because Funny Girl is often thinking of the next funny thing she's going to say, she's not always the best listener.

The Drama Queen

Life is so much more exciting with the Drama Queen around. For her, the world is a stage, and she will make every scene in her life thrilling and theatrical.

Attitude: The Drama Queen wants information about everybody! When you see her in the hallway, she will be walking next to a friend and downloading dirt about "who did what to whom."

Trademark Line: "I shouldn't say anything, but . . ."

Nicknames: The Inside Scoop, the Grapevine.

Likes: Exaggerating and freaking out, no matter what the topic is: "Oh my GOD, I love gum! It's SOOO good!"

Disturbing Fact: Since the Drama Queen will say bad things about *other* people behind their backs, remember that she will probably say bad things about *you* behind your back.

Useful Fact: Because the Drama Queen loves drama, she will *create* the drama herself if there seems to be a shortage.

The Leader Who Makes a Difference

She's going to be part of the solution!

Attitude: Go, go, go! The Leader Who Makes a Difference isn't bossy; instead she leads by example.

Trademark Line: "Let's do it!"

Nicknames: President [*insert-her-name-here*].

Likes: Devoted to making the world a better place, the Leader is going to house the homeless, feed the foodless, and clothe the . . . never mind.

Dislikes: People who are downers.

Interesting Fact: The Leader might be more of an *authority figure* for her friends than their own teachers or parents. This isn't a bad thing. Dedicated Leaders are actually sincere, which is one reason they're so special.

The Boy-Crazy Guy Magnet

Some girls prefer to hang out with guys.

Attitude: Boys rule.

Fashion: Whatever jacket her current boyfriend has.

Trademark Line: "Oh look, there's Mark! Gotta go!"

Interesting Fact: The Boy-Crazy Guy Magnet is somebody who doesn't like to be alone.

Strange Fact: Although you may be surprised, the Boy-Crazy Guy Magnet may be unhappy that she doesn't have more girlfriends. A girl who is *really* boy crazy *might* still be finding her own identity.

The Silent Genius

If a brain surgeon and a rocket scientist had kids, this would be the result!

Attitude: The Silent Genius likes to observe the world around her; she may take notes in a journal or doodle artwork compulsively. Whether she gets good grades or not, she has her own brilliant insights.

Fashion: The Silent Genius often doesn't care about fashion at all.

Nicknames: Study-aholic, Brainiac.

Likes: The Silent Genius may focus on schoolwork or her own creative projects as opposed to being social.

Fun Fact: By concentrating on her mind and education while young, the Silent Genius is often the most successful girl later in life.

The Cling-On

Static electricity has nothing on her.

Attitude: It's hard for a girl to know where she belongs in middle school and high school. Because of this, some girls end up trying way too hard to stick with a social group.

Aliases: The Agreeing Machine, the Wanna-Be, the Copy Cat, the Yes Girl.

Clothing: What's everyone else wearing?

Least Favorite Holiday: Independence Day

Trademark Line: "What are you guys talking about? Where are you going? Can I come?"

Good to Know: Because of her social insecurity, it is easy to be tough on the Cling-On. *Don't be.* She may be cool one on one; give her a chance to show her real personality.

Studies really do show that the social groups girls are in will eventually play a huge role on their grades. Who you hang out with will influence how hard you work at your education.

The Imaginary Friend

When the pressures of having actual friends are too much, just make up your own!

Attitude: Should be pretty good. After all, if the Imaginary Friend has a bad attitude, it's *your* fault!

Note Writing Tip: If you write your Imaginary Friend any notes, it is usually better to use invisible ink, so nobody who's "real" thinks you're nutty.

Fun Fact: Imaginary Friends don't argue much. If your Imaginary Friend does argue with you, it may be time to end the friendship. If you're not sure how to do this, just use your imagination.

Best Friend Test

So, she's your best friend, huh? We'll see about that right now!

1. When is her birthday?

2. What makes her really mad?

3. What is her favorite food?

4. Where was she born?

5. What is her middle name?

6. If she could be an animal, what kind would she be?

7. What is her blood type? (JK)

8. Who does she want to marry?

9. What does she want to be when she grows up?

10. How many pairs of socks does she own?

After checking with your friend to see how you did, see the scoring guide below!

Scoring:

1–3 correct: Liar! You don't even know her!

4–6 correct: You might be her good friend, but her BEST friend?

7–9 correct: You ARE her best friend!

10 correct: You are either a genius or a stalker! ☺

The Friend You Should Make Today

It's easy to look at people and pick apart what's wrong with them. If it seems like everyone has something wrong with them, that's because it's true! There are no perfect people, so judging them by their outside image is judging them unfairly.

Here's what's amazing—only about half of all girls say they liked their best friends the first time they met them. This means that half of all girls *didn't* like their best friends when they first met! If you get to know any "type" of girl, you start understanding how unique she is. She's not weird, she's funny. Or maybe she's not stuck on herself, she's just shy. You'll never know unless you give her a chance.

Sisterhood is powerful! Try to think good thoughts towards other girls, even if those girls are really different than you. Growing up is tough for everybody. If girls stuck up for each other more and dissed each other less, you *know* the world would be a much better place.

"One who looks for a friend without faults will have none." ~ *Hasidic proverb*

Cliques (Pronounced *Clicks*) and Popularity

Social groups, or "cliques," are never more important to a girl's world than during fifth through eighth grades. Cliques do exist in high school, college, and even the adult world, but it's in middle school that girls start to get used to the idea of being in a social group.

Maybe you don't need that many friends. Having *one* best friend keeps things simple, because you don't have to spend a lot of time figuring out what to do together. On the other hand, if you have *two* best friends, the three of you will always have something to talk about . . . namely, each other!

We're ALL friends! Elizabeth is best friends with Hannah. But she's also best friends with Isabella, Maddy, and me. But Maddy and me are really best friends, along with Maria and Isabella. Actually, Maria doesn't think Isabella is her best friend, but Isabella thinks Maria is HER best friend. Maria thinks that Hannah is her best friend, but as you know, that's actually Elizabeth. See?

But if you have a *lot* of friends, things will always be complicated and they'll never be boring! Girls like the security of being in a group at a time when everything seems topsy-turvy. But hanging out with a group of friends often brings up issues of popularity, both within the group and with other groups. Popularity (whatever that is!) often belongs to the girls who are most admired or most feared (or both!).

You may think that you're *not* in a clique. And maybe you're right! But if you've had the same group of friends for a long time, that's pretty much what a clique is.

But cliques aren't necessarily *bad.* A clique can be a blessing because growing up is tough to do, and it's nice to have the support of good friends who are going through the same things you are. Plus, you can have a few good friends in the clique and then other, more casual friends also. As the friendships shift and little arguments break out between people, you can shift your friendships around a little and still have the safety of the group.

WARNING: Don't ever go to a horror movie with a bunch of your friends! This would be a *Sick Chick Flick Clique.* Many states have outlawed these groups. ☺

But cliques can become a curse if gossip, rumors, backstabbing, and jealousy become a part of the way the group operates. This is pretty weird because girls are in cliques because they *want friends,* so why would they want to hurt anybody? If you're wondering if your clique is good or evil, think about how you feel away from it. Do your friends make your life *better* or more of a drama? Do you feel as strong *away* from your friends as you do *with* your friends?

Questions That Girls in Cliques Ask Themselves

"What's **my** role in this group?"
"Who took my lip gloss?
"Do I have too many friends?"
"Which one of us is prettiest (or smartest, best dressed, nicest, etc.)?"

If a clique fight breaks out, it can get ugly. For some reason, a girl in a clique fight will try to create an "army" for herself. Somehow the winner will be the girl who has more girls on **HER** side.

If someone tries to recruit you into her **Clique Army,** avoid her, or if it's remotely possible, try to make peace. (You just *know* the fight is over something stupid like a miscommunication, or an argument about whether pink is cooler than black.)

Some cliques seem to exist only to tell the secrets of other people. Even though this is clearly wrong, it's hard to resist a secret. There is something about things that are supposed to be "secret" that makes them more interesting. Even the most boring story is suddenly glamorous and charming if it is a *secret*!

Are You in a Clique?

1. **WATCH** how people come to your group. Is it easy for a person to join your group at lunch without it being a big deal? Is it possible for a person to leave your group without there being any drama?

2. **LOOK** at the people in your group of friends. Is it possible that any of the girls like the other members of the group just because of their clothes, looks, or popularity?

3. **LISTEN** to the conversations that the people around you have. Is most of the talk about appearances? (How to look good, who looks good, who doesn't look good, hey I look good, etc.)

Secrets!

"Secrets, secrets are no fun
Unless you share with everyone!"

~Lynn Adair

Many experts think that the ability to keep a secret is the sign of a healthy mind. Starting about the age of six or seven, kids begin to understand the idea of keeping a secret, and in some cases, the idea of being trustworthy. So don't expect a little kid to be able to keep a secret. They just don't get it! A seven-year-old girl named Laura said it all: "I know what a secret is. It's something you only tell *one* person at a time!"

We think there are three kinds of secret keepers:

The Vault: This girl can keep a secret, and she *does*! If a secret goes in, it will never come out again. She is a very rare breed. If you have a "vault" for a girlfriend, you're fortunate. When you're going to pop unless you tell someone something, this is the girlfriend to talk to.

The Piggy Bank: These girls can keep a secret, but if someone pressures them, they will "break" open and spill their change—we mean secrets—all over the place. Although some of us are stronger Piggy Banks than others, most of us are in this category.

The Open Door: This girl will keep a secret for up to an hour sometimes. Then she just can't help herself! But if you're lucky, she might only tell her secret to one person at a time.

Which one are you? If you're honest with yourself, and you don't want to get in trouble, just 'fess up next time someone is getting ready to spill the beans!

TIP: If you really are going to explode unless you tell someone a burning secret, and there are no Vaults available, try a pet. Most animals are trustworthy, although guinea pigs do have a bad reputation. You could also tell a parent or someone who lives in another town. That way the secret is *out* (whew!), but nobody will *find out* (probably).

One thing we've always wondered about is when one of our friends wants to know one of *our* secrets. Sometimes a friend will even say that she has a "right" to know your secret. This has always cracked us up—unless the secret has to do with a life-or-death situation, or the person is a law enforcement officer, nobody has a right to know *your* secrets!

 "Eavesdropping" **means** *to listen in on a conversation you're not a part of.* In England during the 1400s, eavesdropping was a crime that a person could be thrown into jail for!

Gossip

"The less you talk about others, the more people will listen if you do."
~*Ebola Jones*

Gossip is what happens when two or more people talk about someone who isn't there. You already know that gossip is *bad*, but it is also unavoidable. Girls just love to talk about other people! Check out these amazing gossip facts:

 85 percent of gossip is about friends or acquaintances. (So you can plan that people are going to gossip about *you* sometime soon!)

65 percent of gossip reflects badly on the person being talked about. (So 35 percent of gossip is *positive* or *neutral!*)

55 percent of gossipers pass on to others whatever gossip they hear. (The juicier the gossip, the more likely it will be passed along.)

 28 percent of gossipers tell four or more people their gossip. (This is how gossip can start off true but quickly get exaggerated or changed.)

Studies also show that people who are in a positive mood or who have high self-esteem usually pass along *positive* news about others. People who are feeling low tend to spread *negative* gossip about others.

Gossip is really addictive. This might be because everyone knows that gossip is almost *never* accurate. So hearing some gossip is sort of like getting a piece in a puzzle. If you can just get enough pieces, you can solve the mystery of what really happened!

How do you avoid gossip? You can't. It's *impossible*! BUT you can try to avoid contributing to negative gossip. Let's say you're in a big group of girls. The gossip starts, and you're being practically invited to say something bad about another person behind her back. Here are some good neutral things to say:

"I don't know her very well."

"Who wants gum?"

"It's none of my business."

"Has anyone seen my loofah?"

"She has her life, and I have mine."

Or, just shrug and roll your eyes.

FUN STUFF TO DO

"Anything, everything, little or big becomes an adventure when the right person shares it."

~**Kathleen Norris**

It used to be that all girls grew up to be homemakers, mothers, and cooks. But nowadays, girls can also grow up to be astronauts, police officers, doctors, senators, even mailmen. Or should we say mail*women*. (Okay, *letter carriers*!) A girl can be whatever she wants to be! ☺

Hobbies

Trying new things (or old things in a different way) is what life is all about. If you don't already have a hobby or interest that makes you unique, get one! It could be related to cooking, sports, music, collecting, crafts, writing, painting, photography, community service, or anything you can imagine. Just try something *new*. Having a unique interest will set you apart from the pack and allow you to enjoy your "alone time" so you won't spend it worrying about what everyone else is doing.

Special Note: Social media is, like, the LEAST unique interest anyone can have.

Maybe you are interested in things that some people might think are stereotypical for girls. Take it to the next level! Be creative. Do you like buying clothes? Try *making* them! Maybe you will want to grow up to *design* them. Do you like to sing? Get a karaoke machine or join a choir. Maybe you will grow up to be a performance artist (okay, we all know you want to be a rock star!), or maybe you will teach voice lessons or become a speech therapist. If you think jewelry is fun to wear, take a class in designing and creating it. You can even start your own business selling it.

If you start by thinking about what you **LOVE** to do, you're probably on the right track to finding your hobby. We're assuming that you know about classic activities like Cat's Cradle (and other string games), face painting, tie-dyeing T-shirts, and outer-space exploration. ☺

Activities

While you're figuring out your new passion, take a look at some of the following activities. We have listed them from the easiest to the most challenging.

Arm Shortening

Talk about being limber!

You will need: A wall, an arm, a hand at the end of the arm, fingers.

1. Face a wall. Stand up straight!

2. Extend an arm and move your feet until your fingers *just* touch the wall.

3. Keeping your arm straight, bring it down and behind you.

4. Now bring your arm back up to its original position. *It's shorter!*

Want to know why this works? (Come on, you do, don't you?) See the bottom of the page.*

The Ultimate Makeover

How much do you trust your friends?

You will need: A friend who is a good sport, makeup supplies for the face (no mascara!), a blindfold.

This is a super-hilarious idea. You need at least two girls to play, although audience members will get a huge kick out of it.

The two girls sit and face each other. One girl will apply makeup to the other's face, but the trick is that the girl applying the makeup has to do it blindfolded! That's why it's important that the makeup be safe to use on the face, especially if it accidentally gets on the lips or eyes.

The audience can gather around and watch (no hints!) as the blindfolded girl applies makeup. When she's done, the two girls switch roles, but nobody is allowed to look in the mirror until both are done. *Then* they can look!

Option: A different version of this game is getting a supply of hair clips, barrettes, combs, and brushes and having the girls do each other's hair.

---

* You unconsciously lean toward the wall while bringing your arm back and then forward again.

Quick Summer Fun!

If you have access to a swimming pool, drag a kid's inflatable pool over to it. (Just blow it up, but don't put any water in it.) You can use the inflatable pool like a boat inside the larger pool!

Multitasking

A new twist on doing two things at once!

You will need: A foot and a hand.

It is commonly believed that girls are better at multitasking than boys. Let's test that! Sit down. Lift your right foot off the floor. Start making clockwise circles in the air with your foot.

Good! Now keep circling your foot and hold your left hand in the air in front of you. Pretend to make a number "6" using one of your fingers in the air in front of you.

Now put the two parts together! Circle your right foot clockwise and make a "6" in the air with your left hand. Tough, huh? If you're like most girls, your foot will change directions even though you don't want it to. Try experimenting with different hand-and-foot combinations and directions.

Money Magic

This trick will make you richer! (In a very general, nonmoney way.)

You will need: A dollar bill, two paper clips.

Take a dollar bill (or any other denomination) and fold it as the illustration shows. Then put the paper clips on the bill as shown. Tell your audience to get ready, and then quickly pull the ends of the dollar bill apart from each other. The paper clips will fly up and when they come down, they will be magically connected!

Yawns on Demand

Just open wide . . . soon everyone else will too!

You will need: A mouth and a group of people.

You know that people yawn when they are bored or tired. There are other reasons to yawn; lots of us yawn when we're nervous! But strangely, people also yawn just because they saw someone else yawn first. (You may even yawn just *reading* about yawns!) These are called *contagious yawns.*

One out of two people who see someone else yawn will usually open wide and yawn themselves. To test this theory, try yawning in a subtle (but noticeable) way when you are with a group of people. See if anyone else then yawns in the next thirty seconds.

Now, here's the cool part. People who imitate someone else's yawns (without thinking about it) are more *empathetic* than most. That means that they are *sensitive* to other people and their feelings. Watch who yawns and make a mental note: they are *sensitive*!

Make a Dork Album

Celebrate your inner dork!

You will need: Embarrassing pictures of yourself and/or a friend, a small picture album.

Get on the computer and round up the worst, least flattering photos of yourself you can find. You know, the pictures where your eyes are closed, where you didn't know someone was going to take a picture, where you just woke up in the morning, or where you made a horrible face on purpose but then were surprised at just how horrible it was . . . *those pictures*! Sort through them and pick the cream of the dorkiest photos.

Once you have your All-Star Lineup, print out the photos and fill a small photo album with them. This will provide you with laughs when you may be taking life too seriously. These also make *great* gifts for friends! You can make them a Dork Album of just your friend, just you, or both of you together.

Dress-Up Day!

Tired of playing a joke on one person at a time?

You will need: Friends.

Persuade all your friends that they simply *must* dress up in a certain style on a particular day. It could be Hawaiian or 1960s or mismatched clothing—but have a theme and really push for it.

Then when the "Dress-Up Day" rolls around, just wear your regular clothing. When you see your friends at school in their floral shirts or tie-dye, they will be surprised. "Why aren't you dressed up? This was YOUR idea!" they will ask. Act very casual and say, "I changed my mind." Their expressions will give you laughs for a long time. (Hopefully, they won't be mad at you for a long time, too!)

Chain, Chain, Chain . . . Chain of Daisies

Organic jewelry has never been better!

You will need: Daisies, a pocket knife. (Other long-stemmed flowers can also work, even dandelions.)

You can make a *daisy crown* with this method, which may be the coolest thing of all time. Other possibilities include daisy belts, daisy bracelets, daisy anklets, and daisy chokers. ("Hey, get these daisies off of me!") You may need as many as 35 to 40 daisies for a belt, but fewer for other daisy chains.

Cut a daisy stem so that it's about 3 to 4 inches long. Cut a small slit about halfway down the stem; then do the same thing with the remaining flowers.

Take a daisy and stick its stem through the hole of one of the other daisies. Then take another daisy and put it into the hole of the daisy you just stuck through the first one. Keep doing that! Work your way along, testing for length and straightening the stems, until you only have one daisy left. Then hook that into your first daisy. Put on your crown and find something to use for a throne. The woodland creatures will soon be there to pay respect and compliment you on your beauty.

Note: *Don't use roses for this. Think of the thorns!*

The word *daisy* originally meant "day's eye." So that means the petals are the flower's eyelashes! Cute!

Fortune-Teller Note

What? You've never made one of these?

You will need: A square piece of paper, a pen or pencil.

1. In case you've never folded up a fortune-teller, here's how to do it:

2. First up, get a square piece of paper. Then just fold it in half. Now unfold it.

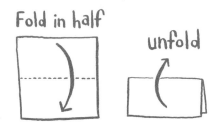

Fold in half   **unfold**

3. Fold each of the four corners of the paper to the center point. Leave them folded down, and turn the paper over.

4. On the back side of the folded piece of paper, take each of the four corners and fold them down to the center point. Then number each of the eight triangular folds.

Fold 4 corners into center

5. Now you need eight **FORTUNES**. You need to invent these. In addition to "yes" and "no" type answers, you may want to have some "maybe" and "random" fortunes. For example, you could have fortunes that read:

flip over and fold 4 corners into center

We sense an answer in the air . . . what does the wind whisper?

The future holds great promise.

Who're you kidding, sister?

Popsicles are good!

Go ask the Magic 8 Ball!

Possible but not probable.

You know the answer in your heart.

Absolutely yes.

Not a chance!

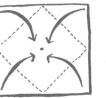

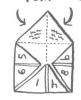

number each triangle

Label with fortunes

Write these fortunes under the triangles with the numbers.

6. Then turn the paper over and write the name of a color over each of the squares. Presto change-o! You're ready to start fortune-telling!

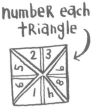

flip over and Label with colors

Show a friend the colors she has to pick from. After she picks one of the four colors, turn the "color" side of the fortune-teller down. Stick a thumb and forefinger into "pinching position" on each side.

You will start spelling out the color, opening and closing the fortune-teller with each letter. Once you finish, have your friend pick one of the four numbers that are revealed on the *inside* of the fortune-teller.

Again, open and close the fortune-teller as many times as the number she picked. Your friend again picks one of the four visible interior numbers, and this is the fortune that you peel back and open. If you follow all these steps, we can say with certainty that the future holds great promise. ☺

It's Different for Girls!

This experiment often demonstrates the natural superiority of girls!

You will need: One male human (*ten years old or older*), one female human (*ten years old or older*), one or two lip gloss, ChapStick, or lipstick containers.

1. Have your girl and boy volunteers kneel down on the floor. Make sure that they keep their legs together.

2. Now, have both of them bend forward and put their elbows up against their knees. Their forearms should extend *forward* from the knees, and their palms should be flat against the floor. (Their legs should still be together.)

3. Place the lip gloss containers (or whatever you're using) upright at the end of their fingers.

4. Okay, now you're ready! Have both of them now kneel up straight with legs still together. Have them clasp their hands behind their backs, above their waists.

5. Now tell them this: "Keeping your arms and legs in position, lean forward, knock the lip gloss container over with your nose, and return to the kneeling up position."

Watch! The odds are very high that the girl can do it. The odds are very high that the boy can't!

The reason this happens is because girls tend to have their body weight down lower than boys. They can balance better!

Dollar Ring

How to make a bling-bling ring!

You will need: Any U.S. paper money.

If you're looking for a fun way to "wear" your lunch money, this is it. Girls have been using this design for a long time; it dates back to at least the 1930s!

1. Take a dollar bill (the crisper, the better) and fold the white border on the top and bottom over to the front side.

2. Then fold the bill exactly in half, lengthwise. Okay? Now do it again! (So you fold the bill in half twice lengthwise.) The big **ONE** insignia should be framed by your fold.

3. Hold the bill in front of you. On the left end, fold the white border of the end back and away from you. Good! Now make another fold the same way that frames the picture of the ONE.

4. Start turning the folded bill into the shape as shown; you may want to wrap it around your finger to give it the shape you'll want. Make sure it looks like the picture!

5. With the folded end on the left, make a fold so that the right-side of the bill bends straight *up*. Then wrap and fold it over and *down* as the picture shows.

6. You're almost done! *Loop* the folded end (on your left) around in a circle so that the symbol of the **ONE** ends up right in front of the folded area that you made with step 5. There should be a little tail hanging down below it.

7. Take the tail and wrap it up and behind the folded symbol

of the **ONE.** Then keep going around and fold it over the top. (If it's really long, you may need to wrap it a little around the bottom too.)

8. Tuck that last little fold to the right of the symbol **ONE** into the gap between the folded "badge" and the ring itself. This holds the whole thing together!

9. Walk around like you're cool!

TIP: Don't wear your ring around any area with mean people who might want your pretty jewelry!

Black Light Freak-Out

It doesn't seem like this would work that well. It does!

You will need: A black light, liquid Tide, a bubble blower.

The human eye can't see "black light." You can buy *black light* light bulbs; they are sometimes used for taking night photographs or for cool tricks like this. Tide detergent has a fluorescent chemical in it that shows up under black light really well. So here's what you do:

Mix 1/3 cup of liquid Tide with the same amount of water. Turn on your black light. Dip your bubble blower into your mixture and blow bubbles. They will glow and look purple-freaky! This is a great thing to do at slumber parties and on Halloween.

Soda Blast!

It's dramatic and it's safe.

You will need: A bottle of diet soda (20 ounces minimum), some Mentos breath mints, a pipe or test tube or cardboard roll you can stack the Mentos in.

For best results, let your soda sit at room temperature for a day before you use it, and do not jostle the bottle around. You will want to do this activity outside. The bigger the soda bottle you're using, the more room you will need.

To begin, unroll your Mentos package. Your goal will be to dump all of them into the soda bottle at the same time. The best way to do this is to stack them inside a test tube or short piece of pipe. Hold a small card under them so they don't fall out.

Now slowly open the bottle of soda. Position your stack of Mentos directly over the mouth of the bottle. Remember, you want them all to go in together. When it's all lined up, slide the card away from the bottom of the stack and let them fall in. Then stand back. The contents of the bottle will erupt straight up in an amazing way!

How does it work? All the carbon dioxide in the bottle is attracted to the Mentos. The little bubbles combine to make big bubbles, and the big bubbles combine to make an eruption. There will probably still be soda in the bottle after your blast goes off, so if you have more Mentos, you can do the trick again with the same container of soda.

Journaling

Does calling it a "diary" make it less cool?

You will need: Uh . . . a journal? Your favorite pen.

> *". . . in the end, I always come back to my diary. It's where I start and finish."*
>
> **~Anne Frank**

As they get older, many girls start looking inward and thinking hard about their lives. They ask the important questions: *Who am I? Who are you? Where did I leave my favorite pen?* This is a time of life when you need a place to record your wishes, secrets, and feelings for yourself.

A journal can be an amazing document to look back over and see what was important to you last year or five years ago. You're basically making your own time capsule! Whether you think you're a good writer or not *doesn't matter*. The journal is for **YOU**, although we bet you'll eventually want to share parts of it with others.

Where you actually write may matter. Although it's easy to write on a computer, there is something really personal about a journal that is handwritten. Here are some different ways you can approach your journal:

Absolutely Creative Journal: Poems, doodles, ideas, sketches, made-up languages, and glued-in collages collide in a beautifully messy work of art and you.

"Get the Bad Juju Out" Journal: This is perfect therapy. If you pour all of your insecurities, fears, and hatred out into your journal, guess what's left inside you? Nothing but good stuff!

Decompression Journal: By writing down the day's events, you can process through them and gain perspective. Keeping a journal like this is like having a front-row seat at the movie of your life.

Gratitude Journal: Think about what you have to be grateful for, and write about how, even during the tough times, life is good.

"Be thankful for what you have; you'll end up having more. If you concentrate on what you don't have, you will never, ever have enough."
~**Oprah Winfrey**

Journalistic Journal: Once you've been writing for a while, you may want to encourage your friends to give you writing or artwork they've done and put it into a shared blog. (And since Google provides free blogs, don't pay for one!)

Or, you can just combine all of the above ideas into one journal! Try to make time for writing, but don't feel like you need to make an entry every day. That can turn what should be a fun, creative outlet into a chore. ☹

And remember: Just like school yearbooks, the *longer* you have your journal, the more priceless it is!

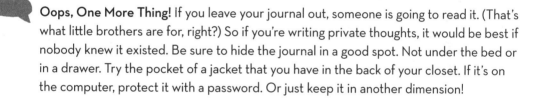 **Oops, One More Thing!** If you leave your journal out, someone is going to read it. (That's what little brothers are for, right?) So if you're writing private thoughts, it would be best if nobody knew it existed. Be sure to hide the journal in a good spot. Not under the bed or in a drawer. Try the pocket of a jacket that you have in the back of your closet. If it's on the computer, protect it with a password. Or just keep it in another dimension!

The Magic Jar

You will need: A small glass jar with a metal lid, "light" corn syrup, glitter, beads, plastic figures and doodads, glue (*better if it's waterproof*), creativity. *Optional:* Food coloring.

Who doesn't love snow globes? You shake them and watch the little snowflakes come swirling down . . . so pretty! And now, you can make your own version of the magic globe.

The scene that you want to create *inside* of the jar needs to be glued down on the *inside* of the metal lid of the jar. Your scene might be made up of little plastic snowmen, doll heads, lost pieces from board games, or costume jewelry. Provided the items are plastic, they should be fine. So, glue them down to the inside of the lid in whatever arrangement you like.

While the lid dries, put the stuff that you want to "float" in the air into the empty jar. Whatever glitter or beads strike your fancy!

Next, pour an equal amount of light corn syrup and water into the jar. Fill the jar fairly full, but not quite all the way. (If you want to put in a little food coloring to make it look like sky or water, now's the time.)

When you're ready for the moment of truth, put glue around the rim of the jar on the inside of the jar's lid. Screw it on tight, and then leave it alone. It has to dry, so let it! Once it *is* dry, prepare for instant holiday dazzle. Pick up the jar, shake it . . . and let the magic begin!

> Big glass beads with flat backs look cool on everything. Get some Super Glue and glue some of these to things in your room. We bet you love it!

Magic Bubbles

This is the coolest bubble activity of all time.

You will need: A bottle of bubbles with bubble blower, a decent-sized cardboard box, a plastic garbage bag, dry ice, work gloves.

WARNING: Don't ever touch dry ice with your skin! Dry ice is so cold (minus 100 degrees F), it will stick to you and freeze. It can severely damage and scar your skin.

All you have to do for this simple and amazing activity is line the inside of your cardboard box with the plastic garbage bag. Then put on your gloves and put the dry ice in the box.

Now start blowing some bubbles and blow them *into* the box. The bubbles will act very unusually; they won't rise *or* fall, they will just hover in the box, changing colors and combining with each other. (This is because dry ice is made of frozen carbon dioxide and the bubbles are lighter than the carbon dioxide gas that is being released.)

 BONUS: When you are done with the dry ice, try breaking off a piece (with your gloves on) and putting it in a glass of water for that cool "scary potion" effect! You can also use dry ice to put into balloons . . . after you put it inside the balloon, tie off the end of the balloon. The balloon will be "blown up" by the dry ice! Cool!

Mehndi (*MEN-dee*) Painting

Give yourself a nonpermanent tattoo!

You will need: A friend, henna powder, tea, lemon or lime juice, sugar or honey, a nonmetal bowl. You also need either a pastry bag or a large plastic ziplock bag.

Ancient Indian body painting is amazing. You can do it yourself, or there are probably artists in your area who can help you get started if you prefer. Henna is used as a skin and hair dye. You can find henna in organic food stores, beauty stores, Indian shops, and many other places. The henna you buy should look like a *green* or *brown* powder. Not black! And the fresher it is, the better it works.

Follow the directions that came with your henna, but also be willing to experiment. You will want to mix your henna and let it sit for a few hours, or even overnight.

Although "recipes" vary, mix the henna powder with some tea and lemon or lime juice in a bowl to make a watery paste. Henna experts are

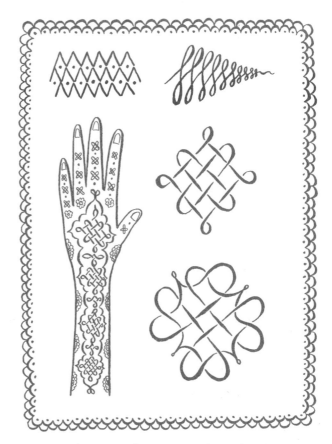

reluctant to give exact amounts, but try starting with a ratio of 2 to 3 (powder to liquid). One way to do it is to make a cup of strong tea and add a little sugar. Then pour some of the tea and lemon juice into the henna powder.

Don't make your henna mix too thick, because the henna mix will "set up" a little bit after you're done. It should be like watery mashed potatoes, with *no* lumps or air pockets.

Once you're done mixing your henna, loosely cover the mixture with cellophane. Some people let the henna sit overnight, but once the surface is darker than the part underneath, the dyes are being released.

When you're ready to paint, either fill up a pastry bag (those things chefs use for frosting) or make your own. Just cut off a tiny bit of the corner of a ziplock freezer bag and carefully pour the paste into the bag. Holding the mix in the bag, squeeze it so that one end makes a small tube. Then start squeezing it out that small corner hole!

If your henna mix is the right consistency, you can also paint it on with a small brush. You can make whatever design you want; there are many good books and websites that can give you ideas.

Squeeze or paint the design you want out onto your friend's hand or foot. (If you want to practice with an area nobody will see, try shoulders, backs, or legs.) Many artists dab the henna with a cotton ball dipped in a mix of lemon juice and sugar to help it set up more quickly.

Although mehndi *should* dry for four to six hours, you can do faster versions. (But try to leave the design on as long as possible.) If you don't wash it with water for another four hours, it can last for as long as two to three weeks.

 You can also body paint with glow-in-the-dark paints (craft stores have nontoxic ones) that look really cool in the dark and under black lights. If you want a less permanent body or face paint, mix a little lotion with dry tempera paint.

Crayons!

You might be surprised to learn that these rods of colored wax are more interesting than you think. For example, you know that waxy smell that you get when you open a box of crayons? That smell is beef fat. Processed *beef fat* (called *stearic acid*) is an ingredient in many crayons. The smell of crayons is so well known, a university study found it to be the 18th most recognized odor in the nation! (The smell of peanut butter was number two.)

The most famous crayons are probably Crayola crayons. "Crayola" is a word that means "oily chalk." Crayola crayons started out with eight colors in 1903. Today there are 120 colors. Some of the colors available that you may not have heard about include Outer Space, Manatee, Fuzzy Wuzzy Brown, Dandelion, Eggplant, and Macaroni and Cheese—and you can get them in glow in the dark if you want!

Survey Says! A poll of 25,000 Americans found the favorite crayon color of the American people: **blue!**

"I alone cannot change the world, but I can cast a stone across the waters to create many ripples."

~**Mother Teresa**

Make the World a Better Place

It's time to cast a stone!

You will need: To save the world. (Or at least your hometown.)

This is the most important activity **anybody** can do. When you showed up on this planet, there were problems all over the place. Nobody is blaming you for them, but before you leave, it would be nice if you could help make the world a better place than it was when you found it.

You may already be a member of a club, organization, temple, or church. Maybe you're in Girl Scouts or a Big Sister program. If so, start looking for opportunities to help out. Decide what kinds of issues are important to you. Check the "Girl Power" chapter for more ideas. There are also little random things you can do to make the world better, like smiling or giving someone a compliment. Maybe you've seen the bumper sticker **Commit Random Acts of Kindness.** That's a great idea!

Besides the good feeling you can get from helping others, making the world a better place also looks great on college applications! Keep track of what you did and when—we guarantee *someone* will be very impressed.

If this sounds like too much for you right now, that's okay. But get around to it sooner or later. We *know* you don't have anything better to do . . . **Nobody does!**

HOLIDAYS

"Celebrate the happiness that friends are always giving.
Make every day a holiday and celebrate just living!"
~**Amanda Bradley**

A wise person once pointed out (in a book sort of like this!) that every day of the year is special for *someone*. For instance, think of your birthday. That's your *special* day when we celebrate how unique you are. (Never mind that 20 million other people have the same birthday as you!) Here are some other very special days that you might not know about.

 Always make it a point to say "Thank you!" to your mother on *your* birthday. If it wasn't for her, you wouldn't have much to celebrate!

All of the following holidays are honest-to-goodness real, live holidays!

January

January is **International Creativity Month, It's Okay to Be Different Month,** and **International "Get Over It" Month.** It contains **"Someday We'll Laugh about This" Week** and **National Fresh-Squeezed Juice Week.** January's flower is the snowdrop. Its gem is the garnet.

January 1: **Get a Life Day**

January 3: **Drinking Straw Day**

January 4: **Trivia Day**

January 5: **Great Fruitcake Toss** in Manitou Springs, Colorado. This is a day for tossing, hurling, and launching leftover fruitcakes in a competition!

January 7: **"I'm Not Going to Take It Anymore" Day**

January 8: **Women's Day** (in Greece). Women do absolutely no housework this day; instead they hang out in cafés and go shopping. Men are supposed to work in the home, vacuuming and cleaning. If any men are caught outside, they may be drenched with water!

January 12: **National Handwriting Day**

January 16: **National Nothing Day**

January 18: Pooh Day. Birthday of A. A. Milne, the author of the *Winnie the Pooh* book, among others.

January 20: International Women's Day

January 21: Squirrel Appreciation Day and **National Hugging Day**

January 22: Answer Your Cat's Question Day

January 23: National Compliment Day

January 25: Opposite Day

January 27: National Chocolate Cake Day

January 28: National Kazoo Day and **Bubble Wrap Appreciation Day**

January 31: Backward Day

February

February's **International Boost Self-Esteem Month** and **National Bird Feeding Month.** It contains **International Flirting Week, Get Paid to Shop Week, National Pancake Week,** and **International Friendship Week.** February's flower is the violet, and its gem is the amethyst.

February 3: Girls' Festival Day (in Japan). At this festival (*Hina-matsuri*), all families with daughters invite people over to wish the girl good fortune and maybe give her presents. How cool is that?

February 7: Love Your Robot Day

February 9: Alice Walker's birthday (born 1944)

February 11: Bun Day (in Iceland). A day to celebrate hair buns, hamburger buns, and sticky buns. ☺

February 12: International Pancake Day

February 14: International Quirkyalone Day (Yeah, yeah, it's also **Valentine's Day**)

> If you have a special someone, Valentine's Day can be the greatest day of the year. But if you wish you did but don't, it can be the hardest day. Maybe it's best to expect nothing—then if something good happens, it's a surprise! And if it doesn't, who cares!

February 15: National "I Want Butterscotch" Day and **National Gum Drop Day**

February 20: Battle of the Flowers (in southern France). A day to throw flowers at anyone you want!

February 22: World Thinking Day

February 26: For Pete's Sake Day

March

March is **National Women's History Month, National Kidney Month, International Listening Awareness Month,** and **Optimism Month.** It contains **Celebrate Your Name Week, National Procrastination Week,** and **International Brain Awareness Week.** March's flower is the daffodil. Its gem is the aquamarine.

March 2: **Babysitter Safety Day** and **Read Across America Day**

March 3: **I Want You to Be Happy Day**

March 4: **Ding Ling Day** (in China). Ding Ling was a female Chinese author (1904–1986) who worked for equal rights for women.

March 8: **Uppity Women Day** and **International Women's Day**

March 9: **Backstabbers' Day**

March 12: **Girl Scout Day**

March 13: **Earmuff Day**

March 14: **White Day** (in Japan). On this day, boys and men who got candy or gifts from girls on Valentine's Day return the favor. Their gift should be slightly better than the one they received, and it's wrapped in white.

March 15: **Act Happy Day**

March 16: **Everything You Do Is Right Day** and **Lips Appreciation Day**

March 18: **Forgive Mom and Dad Day**

March 21: **Absolutely Incredible Kid Day**

March 29: **Happy Day.** Four words: *Don't worry, be happy!*

March 30: **I Am in Control Day**

April

April is **National Grilled Cheese Sandwich Month, Couple Appreciation Month,** and **National Smile Month.** April contains **Egg Salad Week, Wildlife Week, National Karaoke Week,** and **National TV Turnoff Week.** April's flower is the sweet pea, and its gem is the diamond.

April 1: Call us crazy, but this seems like a good day for a practical joke. See page 258 for ideas!

April 2: **International Children's Book Day**

April 7: **No Housework Day.** If someone suggests you do some housework, quote the philosopher Baruch Spinoza: "Nature abhors a vacuum."

April 9: **Name Yourself Day**

April 10: **Siblings' Day**

April 12: **International Teens Against Zits Day**

April 17: **Children's Day.** In Turkey, kids take over the government and get free ice cream and movies—all day!

April 20: **Look-Alike Day**

April 21: **Kindergarten Day**

April 22: **Earth Day**

April 26: **Hairball Awareness Day** and **Hug an Australian Day**

April 30: **Hairstylist Appreciation Day**

May

May is **More Than Just a Pretty Face Month, Creative Beginnings Month,** and **National Book Month.** May contains **National Stuttering Awareness Week, Be Kind to Animals Week,** and **National Wildflower Week.** (And don't forget that **Mother's Day** is always the second Sunday in May!) This month's flower is the lily of the valley and its gem is the emerald.

May 1: **Mother Goose Day** and **Save the Rhino Day**

May 3: **Lumpy Rug Day**

May 5: **Cinco de Mayo!** More avocados are sold on this day than any other in the United States.

May 6: **No Diet Day**

May 8: **No Socks Day**

May 9: **Lost Sock Memorial Day**

May 10: **Trust Your Intuition Day**

May 16: **International Sea Monkey Day** and **Love a Tree Day**

June

June is **National Iced Tea Month.** It contains **National Hermit Week, National Hug Week,** and **National Forgiveness Week.** The first week of June contains **World Environment Day.** And don't forget that the third Sunday in June is **Father's Day**! June's flower is the rose. Its gem is the pearl.

June 1: Child Protection Day. To celebrate,
babies compete in a crawling race in Lithuania.
(Really.)

June 4: National Hug Your Cat Day

June 8: Best Friends Day

June 9: Donald Duck Day

June 11: National Hug Day and **National Taco
Day.** You can hug anybody on this day, not
just cats. (And the beauty of Hug Day is
that after you get one hug, refills are free!)

June 15: Smile Power Day

June 18: National Splurge Day

June 19: Join Hands Day

June 22: Mirthday!

June 23: Let It Go Day

June 27: Leon Day. It is exactly six months till Christmas on Leon Day. ("Leon" is "Noel"
spelled backwards.)

June 29: Waffle Iron Day

July

July is **Cell Phone Courtesy Month.** It contains **Copious Compliments Week, National Baby
Food Week,** and **National Salad Week.** July also includes
National Nude Recreation Week and **Spam Festival Week,**
but don't hold that against it. July's flower is the water lily
and its gem is the ruby.

July 2: I Forgot Day

July 3: Compliment Your Mirror Day

July 7: Father-Daughter Take a Walk Together Day

July 10: Ima Hogg's birthday. Ima Hogg (1882–1975) was the
daughter of a Texas governor; she preferred to be called
Miss Ima. She made up for the crummy name her dad gave
her by giving generously to charities and starting many community projects.

July 19: Cow Appreciation Day

July 21: National Ice Cream Day

July 31: J. K. Rowling's birthday! Joanne Kathleen Rowling (born 1965) came up with the idea of Harry Potter during a train ride in 1990. Her first Harry Potter book came out eight years later, and she is now one of the richest women in the world. Go J. K.!

August

August is **Admit You're Happy Month.** August contains **National Friendship Week, National Smile Week, Simplify Your Life Week,** and **Kool-Aid Days** (the second weekend of the month). August's flower is the poppy. Its gem is the onyx.

August 1: "Pretty Is as Pretty Does" Day

August 4: National Sisters' Day

August 6: Fresh Breath Day

August 9: Book Lover's Day

August 13: Left Handers Day

August 15: National Relaxation Day

August 18: Bad Poetry Day

August 22: National Punctuation Day

August 25: Kiss-and-Make-Up Day

August 26: Women Get to Vote! See the "Girl Power" chapter for more information on this.

August 27: Just Because Day

September

September is **Hat Month, National Chicken Month,** and **National Literacy Month.** September contains **Biscuits and Gravy Week** and the fourth Saturday of September is **International Rabbit Day.** September's flower is the morning glory and its gem is the sapphire.

September 5: Be Late for Something Day

September 6: Read a Book Day and **Do It Today Day**

September 11: No News Is Good News Day

September 13: Blame Someone Else Day

September 15: Women's Friendship Day and **Respect Your Elders Day**

September 16: Collect Rocks Day

September 22: Elephant Appreciation Day

September 24: Buy Nothing Day

September 28: International Very Good-Looking, Smart Woman's Day

October

October is **National Cookie Month, National Popcorn Poppin' Month,** and **Liver Awareness Month.** It also contains **National Pet Peeve Week.** The first Saturday in October is **Frugal Fun Day,** a time to have cheap fun. October's flower is the calendula (!) and its gem is the opal.

October 7: World Smile Day

October 9: **Alphabet Day** (in Korea)

October 11: World Egg Day

October 13: Skeptics' Day

October 22: National Color Day

October 25: Sour Day

October 26: The Most Unproductive Day in the World

October 29: Laugh Suddenly for No Reason a Lot Today Day

October 30: Haunted Refrigerator Night

October 31: National Knock-Knock Day. Oh yeah, this is also **Halloween**!

Halloween

WARNING: Ninety percent of parents admit they steal candy from their kids' bags. (The other 10 percent lie.) So keep an eye on your candy! And if you're not sure what to be for Halloween, go to school dressed as one of your teachers. This is (almost) always funny! ☺ To learn more cool stuff about this holiday, read "Halloween" in *The Big Book of Boy Stuff.*

November

November is **"I Am So Thankful" Month,** and it contains **National Fig Week** and **National Children's Book Week.** The Friday after Thanksgiving is **Buy Nothing Day.** November's flower is the chrysanthemum. Its gem is the topaz.

Question: What do you get when you cross a turkey with a centipede?
Answer: Drumsticks for everybody!

November 1: Vinegar Day

November 3: Culture Day

November 8: Cook Something Bold and Pungent Day

November 10: Sesame Street's anniversary! On this day in 1969, a crazy kids' show with puppets, people, and songs made its debut. (This holiday is sponsored by the letter "Q.")

November 11: Corduroy Appreciation Day

November 13: World Kindness Day

November 14: National Teddy Bear Day

November 17: Homemade Bread Day

November 21: World "Hello" Day. Say "Hello" to 10 people you don't know!

November 29: "Sinkie" Day. A "sinkie" is anyone who grabs a food item and then eats it over the sink. There are a lot of us out there!

December

December is **Read a New Book Month.** It contains **National Hand-Washing Awareness Week, Cookie Cutter Week,** and **"It's About Time" Week.** December's flower is the poinsettia and its gem is turquoise.

December 4: Wear Brown Shoes Day

December 5: Bathtub Party Day

December 9: Boring Celebrities Day

December 11: Day of the Horse

December 16: National Chocolate-Covered Anything Day

December 20: Underdog Day

December 21: Humbug Day

December 23: Festivus! This holiday was invented by a man named Dan O'Keefe and was made popular on an episode of the TV show *Seinfeld*. Festivus was intended to be a holiday that required no shopping. The only Festivus decoration is a bare metal pole, which can be stuck in a pot or hung from the ceiling. Because it is bare, one of the mottos for Festivus is "It's time to decorate the pole! We're done!" Because Festivus is a time to complain about important things, a holiday card might read, "I have a problem with you people." The holiday should also include feats of strength. As a matter of fact, Festivus is not over until the head of the household is wrestled to the ground and pinned.

Ben & Jerry's made an ice cream flavor named Festivus in 1999. It was ginger flavored with pieces of gingerbread cookies inside.

SPORTS AND GAMES

*"**Tomboy.** All right, call me a tomboy. Tomboys get medals. Tomboys win championships. Tomboys can fly. Oh, and tomboys aren't boys."*

~Julie Foudy, Olympic gold medalist, two-time World Cup soccer champion

Hey, stretch out a little and take this quick fitness quiz:

* Try to do a sit-up. If you can do it, good for you! *(25 percent of girls can't.)*
* Try to touch your toes without bending your knees. *(No bouncing! 40 percent of girls can't do it.)*
* Try doing two push-ups. *(70 percent of girls can't.)*
* Run 73 miles. *(Hey, wait a minute!)*

If you couldn't do the first three challenges above, you are now legally required to read this chapter. *Attagirl!* And if you set this book down (or set it on fire) you'll be in BIG trouble! After all, girls spend over 7½ hours every day on "media" (cell phones, computers, TV, etc.). Now guess how much time they spend a day on sports and exercise! Give up? Less than an hour.

There are so many *great* reasons to play sports and get exercise, it's impossible to list them all. But here are three:

Research Shows that...

Athletes get better grades.

Exercise is great for your muscle tone and skin.

Training and practice help you focus mentally.

That's why it's so amazing that many girls don't play *any* sports. If a girl hasn't played sports by the age of ten, there's only a 10 percent chance she'll play sports (or exercise regularly) by the time she's 25. And among younger girls that *do* play sports, many drop out of their programs once they turn 12 or 13.

Maybe part of the problem is that throughout history, people thought it was "not proper" for girls to be active or play sports. What a crock! The Olympics are a good example. The ancient Greeks invented the Olympic games over 2,000 years ago, and women were NOT allowed to compete. Not only that, women were not allowed even to *watch* the games. The fact that the men competed naked probably had something to do with this. ☺

More recently, when the "modern" Olympics started, women were allowed to compete in *some* events. But in the 1928 Olympic Games, some of the women running the 800-meter race collapsed afterwards. They had tried so hard to win that they were tired. Nowadays, we call that "good effort." In 1928, people called it "unladylike"! So all races longer than 200 meters were outlawed for women at the Olympics for the next thirty years. *Can you believe it?*

There was even a theory at the time that if women took part in sports, they'd become "old too soon." One doctor wrote that "women are not . . . built to undergo the strain that men are capable of." Hmmm, he must have forgotten about childbirth!

> *"Sometimes I fall, but landing every jump isn't the point. It's the attempt. It's the effort."*
>
> ~*Sarah Hughes, figure skater*

As recently as 1967, men chased after a woman running in the Boston Marathon. They were trying to rip the contestant number off her back because she was "breaking the rules" by running 26 miles with men. After all, everyone knew that girls couldn't run that far! (Starting in 1972, the Boston Marathon officially began to allow women competitors.)

Although things have improved since then, even today, there are some activities that girls aren't allowed to take part in. Take a look at what we mean:

* *Tag* was banned from an elementary school in Santa Monica, California. WHY? The school's newsletter explained that this was because in Tag, there has to be "a 'victim' or 'It,' which creates a self-esteem issue." *"Tag! You have low self-esteem!"*
* The National Association for Sport and Physical Education has outlawed both *Duck, Duck, Goose* and *Musical Chairs* at school. WHY? Because any sport that "eliminates kids" is not good.
* *Running* was banned at an elementary school's playground in Broward County, Florida.

A school board member said that "to say *no running* on the playground seems crazy" but lawyers changed her mind.

* *Archery* was banned from some high school gym classes in Florida. WHY? Because someone might get shot with an arrow—maybe even in the pancreas. *Wait . . . that rule actually makes sense!*

Now think about the way girls act when they play sports. Research shows that when girls are playing sports with NO boys around, they play hard and try to win. But if boys are in the area, many girls basically stop trying. How strange! There's no law that says you can't be a girl and still be competitive! If a boy is playing with you in your game, try playing *harder,* because you have an advantage. Boys sometimes underestimate a girl's mad athletic skills, which makes it easier for *you* to win!

Stick With It

Chess is a very competitive game, and terrific for *mental* fitness. But only 5 percent of the world's top players are women. One of them, a woman named Xie Jun, was asked why this was. She basically said, "Girls get interested in boys and stop playing chess." Can you believe that? (Luckily, more and more girls are playing chess these days.)

If you are interested in something, *stick with it!* Don't stop playing a sport because a guy you might like is around. Boys appreciate girls who are fit and healthy. And don't worry about a guy seeing you all sweaty. If he likes you too, he'll be cheering you on! The cool guys are interested in girls who are themselves, anyway. Keep your identity! (We're not saying you should exercise just to get attention from boys, but it can be a nice side benefit.)

How to Throw Like a Girl Who's Not "Throwing Like a Girl"

Before we go any further . . .

One of the worst insults a boy can give another boy in sports is to say, "You throw like a girl." How sexist! The stereotype behind the insult is that a girl throws so awkwardly, the ball ends up traveling 10 feet in the wrong direction. This kind of "girl throw" can look like the girl is *pushing* the ball, not *throwing* it.

If that describes the way *you* throw a ball, check out the tips on the top illustration on the following page:

You will need: A ball, a friend to play catch with as you practice.

The next three steps (shown in the illustration below) happen one after another quite quickly:

When you're done throwing the ball, you may find that it went somewhere you didn't want it to, like behind you or off to the side in some weird direction. That just means you need to practice! Keep practicing, and someday, when someone says, "You throw like a girl!" it will be the coolest compliment a girl could receive.

Hold the ball with your fingers, not your palm.

direction the ball will go

Keep your wrist loose!

Turn sideways with your throwing arm on the opposite side of the person you're throwing to.

Feet are shoulder width apart.

Snap your wrist forward at the last second.

Keep your elbow high.

Let your arm follow through.

Raise arm up and reach toward target.

To throw a football, just get your fingers between the ball's laces. (Your little finger should be at about the middle of the laces.) As with a softball, hold the ball with your fingers, not in your palm. Follow the rest of the throwing tips above.

Push off with your back foot.

Step forward with your front foot.

Why Girls Are Better Athletes Than Boys

"I don't have to be enemies with someone to be competitors with her."
~Jackie Joyner-Kersee, Olympic gold medalist and maybe the greatest female athlete of the twentieth century

The reason girls are better athletes than boys has nothing to do with ability. It has everything to do with ATTITUDE. Girls believe in *cooperation, teamwork,* and *sportsmanship.* Boys believe in *winning, looking good,* and *trash-talking!*

As an example of this, our spies have discovered the following secret sports agenda written by a boy from your school. You will be *shocked* at how it shows the ways that boys think about sports.

Today's Secret Sports Agenda

1. Meet Timmy at the gym.
2. Crush Timmy in a game of **H-O-R-S-E**. Then beat him at **P-R-E-T-T-Y-P-O-N-Y** and **M-E-N-I-N-G-I-T-I-S**.
3. Beat Timmy in a game of **One-on-One**. (Unless I count Danny as **one-half**! *Ha ha!*)
4. Game of **Tip-In.** I win. (Hey, there is an "I" in "WIN" and I *always* WIN!)
5. Get out towels to wipe gym floor clean from Timmy's bitter tears.
6. Trash-talking and celebrating.
7. Get a Slurpee. Think about how great I am. (This may take a while.)

We're sorry you had to see the ugly truth about boys, but it was for your own good.

Most girls know that winning is *not* the most important thing in sports. If you won every single game you played, you wouldn't bother playing because there would be no point to it. A good sport knows that the important question is not "Am I winning?" but "Am I having fun?" If the answer is "yes," it does not matter whether you lose a game or not.

After a game is over, congratulate the other team's players if *they* won, and be polite to the losers if *you* won. A good thing to say to a losing team is just "Thanks for the game." (It doesn't make any sense to say "Good game" if you just beat them 58 to 6 in basketball!)

Rock Skipping Tip: Scientists have found that to make a rock skip best, look for a flat rock with small holes in the surface. Then throw it at a 20-degree angle at exactly 25 miles per hour. (Bring a radar gun and protractor with you if you need them.)

Practice, Practice, Practice

"What separates a winner from the rest of the pack is not raw talent or physical ability; instead it is the drive and dedication to work hard every single day."

~Linda Mastandrea, wheelchair athlete

Although a lot of good athletes have natural ability, most of us have to *practice, practice, practice.* (Watching excellent athletes and keeping a positive attitude also helps.) But no matter what sport you play, your confidence and abilities will grow in relation to how much you *practice.*

Which Athlete Type Is Most Like You?

Fiery Competitor: These girl athletes are competitive, and they let it all hang out. They can be heard shouting encouragement from the bench or sidelines when they're not playing. Fiery Competitors aren't afraid of stress and they like highly skilled sports.

Not Afraid to Be Alone: This athlete is self-motivated, and she's also not afraid to perform. But she doesn't need a lot of chatter or crowds, and she hates ball hogs.

Social Player: As long as she can do some talking while she plays, this athlete is happy. Relationships are all-important for her, and she needs a sport that allows for that.

Quiet and Thoughtful: This athlete is an easygoing girl and is not a big fan of high stress sports. But she can be a good team player and is a coach's dream.

If the Shoe Fits . . .

Now see what sport is a good fit for you! The following is not a complete listing of ALL sports, but it might be a good place to get ideas.

"Confidence, self-esteem, time management, discipline, motivation—all these things I learned (whether I knew I was learning or not) through sports."

~*Mia Hamm*

Soccer

Athlete Types: *Fiery Competitor, Social Player, Quiet and Thoughtful*

Your main goal (Get it—*goal?*) should be to grow up healthy. If you want to meet that goal, play soccer! One of the most important things that should take place for a girl is good development of her "bone mass," which is the density and minerals present in her skeleton.

Soccer really is one of the best sports for your bone mass because of its unique combination of jumping, changing direction quickly, kicking, and sprinting. These all really help your bones. *Goal!*

When soccer got its start back in the Middle Ages in England, the games used to involve *hundreds* of players at once. There was no out-of-bounds and full body contact was legal. Because so many people took part in the game, it was feared that there would not be enough archers to defend England if the country were attacked. So starting in 1314, four English kings outlawed soccer.

Obviously, the game became legal again, and soccer is now the most popular women's sport in the world. Still, you won't be surprised to learn that women weren't allowed to play the most popular sport in the world at the Olympics until 1996!

 In 2003, a professional soccer game in Ireland had to be cancelled because of thick fog. One team's goalkeeper, Richard Siddall, was left on the field when everyone else had already left; nobody told him the game was cancelled! Siddall couldn't see through the fog, so he stayed in the goal, afraid that the ball would be kicked at him any moment.

Skateboarding

Athlete Types: *Fiery Competitor, Not Afraid to Be Alone, Social Player*

Some people might think that skateboarding is a "guy" thing, but since more than 25 percent of skaters are girls, that seems like a myth. Another myth about skating is that it isn't really exercise. To that we ask: "Have you seen many chubby skateboarders?"

Although it's not necessary to do tricks to be a skateboarder, you should probably know what some of the most basic ones are. When you're skateboarding, if you're right-footed, you will probably put your right foot toward the front of the board and push off with your left foot. If you can, try switching your feet and riding with your left foot on the board. This is called "goofy-foot," and it allows you to try different tricks and to feel more comfortable on the board.

The first trick a skater usually learns is the *Ollie.* An Ollie is when the skater kicks the front part of the board up off the ground and then lands on it again. To do this, she needs to have her back foot pretty far back on the board (to press down) and her front foot behind the front wheels (so there's less weight there.)

There are all sorts of other flips, shoves, grinds, board slides, grabs, and stalls to try to master, but just keep in mind that when it gets down to it, a skateboard really is transportation. You don't need to get hung up on tricks to enjoy yourself on a board!

Outdoor Sports

Athlete Types: *Quiet and Thoughtful, Not Afraid to Be Alone*

An athlete doesn't *have* to compete with other people. For example, just getting out into the great outdoors is a terrific way to get exercise. Whether it's jogging around a track, hiking on a trail, surfing, or cycling, everything's better in the fresh air.

Let's look at running. All you need are some shoes and yourself. But you don't have to run alone; it's a great exercise to do with others too. And there's a huge variety of distances and routes you can run. Running not only helps with your strength and endurance, it's also great for your body's overall health.

If you're just getting started with running, distance and speed aren't important at all. Just listen to your body and go for as long you can. Or, if you don't like running, a fast walk is easier on the joints and has the same benefits. Hoof it through your neighborhood, explore a city, or go hiking in a park. And hey, there's also rock climbing, windsurfing, waterskiing, snow skiing, snowboarding, or kayaking, just to mention a few.

Maybe you like the *idea* of the outdoors, but it's just too cold outside. *Brrr!* Try "fake" outdoor activities like indoor rock climbing, stationary bike riding, or surfing in your bathtub.

Tennis

Athlete Types: *Quiet and Thoughtful, Fiery Competitor, Not Afraid to Be Alone*

Tennis has some of the cutest outfits of any sport. And no wonder! The game was invented by those famous *fashionistas*, the monks. About a thousand years ago, French monks used to play a game called *jeu de paume*. In this game, a monk would get ready to serve a ball to his opponent, but before he did so, he'd yell, "Tenez!" It was to make sure that the other person was ready: *tenez* is French for *attention*. (Yes, this is where tennis got its name.)

Anyway, French people played *jeu de paume* for centuries, but it took an Englishman named Walter Wingfield to write out the rules for it. Wingfield tried to rename the game *sphairistike,* which was not very catchy. (Wingfield also thought that tennis could be played on any surface, including ice. This gives a new meaning to "*brrrr*eak point.")

Tennis is great exercise for your legs and heart, and it is also good for your foot-work, which could make you a better dancer! This is also one of the few sports where the top women players get as much (or more) attention as the men do. (Other related sports you might want to consider are badminton, pickleball, racquetball, handball, squash, and even Ping-Pong.)

You can see the Problem!

Look Out! After the match is over, be careful! This is when most tennis injuries occur. You see, the winner tries to leap over the net to shake hands with the loser. And then the winner's foot gets caught in the net, and, well, *ouch*.

Can you name the outdoor competitive sport with players competing directly against each other that has more officials than players? That's right, it's tennis! (How'd you guess?)

Volleyball

Athlete Types: *Quiet and Thoughtful, Fiery Competitor, Social Player*

"You can be an athlete and be strong—and also be a girl."

~Gabrielle Reece

If you want to take out some aggression, spike a volleyball! Volleyball is an exciting sport with lots of breaks in the action, and lots of girls take part in it. It is the third most popular high school sport in the United States, and beach volleyball and college-level volleyball have also evolved into really popular sports.

Unlike other competitive team sports like basketball, there is never any physical contact with the players on the other team in volleyball. This is nice if you prefer not to bounce off of other people! But volleyball can still be an aggressive sport. There are still lots of opportunities for dramatic plays, saves, blocks, dives, and spikes.

Sports Bras

Don't let discomfort stop you from playing sports. Just get a good sports bra! You will probably want the type called a **compression bra**. Be sure to try it on before buying one. The bra should have good ventilation and no clasps that dig into your skin. To find out if a sports bra is right for you, jump around a little in it to see if it works properly.

Softball and Baseball

Athlete Types: *Fiery Competitor, Social Player, Quiet and Thoughtful*

This is the number one team sport in the United States. Whether you play girls' softball or Little League baseball, you're going to get good practice with high-skill activities like batting or pitching. (These are great for hand–eye coordination.)

Softball and baseball also get you to use your mind with teamwork and strategy. Because it has a lot of "down" time, softball is definitely one of the more social team sports. If you want to get as much exercise as possible, become a pitcher. They burn more calories than any of the other players!

 Want to be the coolest player on your team? Bring gum or sunflower seeds to a game and share them in the dugout.

Bad Joke Alert!

Q. Why shouldn't you play softball with big cats in Africa?

A. Because they are *cheetahs*.

Water Sports

Athlete Types: *Quiet and Thoughtful, Fiery Competitor, Not Afraid to Be Alone*

Swimming and diving are the ultimate individual sports. Not only do you usually compete by yourself, you can't talk underwater. (Scientists believe that one girl in a hundred can whistle underwater. See if *you* have what it takes!)

There may not be any sport that exercises more muscles in your body than swimming, and it's great for your heart as well. Swimming is sort of like running because it has a huge variety of short sprinting events as well as longer events that require endurance.

One thing that serious swimmers *all* have in common is that they get up *early* in the morning for their workouts. Hitting the water at 6:00 a.m. can be a challenge for some sleepyheads.

 Good News! If you swim a lot and have light colored hair, the chlorine may turn it slightly green!

Swim Strategy Tip! If you are on a swim team, bring a bottle of your own swimming pool's water to any AWAY swim meets you go to. Before your event, pour your bottle of water into the pool. This "friendly" water will help you swim faster!

 Synchronized swimmers have routines that are performed together to music. For a swimming party idea, be creative and put together an "unsynchronized" swim routine that is a disorganized mess!

Before diving or jumping, **ALWAYS MAKE SURE THE WATER IS DEEP ENOUGH TO DIVE INTO.** And don't jump off of anything higher than a regular diving board. (These are usually just a meter over the water's surface.) Once you know it's safe, you can warm up with a nice Cannonball. Extra Olympic points are awarded for creating a big enough splash to get someone wet who *isn't* in the pool.

Once you have mastered the Cannonball, it's time to try its variations.

The Can Opener: This is a Cannonball with one leg extended in front

The Watermelon: A backwards Cannonball

The Hammerhead: A headfirst Cannonball

If you think you can handle it, the toughest of all these Olympic dives is the *Flying Squirrel.* Jump into the water with your arms behind your back, grabbing your ankles!

 Next time you go swimming at your local pool, you may want to keep your head above water. Little kids get in that warm water and just can't help themselves. Experts say that public pools have more pee than chlorine in them.

Basketball

Athlete Types: *Quiet and Thoughtful, Fiery Competitor, Social Player*

Basketball is one of our favorite sports! Maybe that's because it is one of the few team sports that you can practice by yourself. Think about it: you can practice dribbling and shooting anytime, but in other team sports like volleyball or baseball, you have to have at least one other person to practice.

And talk about exercise! Playing basketball takes skills (like using both of your hands) with every kind of body movement there is. In just two minutes of playing basketball, you could be throwing, running, changing directions, and jumping.

Another good thing about basketball is that there's a position for every type of player. It's tough to have a good basketball team without a range of sizes. So if you're a big girl who doesn't mind some physical contact, you can be a superstar!

In 1896, the score of the first official women's basketball game was 2 to 1. One reason was that the rules stated nobody could dribble more than three times.

Canuggling

Athlete Types: *Fiery Competitor, Social Player, Crazy Girl*

Now this is a *really* different sport. "Canuggling" is easy to describe, but hard to do. First, three people get in a canoe. One person stands in the middle and juggles, while the other two paddle. Believe it or not, this is a *sport* because while you do this, you can race other canoes full of people doing the same thing! (No, we did not make this up.)

Figure Skating and Ice-Skating

Athlete Types: *Quiet and Thoughtful, Not Afraid to Be Alone*

"Skating is joy."

~Bonnie Blair

This is a sport people often associate with women. Whether it's ice-skating, figure skating, ice dancing, or ice hockey, they all combine elements of dancing with skating. (Okay, not so much with hockey.) That makes skating one of the most highly skilled sports around. If you've gone skating, you know that just staying up is tough; your whole body is supported by only two thin metal edges!

 Who knew? A "double axel" has nothing to do with cars.

If you are serious about ice-skating, be prepared for a *lot* of practicing. Most competitive ice-skaters practice about 650 hours a year. They compete for around 42 minutes a year. (Compare this to say, a soccer player, who practices about 200 hours a year and competes in games for about 40 hours.)

 Figure skating, gymnastics, soccer, and beach volleyball are among the highest-rated television sports events for women athletes.

Martial Arts

Athlete Types: *Quiet and Thoughtful, Fiery Competitor, Not Afraid to Be Alone*

If you want to develop speed, confidence, and self-discipline, you may want to look into some of the martial arts, like judo or tae kwon do. Plus, one bonus of studying martial arts is you get colored belts as accessories to your outfits!

You don't have to study kung fu death grips to develop your mind-body connection. For example, although tai chi and yoga are not necessarily martial arts, they do share many elements with them. (And they are not *just* for old people, okay?) Martial arts, tai chi, and yoga emphasize flexibility, balance, and stretching. They can also help you become more graceful in your movements, which is always a plus! And you will get terrific muscle tone as well.

 Girls have found that the mental and physical balance these sports require helps them deal with stress and changes in their moods.

Golf

Athlete Types: *Quiet and Thoughtful, Fiery Competitor, Social Player*

Golf is one of the fastest growing sports for girls—about 40 percent of all new golfers are women.

Maybe one reason for golf's popularity is that it doesn't matter what size or shape a golfer is. If she practices, she can do well. Just walking a golf course is good exercise, and the game is so challenging, golfers don't even realize they're getting a workout. It is also a really good game to practice focus, concentration, and self-control.

 The odds of hitting a hole in one are about 13,000 to 1. No problem!

Another advantage of golf is that you can wear a cute outfit! Although blue jeans aren't allowed on some golf courses, most other clothes are fine. Just remember that a round of golf can last around four hours, so it may be chilly when you tee off and hot when you drop your last putt. Bring a hat, sunglasses, and sunscreen.

The biggest downside of golf is that it costs money. You need a golf bag and a bunch of clubs and balls, which are not cheap. You also have to pay to get on the golf course. It's also a very good idea to get lessons if you're a beginner. Try to get some free ones!

 The first woman to play golf was Mary, Queen of Scots. During her rule in the 1500s, she called the young men who carried her bags "cadets" or "caddies." And the name stuck!

Gymnastics (and Flexibility)

Athlete Types: *Not Afraid to Be Alone, Fiery Competitor*

Gymnastics has been around for over 2,000 years. Talk about history! There are four major events in gymnastics, and they all require balance, grace, and strength. Because of this, some people feel that gymnasts are the most *athletic* of all sports participants.

Because of the skills involved with gymnastics, this is also a sport that requires a *lot* of practice. It's not really for the casual athlete. Gymnastics makes it possible to increase your flexibility with training and stretching. Plus, there is evidence that female hormones help make girls flexible! Still, some people are just naturally "extra-stretchy." If you have a friend who is super-flexible, you may call her "double-jointed." This isn't quite accurate as nobody actually has an extra joint in her shoulder or hip.

The joints of your bones have a protective padding called "cartilage." And if a girl has stretchy cartilage, she will also be stretchy. A girl's ligaments also help decide help how flexible she will be. Ligaments are bands of tough tissue that connect bones together. And some people have looser ligaments than others. So if you know someone who can pull her thumb to her wrist or put her ankle behind her head, just sniff and say, "Cartilage and ligaments, that's all it is."

 Jumping on a trampoline is fun!

Squirrel Fishing

And finally, the most fun and exciting sport of all time . . . squirrel fishing.

Ways to Compete:

1. Who can get the most squirrels interested in her peanut?

2. How long does the squirrel stay on the line before getting the nut?

3. How many nearby people think that *you're* a nut?

SquiRReL Fishing!
(It's a Real Sport!)

Supplies: fishing pole (oR a stick with long stRing.)
unshelled peanuts
SquiRRels

If theRe aRe squiRRels neaR wheRe you live, tRY this nutty new spoRt! To get the squiRRels inteRested, spRinkle some loose peanuts aRound the aRea. You'll laugh so haRd that you buRn lots of caloRies with this spoRt.

Tie a peanut to a fishing line.   Wait foR a bite!   She caught one!

DANCE AND CHEERLEADING

"It takes an athlete to dance, but an artist to be a dancer."

~*Shanna LaFleur*

Dancing really can be as tough as any sport, but it's also an *art*. Maybe because dancing is a form of personal expression, we think that girls are usually more interested in dancing than boys. After all, girls will dance with each other, while many boys won't dance at all!

Dancing is important to *all* humans; there are almost no cultures in the world without their own dances. These dances may be for traditional performances or religious ceremonies. For example, in Hinduism, the gods created the universe by dancing! Another use for dancing is storytelling. Hula dancing dates back to ancient Polynesia. The dancers' movements and facial expressions (even their eyes) are used to tell a story. And ballet dancing (which dates back to the 1400s) was originally used for storytelling as well.

 In traditional ballet, the male dancers are *always* supposed to be looking at the ballerina. (And when a ballet calls for an ugly ballerina, a man has to play her!)

Dancing *en pointe*, or up on the toes, was not originally part of ballet. It came about in the early 1800s as a way of making the dancers appear lighter and more graceful. The shoes used to dance *en pointe* have toes reinforced with paper and burlap; a professional dancer will wear out three pairs of these shoes in a week.

 Famous Last Words: Ballerina Anna Pavlova was famous for playing the role of the swan in the production of *La Mort Du Cygne* (the Death of the Swan). Her last words were, "Get my swan costume ready."

Some dancers eventually rebelled against traditional ballet because they thought it was too dainty and "girly." Women like Martha Graham and Isadora Duncan wanted a less formal dance that could allow for more personal expression. In the early twentieth century, these pioneers of dance helped to create a new style called "modern dance."

Martha Graham's new dances were intended to make people *feel* emotions. Shocked audiences sometimes "booed" her performances, but Graham stuck with her style. Her vision ended up starting a revolution in dancing. And since Martha danced until she was 76 years old, she was around to see many of the changes she created.

This opened the door to all sorts of new dance possibilities, and some of them have been pretty wacky. For example, a woman named Jenefer Davies Mansfield once put on a "NASCAR Ballet" production. It had 20 dancers, all wearing race-car outfits prancing and leaping on a racetrack stage. The dancers would leap and run, racing with (and sometimes crashing into) each other. They even had pit crews!

> *"There are shortcuts to happiness, and dancing is one of them."*
> ~*Vicki Baum*

If you think you don't know how to dance, YOU'RE WRONG! All dancers (except the pros) fake it. You don't need to know any moves. Listen to the music and make up your own moves! Or just imitate what the other dancers are doing. One great trick is to mentally pretend that you are a train or a plane or any type of moving machinery. (Well, not *any* type. If you pretend you're a blender while dancing, your friends may have to call 911.)

If you are ever dancing and *run out of moves*, don't panic! Use the same strategy. Just imagine that you are lifting rocks, shielding your eyes from the sun, skipping, boxing, catching a ball, mowing the lawn, taking a shower, surfing, getting rained on, or any other thing you can imagine. Then act it out with your body!

Here are a few other favorite dances:

The "I'm Surrounded by Jell-O" Dance

Look around in confusion as you pretend that Jell-O surrounds you. Then make clumsy swimming motions with your arms and legs as you try to escape from it! Other fun substances to pretend you're surrounded by include outer space, honey, taffy, and fire.

Hippie Helicopter Dance

Although this is a hippie dance that is all about trust and peace, it can also be dangerous! If you are going to dance like a hippie, it is best to do it where there's grass (outside) or a sofa nearby (inside). After all, you might get dizzy and fall down while helicoptering, which can be painful!

Borrow some Grateful Dead from your parents, Phish from your uncle, or String Cheese Incident and MGMT from your hip friend. Put on your peasant dress or tie-dye. Kick off your Birkenstocks. Tilt your head back to look at the stars. (It doesn't matter if there are no stars, because you are going to close your eyes next!)

Stick out your arms and . . . *start spinning*! Spin in rhythm to the music, either clockwise or counterclockwise. Don't go too fast. There's nothing cuter than a girl doing the hippie dance, but there's also nothing more hideous than a girl getting too dizzy and having to switch over to the "Lose Your Cookies Dance."

The Two-Step Mope

When you're in a bad mood and don't feel like dancing, hang your head, leave your arms at your sides, and take a little step to the side, keeping beat with the music. Then take a little step back. Remember to keep a glum expression on your face.

The Body Part Call-Out

For this dance, you don't need a partner, but you do need at least two friends. Pick someone as the Dance Master and spread out a little so that nobody is too near anything. Now put on some good dancing tunes. The Dance Master will call out a body part, such as *right arm*! The dancers now dance, but ONLY with that body part!

The Dance Master will add body parts as the song goes along. And if she wants to, she can subtract body parts to get everyone to stop dancing.

Do the Krump

Many dance moves come from inner-city neighborhoods where creative kids come up with new dance ideas. For example, break dancing got its start with dance competitions in the South Bronx in the 1980s.

Krumping began in the Los Angeles area when a performer named Tommy the Clown invented it to entertain children at birthday parties. Because a clown invented it, krumping is sometimes goofy and a little hard to describe. It combines elements of break dancing, fake fighting, and pretending that you have a severe illness. Krump moves include the *whip* and the *wobble*; there is a lot of chest thrusting, and if you really get carried away with the spirit of the dancing, you are *krumped*!

Q. Why do hula dancers wear grass skirts?
A. Grass pants are too hard to zip up.

Some of our other favorite dances include the following:

Hip-Hop

The Prancing
Unicorn

Jazz

The Electric Slide

Funk

Belly Dancing

The Sprinkler

The Lawnmower

Hand Jive

Cakewalk

The Fandango

The Frug

Hula Dancing

The Hustle

Jive

The Macarena

Rumba

The Shimmy

The Twist

Animal Dances

The Turkey Trot

The Donkey Kick

The Bunny Hop

The Camel Walk

The Chicken Dance

The Chicken Scratch

The Fox Trot

The Funky Chicken

The Jitterbug

The Kangaroo Dip

The Manatee

Be careful, as some of these dances can get you in trouble. Around 1920, a New Jersey woman was sentenced to 50 days in jail because she was caught doing the *Turkey Trot*.

hop

hop hop

Finally, our least favorite dance:

Twerking (please, just don't)

Cheerleading

"We don't live in a democracy, but a cheer-ocracy." ~*from* **Bring It On**

Is cheerleading a sport? Well, you have to be an athlete to be a cheerleader—just try doing a backflip sometime! Cheerleading is being considered as an international Olympic event, and in most high schools and colleges, the faculty member in charge of the squad is called a "coach," not an "advisor."

So maybe it's not that big of a *stretch* to call it a sport that uses dance moves. Heck, the best athletes in your area might be cheerleaders. Of course, there are certain attitudes that some people have about cheerleaders. A cheerleader needs to be outgoing and full of energy. And because they are cheering and smiling *no matter what the score is,* some people think cheerleaders are sort of mindless or fake. Why are they getting so excited about something as meaningless as a game? But it doesn't seem fair to pick on someone just for being positive and energetic!

Besides, cheerleaders don't *just* wave pom-poms around and say, *"Go! Fight! Win!"* (Although we've never heard a cheer that went *"Run away! Give up! Lose!"*) Cheerleaders can be high-flying stuntgirls who tumble, do gymnastics, and dance. It's gotten to the point that cheer-leading squads perform their routines at their own competitions. And the audiences cheer the cheerleaders, not the game. (That's because at those competitions there is no game!)

Cheerleading might even be considered an *extreme sport.* In U.S. high schools, cheerleading injuries cause more days of school missed than football. Out of all girls' sports, more than half of all bad accidents that occur are from cheerleading.

Like other athletes, cheerleaders can't wear jewelry while performing. Many squads also have strict hairstyle guidelines. Bangs and "wispies" can be dangerous because they might get in a girl's eyes while she's trying to catch another girl who's falling through the air. "They're as dangerous as a football player not wearing a helmet," one cheerleading coach said.

Busting an Illegal Move! In Ann Arbor, Michigan, a group of high school cheerleaders witnessed a hit-and-run accident. Because it's easy to forget a license plate number, the cheerleaders began chanting it over and over until it was fixed in their memo-ries. The man who had fled the scene of the accident was later found because of the cheerleaders' skills!

Make Up Your Own Cheers

We have often enjoyed making up our own cheers and then putting together dance routines to go with them. Just pick a theme or mood and come up with a cheer.

The Mean Cheer

(*Yell this cheer with a big, bright smile to throw people off!*)
Kill, kill!
Maim, hate!
Murder-mangle-mutilate!

The Dynamite Cheer

We are dynamite, our team is dynamite!
We're tick-tick, tick-tick, tick-tick, tick-tick,
BOOM! Dynamite! Boom-boom! Dynamite!

Airhead Cheer

(*Pretend you're really vain and not too bright for this one.*)
Totally! For sure! I just got a manicure!
Look up! Over there! That girl has really pretty hair!
Go, go, fight, fight! Gee, I hope I look all right!

LIES, MEAN GIRLS, AND JERKS

"The only thing worse than a liar is a bad liar."

~*Lucy Liu*

Lies

Everyone lies. Sometimes a person has to! For example, you might lie to a friend because you care about her feelings and being honest won't be helpful. As one girl put it, "The truth hurts. That's why I lie." Adults call these kinds of lies "white lies." But whatever color they are, are all lies bad? If a person tells a *kindly fib,* this might be the kind of lie that is okay. And as you know, girls often give each other kindly fibs so that their friends feel better about themselves.

Unfortunately, most lies probably AREN'T kindly fibs. So when and where are you most likely to be lied to? Answer: *When you're on the phone.* A study of liars found that about 30 percent of lies are told during phone calls, and 25 percent happen during face-to-face conversations. Text messaging and chat rooms are where another 20 percent of lies get unloaded. But if you want to know the *truth,* read your *e-mail.* I know, they're hopelessly old fashioned, but the *fewest* lies show up in e-mail messages.

There is a *World's Biggest Liar* contest held each year. Contestants compete by telling stories, and judges decide whose lies are the most entertaining. One year, the winner of the Biggest Liar contest was later accused of *cheating.* See, the liars are supposed to make up their lies on the spot, and this liar prepared notes beforehand. Wow. Can you believe a liar would cheat?

> *The Japanese have a pretty honest society.* For instance, the Tokyo Lost and Found Center has about $20 million in cash turned into it each year by people who find lost wallets and purses. Most of this money makes it back to the original owners! ☺

How to Spot a Liar

Girls are often good at "reading people." This means they can sometimes sense when a lie is being told. How? Below are some of the signs that you may already be able to spot without even thinking about it. BTW, there is no single rule about lying that applies to everyone. Noticing any of the following doesn't *prove* the person is lying. (For a complete rundown of how to spot even professional liars, read *The Big Book of Spy Stuff*.)

Eyes: It's been said that a liar can't look you in the eye. This isn't true. It's possible to lie with normal eye contact. But if the person can't look away from you OR can't look at you, then she MAY be lying.

If the person's eye starts twitching, she's probably nervous about something. Also, some people believe that *right-handed* liars look toward their *left* when they lie and *left-handed* liars look toward their right. Finally, liars often DO blink more than normal!

Voice: It is stressful to lie, so a liar's voice tends to go higher than normal. Liars also tend to talk fast. However, if the liar has to invent a lie on the spot, he will slow way down and look upwards as he searches for the best story.

If the person is *really* feeling the stress, there may be stuttering and a lot of pauses and mumbling. Liars also use "filler words" like *er, um, duh, uh,* or *help me I'm a big fat liar*.

Like, Surprise! A scientific analysis of about 12,000 conversations found that men use "like" more frequently than women.

Fake Smiles and Fake Laughing: It isn't THAT hard to spot a fake smile, because liars only smile with their *mouth*. What we mean is that a true smile affects the whole face, so that the corners of the eyes will "crinkle" up and you can see the smile in the eyes. If a person has a thin-lipped, clenched-teeth smile that doesn't crinkle the eyes, it's probably a fake!

Another giveaway is if the person sucks her lips in OR licks her lips a lot.

As for laughter, a laugh is only real if the person closes his eyes as he laughs. If

Which girl is REALLY smiling?

your suspect starts laughing but is watching you with open eyes when he does, look out! He might be a lying laugher. (Or a laughing liar!)

Micro-Expressions: Most facial expressions (smiles, grimaces, sneers, etc.) only last about a second. But a *micro*-expression is what happens when a person is lying and she is trying NOT to make an expression. These micro-expressions may last one-fifth of a second. Even a good liar will sometimes have these fast little facial expressions, especially when she is asked a question and answers it with a lie. It may be a smile or frown, or a look away.

Body Language: Some liars use much more body language than truth-tellers. They tend to touch, rub, or tug on their ears, nose, and eyes, as well as readjusting their clothes.

But a liar who feels really defensive may have fewer hand gestures than usual, or his hands may go into his pockets and never come out. A defensive liar like this may cross his legs and arms. If he's seated, his legs may bounce and twitch.

Word Use: Liars tend to use phrases like "To tell the truth," "Really," "Honestly," "Actually," "No kidding," and "Seriously" more than usual. Other statements to beware of include:

"Trust me."
"Why would I lie?"
"I swear on my sock drawer."
"I'd never lie to you."
"You can ask anyone!"
"I've never told a lie in my life, and I'm not going to start now."

A person who ends their statement with *"All right?" "Don't you agree?" "You know what I'm talking about?"* or other questions that try to get you to agree with what she said is also possibly lying. Or she may just be insecure.

Finally, a person who is lying uses *contractions* less, and emphasizes their denials. For example, instead of saying "I didn't do it," she will say "I did NOT do it!"

 If a person has *pseudomania,* he has a compulsion to lie even when there's no reason to. Does this sound like anyone you know? They are also called *compulsive liars,* but that is not as fun to say as *pseudomaniacs.*

A survey of people in Italy found that Italians tell between five and 10 lies a day. In that country, the number one lie was, "Don't worry; it's been taken care of." In second place was, "It's nice to see you."

How to Lie

Don't lie! This will save you a lot of trouble. But if you have to tell a *kindly fib,* just avoid the common mistakes listed above. The key to telling a lie is to *believe* it. Sadly, if you tell yourself a lie enough times, it will seem like the truth to you. This doesn't mean that you *pretend* to believe the lie; this means that you *actually* believe it. You're basically brainwashing yourself. Although washing is healthy, brainwashing isn't. *So don't lie!*

A SHOCKER! Despite the song, a liar's pants rarely catch on fire.

Mean Girls

"Mean girls are like milk that gets left out of the refrigerator too long. They started out good, but then they turned sour."
~Amanda Rutabaga

Where do Mean Girls come from? Do they wake up one morning, look in the mirror, and decide, "I'm going to be mean"? Or does a fairy come by and sprinkle magical "Mean Girl" fairy dust on them? Nobody knows. But this section of the book is dedicated to the question: *Bad girls, bad girls, whatcha gonna do?*

Mean Girls are not exactly *bullies.* Of course, there are some Mean Girls who might actually *punch* you. (They are called "Cave Girls.") But since girls are different from boys, girl bullies are often different from boy bullies. For example, Mean Girls can actually be nice when someone is watching. But because they're so sneaky and sly, it can be hard for an outsider to spot Mean Girls being mean.

One Mean Girl technique is to get all her friends to hate her

Mean Boy!

Mean Girl!

"enemy." To get everyone on her side, the Mean Girl might try to "scapegoat" her victim. (A *scapegoat* is someone who gets *blamed* for everything that is wrong, whether it is her fault or not.) Everything the scapegoat does is WRONG. If she has long hair, it should be *short*. If she raises her hand in class, she is a *show-off*. If she is quiet, she is *stuck up*. Scapegoats get harassed with name-calling, cold shoulders, rumors, and teasing. It's so stupid.

 No Kidding! Don't you hate it when a Mean Girl says something mean, and then adds, "Just kidding." Like that helps!

But why do some girls get picked on? It might just be because they are *different* and they dare to be themselves. It's like the Mean Girls are the Perfection Police, and they decide what is okay and what isn't. They will pick on girls who are too smart, or not smart enough, or too pretty, or not pretty enough, or overweight, or really funny or *whatever*. A girl who really is *herself* might annoy a Mean Girl who kissed her brain good-bye just to be "popular."

Someday you may find yourself the victim of a group of Mean Girls. They might say nasty things about you or write anonymous notes that put you down. Sure, we've all been told that *sticks and stones may break my bones, but words can never hurt me.* Mean Girls have proven what a load of baloney that is! If someone says something mean, it can hurt for *years*.

 When **Queen Elizabeth I (1533-1603)** found out who had published a nasty pamphlet about her, she had the authors' right hands cut off. Now there's an idea! (Or not.)

Wait! We Have an Important Question

Have **YOU** ever been a Mean Girl? It's possible, you know! Have you ever treated someone as an enemy for no good reason? Has jealousy or competition ever made you treat someone badly? This is a good thing to wonder about from time to time. It keeps us honest!

For the moment, let's say that a Mean Girl is treating you badly. You can just silently take her abuse, which isn't very healthy or satisfying. Or you can do something about it. Here are some strategies for your action plan:

1. Tell an adult and get help. Sure, he or she would have to be pretty "with it" to know how to help. But still.

2. Avoid the Mean Girls when possible. (Duh!)

3. Be patient and wait for the Mean Girl to either move to another state or to stop being mean. (It's fun to wish.)

4. Let your own *sense of humor* help you.

Having a sense of humor about life might not solve your problems, but it will make things better. If you can laugh at the Mean Girl (and yourself), somehow it relieves the tension and makes the world a better place. Your humor may be shown when you smile to yourself at how lame the Mean Girl is when she is nasty.

You can also use humor for self-defense. For example, if you hear a Mean Girl diss your friend, sincerely say, "Wow, and she always says such sweet things about you." The Mean Girl probably won't get it, but you'll be able to smile and walk away. (BTW, that's why they call these *one-liners*. You use ONE, and then move on while you're still ahead. Don't get into a cut-down contest!)

Comebacks to Save for a Mean Girl on a Rainy Day

* Have you been getting a lot of "get well" cards?
* Your outfit *must* be reversible. Try it inside out. You've got nothing to lose!
* Are you getting dizzy? Because the world is revolving around you really fast.
* You put the *duh* in *dumb*.
* Two words: *fashion roadkill*.
* Nice top. Who shot the sofa?

- Would you like to borrow my baseball mitt so you can catch a clue?
- *Looking at her clothes:* Somewhere there's a horse missing its blanket.
- *The worst thing to say to a mean girl:* You are a total waste of makeup.

Other Useful Terms for Self-Defense

A skinny mean girl is a *"skeletor."*
Mean Girls at the mall are *"hags with bags."*
Other useful words include *Ditz, Girl-Goyle, Thicko, Icky, Fluff 'n' Stuff, Eejit, Ninny,* and *Barbie.*

Mean Girl Strategy Tip

If you're outgoing and don't mind making a scene, just scream "**What is your problem?!**" to a Mean Girl if she is really bothering you. This will be sooo embarrassing for her that the Mean Girl might just avoid you in the future.

Jerks

"No one can make you feel inferior without your consent."
~**Eleanor Roosevelt**

Boy bullies (also known as Jerks or Creeps) tend to be *insulting.* A Jerk usually wants to hurt your feelings or get you angry. Whatever a Jerk says to you, try to *keep your cool.* If you get upset, that's exactly what he wanted. After all, consider the source: A boy who doesn't know anything about you? *Please.* His opinion shouldn't count for anything.

So how should you deal with a Jerk? If a Jerk says something mean to you and you just blush and walk away, that encourages him. He has no reason to leave you alone because you're an easy victim!

All of us fantasize about what we wish we said to the mean person who insulted us. Maybe it would be better to just SAY it and not wish we had. Sadly, there is no perfect thing to say to a Jerk, but try something odd enough to startle him and make him think.

Jerk: Why are you so flat?

Girl: I loaned my chest to a friend of mine. Maybe a friend of yours with a brain will do the same thing for you.

After saying something unexpected ("You look like amphibian poop!"), be sure to walk away while the Jerk tries to figure it out. Other odd things to call Jerks that will buy you some "walking away" time include Pelican Head, Biscuit Pants, Idiot Boy, Dillweed, and Mouth-Breather. You get the idea.*

Special Note

There is a special kind of Jerk who might be mean to you because he has a crush on you. He's just too immature to know how to deal with his feelings. (We know this sounds like a lame movie idea, but it's true!)

If you want a slightly longer comeback, here are two of our favorites:

1. Somebody's been drinking a lot of Nerd Juice.

2. Did your parents have any sons?

 If a smart-alecky boy asks you if you wear "over-the-shoulder boulder holders," ask HIM if he has on an "under-the-butt nut hut." Then watch him back away in fear and confusion.

Of course, there are always adults that might be able to help. Aside from the usual parents, teachers, and counselors, if you can find a way to speak to a Jerk's mother, your problems may be solved. The odds are that if she finds out her little Junior is being mean to girls, he'll be in BIG trouble. If you need to talk to a teacher or your parents to get word to the Jerk's mom, then *talk to a teacher or your parents.*

 Want to get the *last* laugh? Move to Russia. Women there live an average of 13 years longer than men! ☺

Revenge!

Yeah, yeah, we know that every book you've ever read and every adult you've ever known has said revenge is wrong. *And it's true.* But stay tuned for an important news bulletin:

Revenge won't make you a better person, but it CAN make the world a better place.

---

* In case you don't, you could also call a boy bully a *gobdaw, fribble, drongo, chowderhead, muppet, apple-knocker, flapdoodle, gink,* or *parrot face.*

Here's how: There are a lot of really bad things a person *can't* get arrested for. For example, a girl *can't* be arrested for lying or backstabbing someone. So what prevents her from doing that? Hopefully, her own conscience! But if that's not enough, it's probably *the fear of revenge.* Part of what keeps people in line is that someone might "get them back."

Wanting to get revenge on someone who's done you wrong is an instinct. It satisfies a girl's need for justice. It's wrong, but it's also *natural.* So maybe you feel like it's time to get revenge. Here are the guidelines:

1. Nobody can actually get hurt. *Duh.*

2. You can't wait more than a *month* to get revenge on someone. *By then, your foe will have forgotten what she did wrong.*

3. **YOU HAVE TO TAKE CREDIT FOR YOUR REVENGE.** No whispers behind the person's back, and no gossip. *If you can't do this, forget the whole thing.*

Since those are pretty tough guidelines to live by, you may want to try some other options instead. Think about the nasty things *you* may have done to other people before. The odds are, you have been the villain in another person's revenge fantasy! And once you know that, it can help you to feel a little differently about your villain. Maybe you can't forgive her, but at least you can rise above her.

Finally, think about what a great life you have. Don't let some nincompoop mess it up!

Five hundred years ago in China, a girl could take revenge by sprinkling **chopped-up tiger whiskers** in her foe's food. Because tiger whiskers have barbs, the victim would suffer uncomfortable digestion after eating.

112

ICK

"A girl can hide her diary for years, but she can't hide her disgust for one second."

~**Korean proverb**

Things that are sort of disgusting or scary make us want to look *away* from them and at them at the same time. That's why we cover our eyes during a horror movie, and then peek through our fingers. It's sort of like a two-way magnet: it repels and attracts us!

"What is icky?" is sort of the opposite of *"What is beautiful?"* You *think* that certain things are gross or beautiful because you've been *taught* that they are. (So maybe grossness is only skin deep!)

That's why little kids don't think *anything* is gross or disgusting. For instance, two-year-olds don't know what "icky" means. A toddler will put anything in his mouth, and we mean *anything*. To study this, researchers put grasshoppers into milk glasses and offered them to kids of different ages. The two- to three-year-olds just tried to drink the milk anyway. The four- to five-year-olds usually took the grasshoppers out of the glasses and *then* tried to drink the milk. But by age seven, most kids understood the concept of "icky," and they would not drink the milk once the grasshopper swam a few laps in the glass.

But maybe we call the *wrong* things "icky." For example, we are taught not to pick our noses because it's *disgusting*. But a German doctor named Friedrich Bischinger believes that you *should* pick your nose, and also eat the boogers because it "is a great way of strengthening the body's immune system." His theory is that there are lots of bacteria in your nose, and by the time you digest the bacteria, it works like a medicine. (And boogers actually do have Vitamin C in them.) Could it be true? *Nah!*

Earwax

Let's warm up with the lightweight icky stuff. You probably know that earwax is designed to catch dirt and keep it from getting into your ears and creating problems. What we bet you DON'T know is that earwax comes in two different types. Asian and Native American people have "dry" earwax, which is gray and hard. Hispanics, blacks, and white people have "wet" earwax, which tends to be orange and oily. So now you know the earwax difference! (And knowing is half the battle.)

Health

Is your heart in the right place? Some people have a condition called *situs inversus*. This is when a person's internal organs are *reversed*. Instead of having your heart on your left side, it's on your *right* side.

The human body has all sorts of variations, and they're more interesting than icky. For instance, between one and two people out of 100 have an extra nipple somewhere on their body. Huh! And humans are sometimes born with a tail. These are usually removed by surgery shortly after birth.

Bathroom Stuff

What goes on in bathrooms happens behind a locked door for a reason. But sometimes a girl has to yell *through* the bathroom door and ask important questions like: "Who left the seat up?" or "Can you bring me some toilet paper?"

It's very annoying that boys don't put the seat down. But for some reason, not only do most guys like to pee standing up, they also like to pee *onto* or *into* something. If a boy was all alone in a huge field, with only one tree really FAR away, he would hike to the tree and pee *against* it. It must be an instinct!

If you have trouble with men leaving the seat up in your house, you may want to get a German invention called the *Water Closet Ghost*. The *WC Ghost* is installed on the back of the toilet seat. It has a voice that is activated when the seat is lifted. It scolds the person for having the bad manners to lift the seat and reminds him to put it back down when he's done. Almost two million of these have been sold in Europe!

> The German slang word *sitzpinkler* means "man who sits to pee." It also means "wimp."

> It is illegal to NOT flush a toilet in Singapore. Talk about an embarrassing ticket to get!

A woman named Barbara May once invented a portable toilet for vans and SUVs. Called the *Indipod,* this device makes it possible to drive from, say, New York to Los Angeles without using any public restrooms. So if you're "on the go" and you HAVE to *go,* you can GO!

Is your bladder shy? Seven percent of girls and boys have a condition know as "shy bladder." This condition makes it impossible to pee when someone else is nearby. The person can't relax and "let go" unless she's alone. If you ever have a problem with this, try thinking of Niagara Falls. And be thankful you're a girl and that you get stall privacy. Boys with shy bladder have to stand at the urinal with strangers to the left and the right, staring at the wall and trying to pretend those other people aren't there. That *can't* be easy.

> A little less than 50 percent of people get weird-smelling pee after eating asparagus.

Different cultures have different attitudes about pee. In the United States, people avoid it like crazy. You probably wash your hands carefully after going pee, but pee has *no* germs. It's sterile! Pee actually *kills* germs because it has ammonia in it. (Wash your hands anyway, though.)

Other cultures are not as worried about pee; as a matter of fact, some think that it's *good* for you! This theory is called "urine therapy" (thera-*pee*!) and it has been used in India longer than anyone can remember. In urine therapy, people use pee for eardrops, lotion, and even as medicine to be swallowed. (*Gulp!*) Believers argue that pee is good for colds, the flu, asthma, and a number of other problems. Pee contains *urea*, which is a protein often found in lotions, and it's supposedly good for curing acne. As a matter of fact, an old Mexican custom was to use a boy's warm urine on skin rashes.

 The average girl will pee about 7,500 gallons of urine in her lifetime.

We almost hate to mention *poop*, because it isn't ladylike. But it turns out that poop can actually be useful! For example, in Japan, it can be found in beauty products. The Tokyo Sewer Bureau heats and squishes poop until it looks like marble. This "stone" can then be used in bricks, for vases, and even for earrings or necklaces. It is called "metro-marble," but if you want to call it "butt jewelry," we'll understand.

Since we humans have been around for thousands of years, people have needed to wipe "the dew off the lily" for a long time. But toilet paper wasn't even invented until a few hundred years ago! The first toilet paper was made in China, and it measured two by three feet. Either the emperor had a huge butt, or he used a portion and folded it, then used a different portion and folded it. *Toilet origami!*

 The average American girl uses 57 sheets of toilet paper daily.

In the United States, cheap toilet paper on a roll wasn't available until the 1880s. Our question is, **WHAT THE HECK** were people wiping their bums with all those years? As it turns out, your ancestors probably used a lot of moss, grass, straw, and leaves. There were also more creative "wipers" as well. Here are some of them:

 Cold weather folks like Eskimos and Siberians used snow. *Brrrr!!*

 The Vikings used handfuls of wool. Other people in the Middle Ages used "gompf" sticks, which were designed to, uh, *scrape.* (Yikes!)

Early American settlers used corncobs. We have no comment.

French big shots used pretty lace napkins. (What a waste!)

Ancient Romans had a short stick with a sponge attached to the end of it. The sponge was soaked in salt water and then rubbed around. (This actually seems like it would work pretty well!)

Many campers desperate to wipe with *something* have accidentally grabbed the leaves of poison oak. As you know, this results in itching and swelling. Please put this book down now and try not to think about it.

Very Disturbing News: Even though you can buy it at *any* market, 3 percent of Americans *don't use any toilet paper at all!*

Gas

We all know how horrible it is when somebody "hotboxes" or passes gas in an enclosed space. Believe it or not, this is actually against school rules in some places. For example, in Ireland, a boy hotboxed horribly in a classroom. He admitted to being a WMD (Weapon of Mass Distraction) and was suspended from school for two days. (Maybe the most important rule he broke was that you're never supposed to admit it!)

As you know, if somebody passes gas, the guilty party (always a boy!) will deny the gas is his, saying, "She who smelt it, dealt it." We encourage you to use any of these useful comebacks to that lame phrase:

☺ He who rejected it, ejected it.
☺ He who denied it, refried it.
☺ He who contradicts it, made the butt bongo mix for it.
☺ He who disowned it, should atone for it.
☺ He who declined it, land-mined it.

The Devil Made Me Do It! Pumpernickel bread is a German rye bread. The name roughly translates to *farting devil* bread. That's because your body creates a lot of gas trying to digest the *nickels*. (And the *Pumper* is no picnic either.)

Food

So here's the thing. People in certain parts of the world eat lots of things we might find unusual. They might feel the same way about your food, for example mayonnaise or beef. But can we accept their choices and not think of their food as "gross"? For example, in Peru and Argentina, many people consider cat meat a delicacy. If you think that's gross, how is eating a cow or a *pig* better than eating a *cat*?

And if one culture eats cats, you just know that another one will eat dogs. One Native American tribe's name (Arapahoe) actually means "dog-eater." In southern China and Korea, dog is considered a good food for the winter months.

Even though guinea pigs are only a mouthful, people have enjoyed eating them in Peru for the last 4,500 years. Peruvians say that the guinea pig tastes like cat. That seems odd; shouldn't it taste like *pork*? Or chicken? ☺

It's no secret that humans eat different kinds of birds, but you may not know that people also eat birds' *nests*. In Southeast Asia, swifts build nests high on ocean cliffs. The nests are made from moss, seaweed, hair, fish parts, twigs, and mostly from bird spit. We don't know who came up with the bright idea of taking a nest and putting it into a soup, but take our word for it: birds' nest soup is popular *and* expensive. A good bowl of it can cost hundreds of dollars!

Surprisingly, the two foods we've saved for last are from plants. First up is the large and dangerously spiked Southeast Asian fruit called *durian*. This fruit smells so bad, it is illegal to have in Singapore. (It has an odor somewhere between moldy cheese and *really* moldy cheese.) If you break open the 12-pound fruit and survive the aroma, you're ready to eat its pudding-like pulp. It stinks so much that eating the durian has been compared to "eating ice cream in an outhouse."

But perhaps the worst food idea we've ever heard comes from Mark Nuckols, the man who invented *Hufu*. Hufu is sort of like tofu (bean curd) except it is designed to look and taste like, uh, human. Mark came up with the idea of Hufu so that cannibals could enjoy their favorite meat without getting thrown in jail. (He based the flavor of Hufu on cannibal descriptions of what it should taste like.) The Hufu motto: *It's the healthy human flesh alternative.*

Hairballs

Watch your cat cleaning itself. See how it licks its fur carefully? The fur goes into the cat's mouth and gets swallowed. Fur (and hair) cannot be digested, and sometimes it accumulates in the cat's stomach. If enough hair gathers there, it may get to the point where the cat hacks up a hairball on the carpet. *Blech!*

💬 **Missouri's unofficial nickname is the "Puke State."**

More disgusting than this are *human* hairballs. And not just from the clumps that come from cleaning hairbrushes. You see, girls sometimes chew on their own hair. The hair accumulates in their stomachs, and there it is: a hairball. Human hairballs are called *bezoars.* (You may have read about them in *Harry Potter.*)

Sometimes a bezoar will stay in a girl's stomach for years and then come out. There are *two* ways it can come out (and we don't think we have to spell that out for you). Here's the nasty part: because the bezoar has been soaking in stomach acid for a long time, when it finally shows up, the hairball can be rock hard. As a matter of fact, people used to think that bezoars *were* rocks. Since large rocks don't normally come out of flesh-and-blood girls, bezoars were believed to be magical. They were supposed to be able to cure poisoning and even baldness!

(If you want more of this revolting—but educational!—material, see *The Big Book of Gross Stuff.*)

NICKNAMES, HANDWRITING, WORDS, AND DOODLES

"A wife should no more take her husband's name than he should hers. My name is my identity and must not be lost."

~Lucy Stone

Even if you gamble away everything you own playing Candyland, you will always have your name! That is, unless you gamble your name away too . . . but then you would be a *nameless soul,* wandering about without purpose. But *with* your name you have a purpose: to be yourself!

Names are very important to us. Even the quietest kid will correct the teacher if her name is mispronounced during roll on the first day of school. Odds are that *your* name has a rich history and a cool meaning. For example, Olivia is a pretty popular name. Who would have guessed that *Olivia* is the Latin word for "olive"? Amazing! Or how about *Samantha*? This is an ancient name from the Middle East that means "good listener." Cool!

When someone tests a new pen, the odds are almost 100 percent that she will write her name with it.

Try looking up your name to learn about it. Also, since your parents picked your name, you should find out why they picked the name they did. Ask them! They may pretend they don't know the information you want, or they might even pretend not to know you. Be persistent!

You: Why did you pick my first name?

Your dad: I don't remember.

You: I see. Can you give me an example of something else you can't remember?

Your dad: Uh . . . what?

You: Did you like the sound of my name?

Your dad: Yes. Your name rhymes with platypus, and that has always been one of our favorite animals.

Other good questions to ask:

What were the discussions about your name like? Were there *arguments*?

What were some other *possibilities* for your name? (These are always interesting!)

What would your name have been if you were a *boy* instead of a *girl*?

A Native American tribe called the Cree names their babies after the first animal the parents see once the child is born.

The Most Popular Girl Names

Just like clothes, names go in and out of fashion. What is popular one year isn't popular the next. Sure, sometimes a name has a good run. For example, *Jessica* was the top girl's name from 1970 to 1984. And *Emily* was number one from 1996 to 2007. But then there was an upset, and *Emma* took top spot!

Hmm, I guess that's not much of an upset.

How many girls do you know with the following names? Here are the most recent top ten girl's names in the United States, starting with number one:

Sophia	*Emily*
Emma	*Abigail*
Isabella	*Mia*
Olivia	*Madison*
Ava	*Elizabeth*

Here are the top five girl's names from way back in 1990:

Jessica

Ashley

Brittany

Amanda

Samantha

You want *boys*, too? Okay, here is the most recent list of the top ten boy's names:

Jacob

Mason

Ethan

Noah

William

 There are thousands of girls in the United States named Lexus. But what about Porsche?

The Worst Girl Names

After doing a wide survey, we have concluded that these are the worst girl's names:

Bimberly

Brunhilda

Chinchilla

Crayola

Fern

Hortense

Latrina

Michelina

Mossie

Pepsi

Prunella

Rotunda

Salmonella

Tamale

Velveeta

Yeti

Zona

No Bad Names Allowed

"What's in a name? That which we call a rose
By any other name would smell as sweet."
~William Shakespeare, Romeo and Juliet

There was once a fuzzy little fruit from New Zealand that nobody ever ate. It was called the *Chinese gooseberry*. It was so unpopular that someone decided to change the fruit's name to *kiwifruit*. How cute! Sales of the kiwifruit went through the roof, even though the fruit still tasted the same. It was the *name* that made the difference. (The same thing happened to *Hen's Turd Apples*. As soon as they were called *Orange Pippin Apples*, sales improved. Go figure!)

Denmark has the strictest "name laws" of any country in the world. The Danes restrict parents from giving kids any name considered "unusual." This is to prevent kids from getting teased about their names. There are 4,000 approved girl names that parents can choose from. (The boys list only has 3,000!) Babies sometimes remain nameless for months while the parents try to persuade the government to allow a name not on the approved list. Banned names include Pluto, Monkey, and Anus. (Well, that makes sense!) Legal names include Jiminico, Fee, and Molli. Oh, and the name Tessa is not allowed in Denmark, because *tessa* means "to pee" in Danish.

Celebrity Fake Names

"I arrived in Hollywood without having my nose fixed, my teeth capped, or my name changed. That is very gratifying to me."
~*Barbra Streisand*

People will do almost anything to become famous. Often, one of the first things they do is change their name. Name your favorite actress or music star and the odds are that he or she was born as somebody else, especially if their name sounds too cool to be real. (For example, Vin Diesel was originally Bob Snider.) Maybe their name just changed a little bit, like with Reese Witherspoon. She was born Laura Jean Reese Witherspoon, so she just subtracted a little!

But lots of male music stars go through *big* name changes. Snoop Lion (also known as Snoop Dogg) was born Calvin Cordozar Broadus, Bruno Mars was Peter Hernandez, and Elton John was Reginald Kenneth Dwight. How about O'Shea Jackson, better known as Ice Cube? But our favorite name change is from an artist known as Ginuwine. His original name was Elgin Lumpkin. That's right: Elgin Lumpkin!

You can make up fake celebrity names by imagining what would happen if

celebrities got married and combined their names. If the actress Bea Arthur married the musician named Sting, she'd be Bea Sting! What if Snoop Dogg married Winnie the Pooh? He'd be Snoop Dogg Pooh. ☺

YOUR Celebrity Name

Since celebrities change their names around to make them sound better, here's one way to figure out a new movie star name for *you*. Take the name of the first dog you ever owned. If you've never owned a dog, take the name of the first pet your family ever owned. (Or one that your parents owned, or the name of a favorite neighbor's pet. Be creative!)

Now get the name of the first street you ever lived on. If that street is just a number, like 157th Avenue, go with any street NAME that you have lived on or that is near you.

You now have your movie star name! For example, let's say your first pet was a cat named Sheba, and the first street you lived on was York Street. Your movie star name is Sheba York!

This is a lot of fun to do with your friends. You may get a name that sounds like a rich kid (Willow Huntington), an organic Native American (Lima Cherokee), or a strange fairy tale character (Thumbelina Crispin).

Your Letters

The greatest invention of all time is *language*. Once written language was invented, girls could write down their thoughts and feelings. Thousands of years later, people can read what these girls thought and know more about them. This makes written language like a time machine!

And all you need for this time machine are the letters of the alphabet. Our alphabet is usually called the *Roman alphabet,* and it's been around for thousands of years. It is the most commonly used writing system in the world. We are [CLAP-CLAP] Number One!

Alphabet Discrimination! There are many different alphabets in the world, but Campbell's Alphabet Soup only comes in the Roman alphabet. This is outrageous! We have a dream that someday Alphabet Soup will be available in Hebrew, Greek, Arabic, and Hindi alphabets. Maybe we'll leave the Cambodian alphabet out, though. It has 74 letters, and we're not that hungry!

The Romans thought that each *letter* of their alphabet had important values, so the letters in a child's name were carefully selected because some of the letters were good and some were bad. The letters that were picked to be the *initials* for a name were doubly important because they could affect a kid's future personality.

For fun, write out your *full* name (first, middle, and last) and see how you score in the old Roman system of letter values. Put a face score over the letters of your name as you read the score of the letter, and double-score your initials. If you end up with a good score, you rule! (But if you get a bad score, take it easy . . . We're pretty sure it doesn't mean anything!)

Letter	What It Means	Score
A	A is a first-class letter! The Greeks called it alpha, and it is associated with excellence and beginnings. The use of "A" as the top grade on report cards has been around for over a hundred years in the United States. (The letter "A" can also make a lot of different sounds, like in this sentence: *Was Alicia's pa all pale?*) ☺	
B	B is a good letter, but it's always going to be second best. People with a lot of "B"s in their name are good at compromising and being team players. Try pinching your nose closed and saying "My mom married my dad." (It'll sound like "By bom buried by dad.") ☺	
C	C is *consistent*, but not that great. Heck, it's only average! One thing it has going for it is that it can make more sounds than any other letter in the alphabet. Say *Circus cheese from the ocean* out loud and you'll see what we mean. ☺	
D	The Romans thought D was the letter of lazy people! It shows low energy and lack of motivation. Sorry! ☹	
E	E is the most commonly used letter in writing. It also stands for optimism and looking at the positive side of things. ☺	
F	F is the only letter used in report card grades that stands for something. "Failure!" Rats. Back in Roman days, people thought that "F" stood for violence too. ☹	
G	G is a letter of energy and activity. Some might say "hyperactivity"! For people who like to move and travel, this is a ☺.	
H	If you want to succeed in life, H is the letter for you. It shows ambition and the desire to get ahead. ☺	

Letter	What It Means	Score
I	There is a reason why the word "I" stands for one's own self. It's because I is the most selfish of the letters! Although people who are self-centered may like it, the rest of us say ☹!	
J	The letter J is an indicator of a good memory and a healthy outlook on life. It also shows a person who is fair minded. ☺	
K	*Money, money, money!* The letter K has symbolized cash for a long time. (In slang, "K" refers to a thousand dollars.) Although money can be good, it also reflects greed and being too caught up in possessions. ☹	
L	For girls who like sports or challenging mind games, this is a great letter. L is the letter of being coordinated, both physically and mentally. Keeping your balance is important! ☺	
M	This is a tough letter. On the one hand, the M shows a person who appreciates beauty, but on the other hand, that person may be too hung up on appearances. The "M" is a little too shallow, judging a book by its cover. ☹	
N	N shows a lack of confidence or self-esteem. This letter needs to buck up and believe in itself! ☹	
O	O what a great letter this is! It is also a very feminine letter. It shows deep emotion and feeling, and a strong sensitivity to other people. Girls with a lot of "O"s in their names make great friends, sisters, and mothers. ☺	
P	The P person is the one who goes along with the crowd. It's the letter that doesn't like to speak up or take risks. ☹	
Q	Q is a good letter for learners and teachers, and any one else who wants to get educated and then pass her knowledge along. (It is also a moody letter, but let's not get hung up on details!) ☺	
R	R U ready for one of the greatest of all letters? "R" is a letter that reflects wisdom, good judgment, and a desire to learn. ☺	

Letter	What It Means	Score
S	S can do a lot of things. Listen to its different sounds: *his, hiss, sure.* Sheesh! Anyway, the top half of "S" is the opposite of the bottom part, so it contains its own opposite, sort of like an alphabetical yin/yang symbol. "S" was thought of as the letter of complexity and goodness. ☺	
T	Even though T is the second-most used letter in writing, being popular doesn't make it good. "T" is a letter that can't be counted on. It's inconsistent and flaky. ☹	
U	U are number one! Well, maybe not number one, but "U" is certainly up there. It is a great letter for a girl, as it is a letter of protection and caring. When picking a babysitter, parents should always go with the girl who has a lot of "U"s in her name! ☺	
V	We don't know if you are a spiritual person, but if you have a V for an initial, you might be. The "V" shows great instincts and an ability to see what others don't. Don't worry, though, it's not *psycho*, it's *psychic.* ☺	
W	W is dependable, but maybe a bit boring. ☺	
X	Ever wonder why X is the letter of the *unknown* in math class? It's because this is the most mysterious letter of all. It is also associated with women, because back when you were inside your mother, something called an "XX sex chromosome" decided that you'd be a girl! ☺	
Y	Some girls don't need to be the center of attention. *Why?* We don't know! But the letter Y is for girls who don't mind being quiet, thoughtful, and a good friend to others. ☺	
Z	Maybe because the letter Z doesn't get used a lot, it shows an appreciation for the weird, strange, and out of the ordinary. ☺	

A to Zed! Even though we pronounce "z" as "zee" in the United States, it is pronounced "zed" in Britain and most Commonwealth countries.

So, how did your name score?

Nicknames

Everyone has to be given a nickname at one point in her life. It's practically a law! Maybe you're a kid who got stuck with a really bad nickname like "Poo-Poo Head" or "Pony Girl." How embarrassing! But still, it's usually better to have a nickname than not. Somehow, nicknames make us seem more colorful and fun.

 About a thousand years ago, the king of Denmark was nicknamed Eric the Memorable. Today, nobody remembers why.

Here are a few ways that you can come up with nicknames everyone will remember.

To make up a nickname, pick a first name from the official state symbols listed on the left. For your last name, pick from the list of cool place names on the right! (All place names are actual countries or cities.)

State Symbols

Apple (*flower, Arkansas*)

Azalea (*wildflower, Georgia*)

Blossom (*flower, Florida*)

Bluestem (*grass, Illinois*)

Boomer (*reptile, Oklahoma*)

Brook (*fish, New York*)

Calico (*cat, Maryland*)

Camellia (*flower, Alabama*)

Chanterelle (*fungus, Oregon*)

Coral (*gem, West Virginia*)

Cypress (*tree, Louisiana*)

Emerald (*gem, North Carolina*)

Dakota (*Sioux word for "friend"*)

Galena (*mineral, Missouri*)

Holly (*tree, Delaware*)

Hope (*motto, Rhode Island*)

Iris (*flower, Tennessee*)

Place Names

Punkydoodles

Stonybatter

Takizawa

Bombay

Trinidad

Sopchoddy

Nimrod

Andorra

Ouagadougou (wah-ga-DOOG-oo)

Jamaica

Twitty

HooHoo

Katmandu

Flin Flon

Climpy

Kyzyl (KE-zil)

Zonguldak

Jade (*gem, Wyoming*)

Jalapeno (*pepper, Texas*)

Kool-Aid (*drink, Nebraska*)

Kukui (koo-KOO-ee) (*tree, Hawaii*)

Laurel (*flower, Connecticut*)

Lavender (*flower, Colorado*)

Lilac (*flower, New Hampshire*)

Lily (*flower, Utah*)

Magnolia (*flower, Mississippi*)

Morgan (*horse, Vermont*)

Niagara (*ship, Pennsylvania*)

Opal (*gem, Nevada*)

Palmetto (*tree, South Carolina*)

Pearl (*gem, Kentucky*)

Poppy (*flower, California*)

Robin (*bird, Michigan*)

Rose (*flower, Iowa*)

Sapphire (*gem, Montana*)

Scarlet (*flower, Ohio*)

Sitka (*tree, Alaska*)

Sunflower (*flower, Kansas*)

Syringa (*flower, Idaho*)

Tabby (*cat, Massachusetts*)

Trilobite (*fossil, Wisconsin*)

Tulip (*flower, Indiana*)

Turquoise (*gem, Arizona*)

Violet (*flower, New Jersey*)

Virginia (*It's a state!*)

Walleye (*fish, Minnesota*)

Willow (*bird, Washington*)

Wintergreen (*herb, Maine*)

Yucca (*flower, New Mexico*)

Samoa

Krypton

Woolloomooloo

Shanghai

Valtimo

Mashpee

Poopó

Odododiodoo

Lucia (LOO-chee-uh)

Weedpatch

Doostil

Calabasas

Affpuddle

Pukë

Djibouti (je-BOOT-ee)

Bora Bora

Willacoochee

Kalamazoo

Glorioso

Vulcan

Mumbles

Wacahoota

Booti Booti

Zimbabwe

Meeteetse

Paducah

Wigtwizzle

Kyrgyzstan (KIR-je-stan)

Coolmeelee

Piddlehinton

Weeki Wachee

Yeehaw

Your *Star Wars* Nickname

Ever notice how all the characters in *Star Wars* have similar futuristic names? Here's how to get yours!

For your *Star Wars* first name:

1. Take the first *three* letters of your last name.

2. Add to that, the first *two* letters of your first name.

For your *Star Wars* last name:

1. Take the first *two* letters of your mother's *maiden* name.

2. Add to that, the first *three* letters of the name of the city you were born in OR the street you live on now, whichever sounds better.

Want to make your last name seem classier? Add a "de" to the front of it, which in France, shows that you have nobility in your family. Example: *Kathy Blanchette* can become *Kathleen de Blanchette*. Fancy!

Looking for a nice summer camp experience? Try visiting charming Lake Chargoggagoggmanchauggagoggchaubunagungamaugg in Massachusetts! It's the longest place name in the United States. This name is pronounced just like it's spelled, like in the popular romantic song:

We took a walk one night and sat on a log
Down by Lake Chargoggagoggmanchauggagoggchaubunagungamaugg
We kissed and then we heard a frog
Down by Lake Chargoggagoggmanchauggagoggchaubunagungamaugg

Everybody sing along!

Doodles

This is an addictive shape to draw. Once you follow these steps, it will be on the margins of all your papers!

In India, girls show their artistic ability by drawing *kolams*. These are simple yet complex shapes that are supposed to bring good luck and health. The way to do it is simple. Just draw five dots across a page. Above and below it, put four dots in the spaces. Above and below those, put three dots, and so on.

3-Step Kolam 7-Step Kolam Complex Kolam

Begin drawing one continuous loop that goes around ALL the dots. After you are done, you can decorate the doodle with symbols and pictures.

Name Quiz

See if you can get these questions about names right. The answers are at the bottom of the page.

1. Which month of the year is the most popular "month" name for girls?

2. What is the only state in the United States with a one-syllable name?

3. Which of these names was recently in the top ten most popular names for girls? *Bimberly, Crayola, Ebola, Elisabet, Mossie, Pepsi, Prunella, Isabella, Salmonella, Velveeta*

4. Megan writes the name of a certain U.S. state on a sheet of paper in all capital letters. She then turns the page upside down and looks at it in a mirror. The reflection reads exactly the same as she wrote it. What is the name of the state?

Answers below!*

Handwriting

Every girl knows that one of the best ways to stay awake in a boring class is to practice signing her own name. There are so many possibilities; which one looks coolest? Which style reflects who you are?

This is what makes "calligraphy" (kal-IG-raf-ee) so interesting. Calligraphy is the art of handwriting beautiful letters and can be done in different styles or fonts. Computers can be used for unique styles too, but learning to handwrite in a font is much more personal and artistic than pulling a paper out of the printer. And if you learn calligraphy, your notes in class will be admired by everyone!

---

* 1. April; 2. Maine; 3. Isabella; 4. OHIO.

Writing notes in class is usually not allowed, but this has such beautiful handwriting. I'm giving you extra credit!

So do you like him or not?

Because handwriting is so personal, it's no surprise to us that the way we write can say something about us. Countries like Germany, Switzerland, and Israel put a lot of faith in handwriting. In France, people often must give handwriting samples for job applications. And in Israel, you may have your handwriting checked just to get an apartment!

The study of handwriting is called *graphology*. It is not scientific, but then, neither are hunches, intuition, or first impressions. Maybe because of this, most of the graphology experts in France are women.

You Be the Judge

If a person writes a few sentences or even a short paragraph on a blank sheet of paper, it can be analyzed. You could probably reach some conclusions yourself! For example, if a girl pushes down really hard with her pen when she writes, she is probably strong willed and determined. But if she barely touches the paper with her pencil, it wouldn't be a surprise to find out she's shy.

Have a friend or family member give you a handwriting sample. Make sure to have the person sign her name at the bottom. (Don't say what the sample is for until *after* you've gotten it, though!) Then see what the handwriting reveals about your subject!

What You See	What It Means
The letters are well-rounded.	This is a balanced person.
The letters are at straight angles.	This person has good energy and might be a leader.
There are little happy faces ☺, hearts ♡, or circles for the dot on the letter "i."	She has a unicorn collection.

What You See	What It Means
The "a" or "o" letters are not all the way closed in.	The writer is talkative.
The "a" and "o" letters are closed in.	She can keep a secret.
There is a good space between the lines of the paragraph.	This is a stable person.
The letters *slant* to the right.	The writer has an energetic, passionate personality.
The letters slant to the left.	The person is timid and quiet.
It looks like the person wrote in a hurry, or it's just messy.	This shows an impatient person.
The lines of the words don't veer up or down.	She is a well-adjusted person.
The person prefers black ink.	This shows a strong personality.
The letters are small and maybe squished together.	She is shy and doesn't like attention. (Probably smart, too!)
There are big letters, or it's written in all capitals, or there are decorations on the letters.	These show a person who likes attention. She also doesn't like to be criticized. (So you may want to skip telling her this!)
There is a good-sized left margin.	The person is flexible and good at adapting.
The style of writing seems to change inside the paragraph.	This person gets bored easily and may be unreliable.
The right-hand margin is small.	She is friendly and open.
The cross on the letter "t" slants down. (Or up!)	If the bar slopes down, the person is a rebel. If it slants up, she has high expectations for herself and others.
There are big loops.	The person is a romantic, imaginative type.
The person has a complete, readable signature.	This shows maturity.

Teachers at a primary school in Smethwick, England, were ordered to always use green ink for correcting papers. Red ink is not allowed because it is too negative and might damage a student's self-esteem!

"Uh..."

If you listen to people (or yourself) talk, you'll hear a LOT of "uh"s and "um"s (and even "er"s). People say "uh" and "um" to fill in space until they can think of the next word they are going to say. Because of this, these are called "filler words."

Men use filler words more than women do. This must be because girls are better at talking than boys, and so they don't need as much filler.

Another interesting thing is that not all cultures use the same filler words. Here are some examples:

Hebrew: *ehhhhh*
Serbian and Croatian: *ovay*
Turkish: *mmmmmm*
Japanese: *eto* (EH-to), *ano* (AH-no)
Spanish: *este*
Mandarin Chinese: *jiege* (JEH-guh)
French: *euh*
Swedish: *eh, ah, aah, hmmm, ooh, oh*

Secret Message Girl

If you don't know how to write in invisible ink yet, here's how to do it!

Technique 1:

You will need: A white crayon, paper, a highlighter (any color but yellow).

If you write a message on *white* paper with a *white* crayon, it is nearly impossible to read. That is, it's nearly impossible until you run a highlighter over it! Then the letters shine right through. Try it and you'll see what we mean.

Technique 2:

You will need: White paper, a small glass or jar, lemon juice, a cotton swab, a mirror.

First, pour the lemon juice into your glass. Lemony! Now just dip the cotton swab into the lemon juice and then use the swab to write your message on the paper. Dip the swab into the juice again if it dries out while you're writing. (If you don't have lemon juice, milk also works for this technique.)

Let your writing dry out; it should become invisible. When you are ready to read the message, hold it up to a strong light or fire and the words will magically appear! Another way to get the message to appear is to have an adult use an iron at low temperature to "iron" the piece of paper. Because lemon juice (or milk) darkens when heated, the message shows up!

Technique 3:

You will need: Water, paper, two bowls, cornstarch, a chopstick (or any pen-shaped piece of wood), a sponge, and iodine (ask your mom if you have some in the house).

Pour 1/4 cup of water into one of the bowls and stir 1 teaspoon of cornstarch into it. Pop it into the microwave for 30 to 40 seconds, stir it, and then microwave again for 30 to 40 seconds more. This is your ink!

Once it cools, take your chopstick, dip it into this mixture, and write your secret message on the paper. As the ink dries, it will become invisible.

Once the message dries, mix 8 to 9 drops of iodine with about 1/2 cup of water in another bowl. Take a sponge, dip it in this solution, and wring it out. Then gently sponge your paper with it. The invisible message will be magically revealed!

Bad Words

"Fear of a name increases fear of the thing itself."

~J. K. Rowling

We guess it's no secret that jerks or mean girls sometimes use a word that rhymes with *witch*. (Just put a "b" where the "w" is.) The thing about "witch with a b" is that it just means an *adult female dog*. And most people like dogs! This word can also mean "to complain" when it is used as a verb. (There is a famous book about knitting called *Stitch 'N Bitch*.) This word can also mean "a type of lamp used in Alaska." But many people only use the word's *slang* meaning, which is "a mean woman." Times change, and words change, too. Some women even consider this word a compliment to their strong personalities. (But you are not one of them.)

 The word *bitchin'* can be used as an adjective for "good" or "cool."

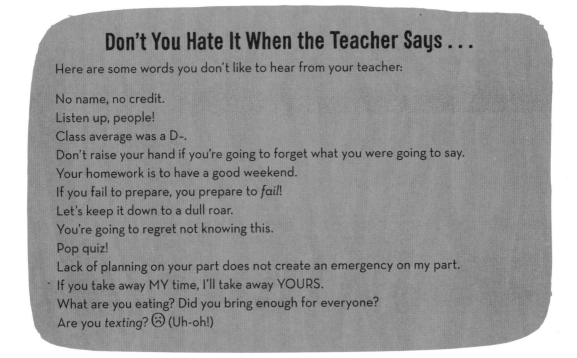

Don't You Hate It When the Teacher Says . . .

Here are some words you don't like to hear from your teacher:

No name, no credit.
Listen up, people!
Class average was a D–.
Don't raise your hand if you're going to forget what you were going to say.
Your homework is to have a good weekend.
If you fail to prepare, you prepare to *fail*!
Let's keep it down to a dull roar.
You're going to regret not knowing this.
Pop quiz!
Lack of planning on your part does not create an emergency on my part.
If you take away MY time, I'll take away YOURS.
What are you eating? Did you bring enough for everyone?
Are you *texting*? ☹ (Uh-oh!)

Speaking of bad words, if a really mean boy ever tells you to go to h-e-[double hockey sticks], tell him you can't because your *passport* isn't ready. That's because there is a real village in Norway named Hell. People go there all the time! (And in the winter, when there are many cold days, it even freezes over.)

BTW, a school in Wellingborough, England, has a school policy that students are allowed to cuss up to five times per class period. Teachers are supposed to keep track of the cussing on the board.

"Allow the Mouth to Rejoice!"

The United Nations is a place where ALL the different nations on the planet come together to try and solve the world's problems. But since there are so many different languages spoken in the world, it's tough for everyone to know what is being said. Translators (people who are good at translating words from one language to another) get to work there.

The problem with translating from one language to another is that if you translate word for word, it won't make sense in the other language. For example, a UN translator once translated "Out of sight, out of mind" from English to Chinese. (This saying means "If you don't see it, you won't think about it.") In Chinese, the direct translation was "Invisible, insane." Not helpful! Translation mistakes like this happen all the time, and sometimes they are pretty funny.

Soft drink companies have had problems translating their ads into Chinese. For example, tales are told of how Pepsi wanted to have the slogan *Come alive with the Pepsi generation!* put on billboards in China, but when they did this, they ran into trouble. That's because the translator had written *Pepsi brings back your dead ancestors* as the new motto!

Coca-Cola's translation problems were even worse. When Coke started to sell its product in China, shopkeepers began making signs to advertise the product. Trying to spell *Coca-Cola* in Chinese resulted in many mistakes; one of them was *Bite the wax tadpole.* Coca-Cola quickly had a new motto written, which translated to *Allow the mouth to rejoice.*

Coors has many ad mottos, including *Turn It Loose!* When the company translated this for its Spanish-speaking customers, it may have become *Suéltalo con Coors.* That would be important, because it can mean the same as *Get diarrhea from Coors!* Yech. We don't think that's the message they wanted to send. And when Clairol tried to shop their new curling iron (called the Mist Stick) in Germany, it didn't sell well. Someone finally pointed out that in German slang *mist* means *manure.* Who wants a manure stick in their hair?

SLANG

*"I thought he was **soo** beyond, but when he wore sandals, I found out he was a hobbit."*

~Venus Frippet

Slang is cool! (SWIDT?) These words can add flavor to your conversations and they're fun to use. What's interesting is that when slang gets used so much, it goes right into the dictionary as a "real" word. That's what happened to words like *derp, squee, selfie,* and *FOMO* (Fear of Missing Out). I know you already know the sitch with a lot of slang, but maybe you can find some new friends on the list below.

adorkable: Adorable and dorky. (Want to just say "adorable"? Go with **adorbs.**)

agreeing machine: A girl who says "yes" to everything to make friends.

amaze-balls: Really good.

aristo-brat: A rich kid who is snotty.

ATM: A friend who spends a lot of money.

babblescent: An adolescent (teenager) who is always talking or "babbling."

bad-lib: Quickly changing (or "ad-libbing") a *bad* word to a *good* one. Example: After Samantha stubbed her toe she bad-libbed, "shh-ooot!" Other good bad-lib words are *sugar, fudge, heck,* and *gafarbawitz.*

bathroomy: A word that describes a girl who uses the restroom much more than the average girl. Example: "Monica is gone again? She is so bathroomy."

be toast: Ruined.

beanie: A pretty girl.

beyond: This means the same as "gorgeous," as in "Those shoes are beyond."

bi-phonal: Being able to talk on more than one phone at a time.

bitchin': Good.

blato: Obvious. Blatant.

bohunk: A good-looking boy.

boo: Boyfriend or girlfriend.

broad squad: A group of girlfriends.

bullhorn implant: A girl with a loud voice has this.

burn the pom-poms: Getting to work and not goofing around. "I finally decided to burn the pom-poms and clean my room."

catfish: A person using fake online identities.

catpause: How long it takes for a girl to leave the room before the other girls start talking about her.

chichi (SHEE-shee): Expensive in a tasteless way.

chimping: Making an "Ooh! Ooh!" sound when looking at photographs of yourself or your friends. Example: "Jenny sha-mailed us photos from the party and we all started, like, chimping."

cling-on: A girlfriend who is like a shadow, never leaving your side.

Ooooh! Oooh! Ooooh!

"Chimping"

co-inky dink: Coincidence!

conked: Having curly hair straightened.

Crayola storm: A girl who wears as many bright colors as she can all the time.

creep-ola: Creepy, bad, off-limits. If your best friend's little brother wants to go out with you, it can be *creep-ola*!

cutiful: Between cute and beautiful.

cutissimo (cute-EES-ee-mo): The ultimate state of cuteness.

dandruff: A girl who "flakes out" and ditches her friends.

de-friend: To break up with a friend. "After what Kylie said, I had to de-friend her."

devastated: Amazed! Blown away! Really impressed!

diss: To disrespect or insult.

do someone a crutch: Do somebody a favor.

down: Being in full agreement. "Want to go?" "Down."

duh-moment: The feeling you get right after you ask a dumb question. "I had a duh-moment after I asked her where she got her birthmark."

eleventeen-year-olds: Any 9- to 12-year-old girl who tries to look older than she is.

ermahgerd: The long form of OMG.

EW: "*Excessive Winking.*" What happens when a girl uses too many "winks" in her messages. Example: *Hi QT!* ☺ *Howz it goin?* ☺ *Ta-ta!* ☺

eye candy: Any attractive person.

eyebrella: Hairy eyebrows.

face-mail: Talking to someone in person.

fake 'n' bake: A tan that someone got in a tanning salon.

felectricity (fee-lek-TRIS-ity): When cat hair sticks to your clothes.

fine: A good word to use when you're tired of arguing with a boy.

five minutes: How much longer you need to get ready. (The actual time may be *slightly* longer!)

frippet: A girl who is a show-off.

froufrou (FROO-froo): Fluffy trimmings, like ribbons, ruffles, and lace. (*Froufrou* is a real word; it came from the rustling sound a girl in a dress makes.)

girl crush: Adoring a super-cool girl in a platonic way!

glossaholic: A girl addicted to lip gloss or ChapStick.

guap: A lot of money.

harsh the mellow: To upset people.

hashtag: Twitter began the use of hashtags (#) to organize subjects and conversation threads. So some people actually SAY it in an ironic or silly way: "That's, like, hashtag awesome."

have a cow: What your parents do when you make one *little mistake*. (They'd actually "have a calf" if this ever literally happened.)

hello-ha: A cute way to say "Hi" with a Hawaiian flavor.

hissy fit: Apparently, angry girls *throw* these, but we're not sure how far. (Actual hissing may occur.)

hobbit: A boy (or girl!) with hairy feet.

homicidal: As you know, if something is "killer," it is *really good*. But if it is "homicidal," it's even better! Example: "Their basketball team is killer, but we are homicidal!"

hottie: We don't really have to define this, do we?

jargogle: To *really* mess something up. (This is a real word.)

jim-jams: Pajamas.

juice: Gossip.

kerfluffle: A mess.

kick it: To hang out.

killer: Really good.

kindergarten nap head: The bad hair that results from an afternoon nap.

kittywhompus: *Really* messed up, worse than a *kerfluffle*.

kumbaya (koom-bye-YA): Taking something to heart and really believing it. Example: "Robin gets all kumbaya about whatever Jason says."

logorrhea: Nonstop talking; diarrhea of the mouth. (Another real word.)

minor ducats (DUCK-its): A small amount of money. "Ducats" were small gold coins used in Europe centuries ago.

Monet (moan-AY): A person who looks good from a distance, but up close, not so much. From the French painter whose artwork is the same way. ☺

moo-juice: Milk. (Okay, so we're immature.)

muggle: Anyone not in your group of friends.

mundane: A normal person.

Nakiesha: Term for any girl who acts like she's a queen. "That Nakiesha walks like she's the homecoming queen."

napnesia: Waking up from an afternoon nap and being totally out of it. Example: "I had such bad napnesia, I didn't even know my name."

newbie: A new person to any group (a.k.a. "nOOb").

nipplecrite (NIPPLE-krit): A girl who doesn't wear a bra, but thinks you should (or vice versa)!

nooj: A guy who is a harmless troublemaker.

Nakiesha

on the DL: On the "down low." This is the secret information only the *truly* hip people know. "On the DL, I like chocolate!"

outie: Either a belly button that sticks out or a short way of saying "I'm out of here."

pack clothes: The type of clothing worn by girls in a certain clique. Example: "Looks like corduroy pants are the pack clothes for today."

pelmet: A very short miniskirt.

pencil beaver: A boy who chews on his pencil or pen a lot.

perflippity: Silly.

prat: British slang for a foolish or stupid person.

quaggle: To quiver, like jelly. (Actually, a real word.)

ridic: Short for "ridiculous."

rude o'clock: What time it is when someone wakes you up and you want to sleep.

sadaddict: A girl (maybe a Drama Queen) who is hooked on feeling sad.

salad dodger: A person who's a bit overweight.

scandal-icious: A juicy piece of gossip.

servant distance: That weird thing that happens when one person is trailing behind the group. Example: "Amelia is always five feet behind us. Why does she do that servant distance thing?"

sherblit: Any cute little thing.

shimmy: To dance.

skimp: A girl who never lends anyone her clothes.

skrunkle: To curl up under a warm blankie and get cozy.

snap: This is a word that can be used any way you want, especially as an exclamation of surprise or approval.

snarky: In a bad mood.

SOOF: "Swear on Our Friendship."

spenny: Expensive.

spiteor (SPIT-ee-or): A person who spits a lot when he talks (a.k.a. splattermouth).

stage-phoning: Loud talking on a cell phone in a show-offy way

stink eye: To give someone a dirty look.

sugar fairy: A girl who's always a little *too* sweet.

tanorexic: A girl who has a tanning disorder. She thinks that she's too pale, and so she tans constantly.

teacher breath: Bad breath, especially if it smells like coffee.

tootles: Depending on who you talk to, either a really cute or really sad way to say "good-bye."

totes: Short for "totally."

trout pout: The weird lips a girl gets if she uses too much lip plumper.

tufty: A cowlick that just won't go away.

uptalk: This isn't slang, but a word for how some girls pronounce regular sentences like questions. So uptalk is like this?

Venus: A beautiful girl.

vidiot: A person who watches too much TV or YouTube.

vocal fry: Like "uptalk," this isn't slang. Rather, it's the low, creaky vibrations that some female singers slip into their music to add style. But some girls started speaking this way too. So instead of saying "very interesting," a vocal fryer says, "Very interesteeeaaaaaaaaang"!

walk of shame: What you have to do if you wear the same clothes two days in a row.

whatever (what-EV-er), or **whatevs:** The perfect comeback line to someone who is annoying you. Or an extremely annoying word to hear from someone you're talking to!

wicked: Really good. Example: "That actress who played the witch was wicked."

ya-huh: A good comeback to "Nuh-uh."

zipperhead: A person with a closed mind.

DOLLS AND STUFFED ANIMALS

"Dolls are just like real life. You buy loads of clothes for them, and still only end up with a few good outfits."

~Penny Nichols

Today's kids have faster-changing tastes than any generation before them. So by the age of seven, many girls have left Barbie behind. But of course dolls aren't *just* for little girls. After all, there is no right or wrong age to play with dolls. Some girls never get into dolls, while others never give them up.

The cool thing about dolls (besides dressing them up and giving them new hairstyles) is that you have to use your *imagination* to play with them. Since the dolls don't usually move or *really* talk, it's up to you to act and speak for them. This can make playing with dolls a whole world of creativity, as dolls trade clothes, go to parties, and solve the world's problems.

Barbie

Barbie really is the *queen of dolls*. Most dolls are lucky to last a year in toy stores before they disappear forever. But Barbie has been around since before your parents were born! She showed up in 1959, and since then, Mattel says it has sold *billions* of Barbies.

A woman named Ruth Handler ran the Mattel Toy Company in the 1950s. Ruth saw a German doll named "Lilli." This doll was a *woman*, not a *baby* doll which was unusual back then. Ruth's daughter, Barbara, was 11 years old at the time, and Ruth wondered if an "adult" doll would be interesting to a girl getting ready to be a teenager.

Ruth named her new doll after Barbara (Barbie!). And while Barbie was originally a favorite with 11- to 12-year-olds, she is now most popular with much younger girls. Preschool girls are one of her biggest fan bases!

Through the years, Barbie has had many versions, more than 40 nationalities, and over 130 jobs:

1959: A star is *born!* (Okay, molded out of plastic, but still.)

1968: *Talking Barbie* came out! She could say six phrases in Spanish or English, like "Would you like to go shopping?" and "I love being a fashion model."

1970: *Living Barbie* came out. Some girls were disappointed because Living Barbie was not actually *alive.*

1979: *Kissing Barbie* was stolen from girls by their brothers because G.I. Joe asked them to.

1980: *Black Barbie* and *Hispanic Barbie* came out. It only took 21 years!

1982: The *Eskimo Barbie* was released. What's next? *Icelandic Barbie?*

1987: *Icelandic Barbie* came out.

1988: *Korean Barbie* hit the stores.

1991: *Czechoslovakian Barbie?* (Many girls were really confused.)

1992: *Totally Hair Barbie* arrived; her hair went all the way to her feet. She was the best-selling version of Barbie ever. *Rappin' Rockin' Barbie—Yo!* also arrived this year. Girls and rappers rejoiced together in wild street parties.

1993: The Barbie Liberation Front removed the voice boxes of Barbies in over 40 states and replaced them with ones from G.I. Joe. Girls were surprised to hear their dolls saying "Eat lead, Cobra" in deep voices. Boys were amazed to hear their action figures say "Will we have enough clothes?"

2000: *Barbie for President* was released. *But she's done this before, running in four other presidential campaigns. What's her platform? Barbie* calls for girls to "B inspired, B informed, and B involved." (But sadly, even *involved* girls can't vote, so Barbie keeps losing these elections.)

2002: *Lingerie Barbie* comes out. Not the smartest idea.

2009: Barbie turns 50. (Dang, that doll is old!)

2011: Wow! Ken and Barbie rekindle their epic romance and . . . *zzzz.*

There have been many complaints about Barbie over the years. Some people complain that Barbie encourages mindless shopping. For instance, *seven* different Barbie Playsets with shopping themes came out in 2003: *Sweet Shoppin' Barbie, Shop & Style Fashion Barbie, Let's Grocery Shop Barbie,* and so forth. Maybe instead of shopping, Barbie could do something more productive with her time, like tutoring Groovy Girls or going to college.

Another sore spot has been Barbie's body. If the original Barbie were the height of an average woman, her bust measurement would be about 39 inches. (That's *big.*) But her waist would only have been 19 inches! (That's *tiny.*) And what's up with those little feet? One Barbie came with a scale that showed her weight as 110 pounds. Most grown women weigh more than that!

Since Barbie didn't seem normal with this body type, she was "reconstructed" in 1998 to be less outrageous.

That's why Mattel gave Barbie an "#unapologetic" marketing campaign. The company says, "As a legend herself, [this gives Barbie] an opportunity to own who [she is] and celebrate what [she's done] and be #unapologetic." Um, okay. (You know she's a doll, right?)

So if you've ever pulled a doll's head off, don't worry. It's normal!

Finally, a study of girls and their dolls found that Barbies were treated worse by their owners than any other dolls. The bad treatments ranged from giving the dolls haircuts with scissors to putting them in the microwave. According to the report, no other toy or brand name created such a response. (The researchers theorized this was because there are so many Barbie types, they don't seem unique.)

In an unusual move, Mattel once started a line of Barbie clothing in Japan for **real** girls. Called "Barbie Couture," the fashion line included $400 miniskirts. Hey, it's the price you have to pay to get *dolled up*. (Get it? BTW, *couture* is a French word that means "fashion.")

One of the most expensive Barbie dolls was called the "Inland Steel Barbie" from 1967. Only four of them were ever made. Recently, a family in Virginia found two of these dolls in its closet and put them on eBay. The opening bid was $7,000!

There have been many "spin-off" characters in the world of Barbie dolls. The most famous is her former boyfriend, Ken. That's right, **Barbie and Ken broke up** (from 2004–2011), so Barbie could date an Aussie surfer named Blaine. But hey, who expects two dolls to have a lasting relationship, anyway?

Ken was named after Barbara Handler's real brother, uh, Ken. Like Barbie, he's come out in many different versions. These have included *Ken a Go-Go, Baywatch,* and *Shaving Fun* versions of the Ken doll. Our favorite Ken was the *Earring Magic Ken*. He wore an earring and dressed in fake black leather and purple fabrics. He also had frosted hair. No wonder he was *Earring Magic Ken*.

In a number of interviews, Ken has said that he really hates it when girls dress him up in Barbie's clothes.

Mattel also released Barbie's younger sister, named Skipper. One version of this doll was *Growing Up Skipper*. This doll was unique because when you pushed her arm back, she "grew" breasts. Skipper also got a slimmer waist and became almost an inch taller when her arm was pushed back. This was supposed to teach girls about their bodies, but when girls pushed their own arms back and nothing happened, they were just disappointed. ☹

 In 1966, Barbie got a little brother and sister who were twins: **Tutti and Todd.**

American Girl Dolls

When American Girl dolls first came out in 1986, they were supposed to be quality dolls that were historical and educational. You've got to like that! Since then, Mattel bought the company, and now makes Barbies *and* American Girl dolls.

The *American Girls Collection* ties American history in with the dolls through a series of books featuring the dolls as characters. They are smart and innocent; one writer describes them as being "talkative without being mouthy, and bright without being eggheaded." In general, these dolls come in a wide range of skin and hair colors, and they are all about nine years old. (But have you noticed the dolls seem younger than the same characters in the books?)

As for the *My American Girl* dolls, their eye, skin, and hair colors can be personalized, and glasses, braces, and jewelry can be added. And since *human girls* can even order American Girl clothing for themselves, a girl can be her doll's look-alike! This is cool and scary at the same time. (Okay, maybe just scary.)

Two American Girl Place stores (in Chicago and New York) have stage shows, doll hospitals, and hair salons where dolls can have their hair done for $15. And at the American Girl Café in New York City, girls can eat with their dolls seated next to them in special booster seats.

Barbie, CSI

Imagine a dollhouse that is accurate down to every last detail. There is wallpaper in the kitchen and little blankets on the beds. And there is a Ken doll lying face down in the living room. He's been poisoned!

Back in the 1940s, a woman named Frances Glessner Lee made incredibly detailed doll-houses. These weren't for play; Frances was a police officer who constructed small crime scenes using dollhouses and dolls. These were used as classroom tools for the police to use as training for crime scene investigation (CSI).

Her "dollhouses of death" were so good, the doors in the dollhouses could be opened with tiny keys. And they were so effective as teaching tools that dioramas like them are still used in universities and police academies today.

Other Contenders!

The **Bratz** might be the opposite of the American Girl dolls. Where the American Girl dolls are doing chores and making the world a better place, Bratz are up to *who-knows-what!* Coming out in 2001, *Bratz* were designed for the 9- to 12-year-old girl who might have "out-grown" Barbie and American Girl dolls. (Girls in this age group are sometimes called "tweens," because they're between little girls and teenagers.)

So how are Bratz different? Well, first of all, they don't seem to care about American history! These dolls also all have huge eyes, pouty lips, and faces with "attitude." (They also have huge heads.) One of the Bratz outfits is a patent leather jumpsuit with high heels. We guess being bratty means you can wear heavy makeup and skimpy outfits!

The Bratz dolls were advertised as having a "passion for fashion." They became popular not just because of their different "looks" and accessories. And Bratz taught us how fashionable it is to have a name that ends in the letter "a." Bratz dolls include Sasha, Katia, Felicia, Dana, Nevra, Fianna, Kiana, Nona, Oriana, and Valentina. *Sheesh.* (Or should we say "Sheesha"?)

There were boy Bratz dolls, too, like Eitan. (Even though only about 12 years old, he had a soul patch!) And of course, there were the younger Bratz, like the Big Babyz. These babyz have a "passion for fashion," so they wore miniskirts while holding bottles for accessories. (We're not kidding.)

Many people have complained about Bratz over the years. This led to the dolls being temporarily discontinued twice. But our bet is they'll be back—after all, it's hard to keep a bad brat down.

Nowadays, the Bratz have to compete with other dolls, like the **Monster High** dolls. These teen girls came out in 2010, and were patterned after monsters like Dracula and Frankenstein. But while Draculaura and Headmistress Bloodgood are kind of cool, the freakiest thing about them might be how THIN they are!

Guatemalan Worry Dolls

In the mystical mountains of Guatemala, girls have magical dolls. They are called *worry dolls* (or *muñecas de la preocupación*) and they have the power to take away all of a girl's worries! Before a girl goes to bed, she tells her worry to one of these small, colorful dolls. Then she puts it underneath her pillow. When the girl awakens, the doll has taken the worry and hidden it somewhere far away. No worries! *Ningún se preocupa!*

Hello Kitty

Although she's innocent and pure, Hello Kitty doesn't seem that impressive at first. She's so darned *plain*. Heck, that cat doesn't have a mouth! How could this creature have so many fans? She likes to have tea parties and make friends . . . but is that it? After a while, this mystery began to bother us, and we had to learn more about this little cat from Japan.

Hello Kitty Facts

Birthplace: London (Even though a Japanese company named Sanrio created her.)

Birthdate: November 1, 1974

Weight: The same as three apples

Hobbies: Practicing the piano, baking, playing in the forest

The Japanese love "cute" things so much, they have a name for their cute culture: *kawaii bunka*. Of course, Hello Kitty is cute for a reason; she is supposed to *make money*. Besides dolls, she has also been marketed on over 20,000 different product types. There are Hello Kitty clothes, purses, pencils, lunchboxes, guitars, candy, surfboards, cell phones, a car, and even Hello Kitty diamond watches (for between $3,000 and $30,000).

 As far as we know, there is no Hello Kitty Litter for cats. Why not?

Hello Kitty may be the only doll that has ever started a riot. In 2000, the 113 McDonald's restaurants in Singapore did a Hello Kitty doll promotion. Over 300,000 people showed up and the dolls quickly sold out, leading to crowd control problems and broken windows. And Hello Kitty is so popular in Taiwan, she was voted the island's third most popular "person" one year!

As we got sucked into learning more about Hello Kitty, we became acquainted with her friends: Mimmy (Kitty's sister), Robowan (the robot dog), Pippo (the pig), Tuxedo Sam (the penguin), Pekkle (the duck), and so on. Sanrio, Hello Kitty's parent company, has made 450 different characters. Most are disgustingly cute.

These are our favorite Hello Kitty characters: Chococat (another kitty with no mouth), and Keroppi (the frog). Keroppi is cool. He has a mouth!

So you can see what happened. We were very suspicious of Hello Kitty, but as we learned more about her and her world, we got interested. Hello Kitty taught us something about life! Sometimes we think something is stupid or lame, when actually we just don't understand it all that well. Once we do, we might like it!

Now if you will excuse us, we need to go pack our Keroppi lunchboxes.

Cabbage Patch Dolls

Designed for toddlers and very young girls, Cabbage Patch dolls were unusual because their logo was a doll's head wrapped in cabbage leaves. Since many children hate vegetables, you might think that the dolls would have failed, but instead they sold very well. Go *figure!*

The neat thing about Cabbage Patch dolls was that since each doll had its own name and identity, a girl could feel like the doll was special and all hers. Cabbage Patch dolls also raised many interesting questions for parents to answer: *Do all babies come out of the dirt? If we plant cabbage, will we find dolls or babies under the leaves? Is Mr. Potato Head out in the garden also?* And so forth. You can see the problem.

 In 1952, a new toy came out. It had different plastic "face" parts (ears, eyes, mouth, etc.) that were supposed to be stuck into a *real* potato. After a while, the company making "Mr. Potato Head" started including a plastic potato.

Fulla

In the Middle East, most girls are Muslim. Although Barbie and other dolls are available there, many Muslim girls prefer to play with a doll named *Fulla*. (She is named after a jasmine plant.) Although Fulla looks similar to Barbie, she comes with black hair (with auburn streaks) and some different accessories. For example, Muslims kneel and pray five times a day, so Fulla comes with her own prayer mat to kneel on. And since some Muslims think a woman's hair should be covered when she's out in public, Fulla has a traditional head covering called a *hijab*. But despite her differences with Barbie, Fulla does have something in common with her. Both dolls are made in China!

 Free Advice! If a kid won't play with her own dolls because they are "always too sticky," don't lend her any of yours.

Doll Day (*Hina matsuri*)

In Japan, March 3 is sometimes known as Doll Day or the Girl's Festival. Families with daughters give the girl really nice dolls as well as a special feast. These special dolls become part of the family's collection and are displayed in the house decorated with peach blossoms.

This comes from an old custom in which everyone in the family made paper dolls of themselves. Then each person's bad luck and little white lies would be transferred to their doll. The dolls were then put in a river so that everyone's bad fortunes and sins could be washed away.

Computer Chip Dollbots

There are now dolls that can talk and even make faces. Sort of scary, huh? We don't know at what point a doll becomes a *robot*, but we're getting pretty close to it. Maybe we should call them *dollbots*.

A dollbot comes with a robotically controlled face, memory chips, scanners, and an artificial voice box, among other electronic gizmos. They know what time it is and can remind their "mommies" about their calendar schedules.

Dollbots can memorize voices, so they know which human they are talking to, and call them by name. The dollbot will act like it is the child's friend. The doll *might* even act like it loves you. (But remember—that dollbot is only *acting*!)

Cinderella

The most famous version of the Cinderella fairy tale is probably the Disney film. It came out in 1950, and has only grown in popularity over time. Its dolls have been huge sellers. Experts note that the peak popularity for girls adoring Cinderella has decreased in age, so that now *two-year-olds* really love her! By the time the girls are six, they're moving on to new heroes.

This might be because princesses have an almost magical appeal to little girls. Parents worry that this is because princesses have so many *possessions* that it seems glamorous to own stuff. ("I want a gown, and a coach, and a royal ball, and a fairy godmother, etc.") So Disney came up with the idea of turning princesses into a *brand*: the Disney Princesses include Ariel (*The Little Mermaid*), Tiana (*The Princess and the Frog*), Belle (*Beauty and the Beast*), Jasmine (*Aladdin*), Merida (*Brave*), Pocahontas, Mulan, Cinderella, and Sleeping Beauty. And the Disney Princess line covers everything from home movies to home decoration and clothing.

A director for Disney Consumer Products explained: "[We look at the Princess] brand as a lifestyle, filling out all the other things girls need in life." So little girls *need* the Princess Fairy Tale Cruiser ($199)? That kindergartener lifestyle is tough to keep up!

But if ALL the little girls are dreaming of being princesses, will they grow up to be disappointed that they are *not* actually royal millionaires? We don't know. But next Halloween, count how many little princesses you see; we bet there are a lot!

 For $12,000 at a Disney park, a woman can have a Cinderella theme wedding. Want Cinderella's Crystal Coach pulled by four ponies? Add another $3,000.

Stuffed Animals

Sock monkeys and teddy bears are so darned cute, it's no surprise that girls everywhere love them.

But maybe the most famous animals ever to get stuffed are the Beanie Babies. These squishy stuffed animals came out in 1993. According to experts, the Babies got their name because they are stuffed with *beans*. This allows the Baby to be put into different cute poses!

At first, there were only nine Beanie Babies, but soon there would be hundreds, and each Beanie Baby came with a short poem about itself. For example, here is the poem (written by a meanie) that came with Cubbie the Bear:

Cubbie used to eat crackers and honey
And what happened to him was funny
He was stung by fourteen bees
Now Cubbie eats broccoli and cheese

The weird thing about Beanie Babies was that *adults* started buying them as collector items for themselves, instead of giving them to, uh, babies. The company that made Beanie Babies would only make a certain number of a Baby type before "retiring" it. And the harder a Baby was to get, the more people seemed to want it! A retired Baby could be resold for thousands of dollars in some cases. (Pretty amazing, since they are just fabric stuffed with beans!)

Adults got so crazy about this, a group of women in England tried to hijack a truck loaded with new Beanie Babies. Luckily, the Babies were saved from these savage criminals.

Even though the Beanie Baby company said that all Babies might be "retired" in 1999—they even put out a black bear Baby named "The End"—Beanie Babies are still being made. And now that they're not such huge collector items, kids can actually play with them.

 Some of the strangest Beanie Babies:

Bali the Komodo Dragon

Buzzy the Buzzard

Cheeks the Baboon

Crunch the Shark

Giganto the Woolly Mammoth

Goochy the Jellyfish

Huggins the Pitbull

Pellet the Hamster

Slayer the Dragon

Squidward Tentacles the Octopus

Stinger the Scorpion

Stuffings the Turkey

ETIQUETTE AND MANNERS

"Manners are a sensitive awareness of the feelings of others. If you have that awareness, you have good manners, no matter what fork you use."

~Emily Post

Etiquette is a fancy word for "good manners" But it isn't enough to say "please" and "excuse me" and "thank you." The thing is, if you care about *other people,* you want them to feel comfortable around you. And if you care about *yourself,* having good social skills will make you feel more confident.

So etiquette is all about being considerate and having self-confidence. You have to admit, that sounds good! By the way, people with good manners are *not* snobs. A snob is someone who makes other people uncomfortable by acting like she is too good for them. Someone with good manners would *never* be snobby.

Here's an **Etiquette Test** for you. Imagine that you are talking with a friend you know pretty well, and you notice that she has something on the tip of her nose. You don't know if it's a booger or what, because you're afraid that if you look too closely, it will gross you out. What do you do?

A. Look away and try to leave as soon as possible.

B. Point and say loudly, "Blimey! You've got snot on your beak!"

C. Look slightly away and say, "You have something on your nose."

D. Rub your own nose with a meaningful look and hope she gets the hint.

See scoring below!*

---

* **KEY:** A. How selfish! B. You are insane. C. You are a thoughtful and caring person. D. Pretty good! (Choice C is better, though.)

Your Home

A good place to start with etiquette is to try raising the level of politeness around your own home. Do you smile and listen to what others have to say? Do you do your part to make your family better?

One way to improve your family's etiquette level is to speak to people as if they are important. (Which, of course, they are!) People who feel they are important will (hopefully) act in a dignified way that will make you proud.

Try giving everybody a title that you use when addressing them. Here are some examples:

Present Title	New Title
Mom	Your Most Beautiful Majesty Whom I Love
Dad	Your Royal and Wise Highness
Sister	Your Esteemed Highness
Brother	Your Most Disrespected Lowness (wait, not helpful!)
Pets	Your Grace
Visiting Friends, Relatives	My Lady, My Lord, Good Sir, Good Madam

How to Curtsy!

A curtsy can be used to show respect to your household royalty.

1. Place one foot gracefully behind the other.

2. Quickly bend slightly at the knees. *No need to bow!*

3. If you have a dress on, hold the edges of it and pull it slightly out as your knees bend. This looks extra-refined and graceful, unless you lose your balance and stagger around. (**WARNING:** Don't do this with a miniskirt.)

Saving Face

"Saving face" means *not getting embarrassed.* Polite girls are careful not to put people *into* embarrassing situations, and they also help people get *out* of them. This is a very important value in many Asian countries. The Japanese even have special agencies that hire out actors and actresses to help people save face. For example, if a woman's family does not approve of her marriage, the bride-to-be can hire actors to play the parts of her family members at the wedding. That way she won't have to worry about being embarrassed by their behavior!

 Young Japanese men going out on a date sometimes hire fake "street punks" from these agencies. The actor playing the "punk" is paid to hassle the couple and then run away when the tough young man (who hired the punk) confronts him!

All of the following situations involve you trying to help somebody save face. Remember to be cool; your tone of voice is very important. Speak in a low, casual tone, like it's no big deal. In other words, you would say, *"There's toilet paper stuck to the bottom of your shoe"* the exact same way you'd say *"Pass the salt, please."*

A Girl's Bra Strap Is Showing and She Doesn't Know!

A girl told us her system she uses with her girlfriends. She makes eye contact with her friend and then meaningfully touches her own shoulder. This means her friend should quickly adjust the strap herself. This will also work with a girl you don't know if she has a clue.

If you *are* friendly with the person, you can always just reach out and adjust the strap yourself (just like you would if the tag on her shirt was sticking out).

A "Friend" Invites You Over . . .

Okay, so maybe she's more of a *frienemy*! Whatever. Anyway, you do NOT want to go over to her house. Our suggestion is to decline politely. The old line of "Sorry, I have plans. Thanks so much for asking me, though," may work. (Don't offer to do it another time if you really aren't interested, though.)

If the girl asks for more details, just blame it on your parents. "Yeah, tonight is a family night" or "My parents want me to do my homework then." (You probably should ask your parents if they mind that you're doing this!)

A Boy's Fly Is Down!

This is tricky, but if you're going to be polite, he really should know. However, if you tell him in a public way, both of you lose face.

There are the usual things you can privately say to him: "XYZ" (eXamine Your Zipper), "XYZ PDQ" (eXamine Your Zipper Pretty Darned Quick!), or "Hey, your barn door's open." But if you don't want to risk it, pull aside a friend who is a boy and tell *him* to tell the "offender."

A Boy You *Don't* Want to Dance with Asks You to Dance

Hey, if you went to a dance, you're there to dance, right? If a guy puts himself out there to ask you, then the least you can do is dance with him at least once. If he asks you more than once and you're not interested, then let him know. Obviously you don't need to dance with someone if you don't feel safe around him, but turning someone down just because he isn't cute enough or popular enough is not good etiquette.

A Boy You *Don't* Want to Go Out with Asks You Out

It takes a lot of courage for a boy to walk up to a girl and ask her to do something with him, *especially* if his friends are watching. As you know from the "Boys" chapter, boys are just as

sensitive as girls. If you really don't want to do anything with him, just say, "No, thank you." It's gentle, yet firm. This is the **BEST** solution. You don't need to lie or be nervous. Just be honest. Don't make excuses, even if he wants them. Your feelings are reason enough. Try to be very direct and clear, so he doesn't get confused. Definitely do *not* say, "Not right now" or "Maybe later." That will just delay the problem and make it worse.

He may not get the message at first because he is distracted by your beauty. Other solutions are to talk about who you're in love with (make sure it's someone imaginary or from another school so that he can't check) or just blame it on your parents. ("My parents won't let me go out.")

SPECIAL ALERT: You know how movies and books have villains that you can't stand, and you sort of hope something bad happens to them? If you make fun of a boy who asks you to dance (or asks you out), then *you* are that *villain*.

Bad Language! Japan is a place where good manners are an art, and women are supposed to be *queens of etiquette*. But at a New Year's Eve festival on a mountain north of Tokyo, they can let it all hang out. When the sun goes down, people walk to a temple in darkness together and they can yell out anything that has been bothering them . . . and even use bad words! "My teacher is an idiot!" "I hate my little brother!" "I have a rock in my shoe!" "!@#$%$#!"

Meeting Somebody

If someone gets a good (or bad!) first impression of you, it will often stick with the person, even if it shouldn't. So always stand up to meet someone, look the person in the eye, smile, and say, "Hi, I'm [insert your name here]." That way you have done your best to make a good impression.

Names are important; it's always better to call someone by name as you're talking to him or her (not to call someone names). It makes everything more personal and friendly. If you meet someone and she doesn't say her name, just ask, "What's your name?" It's better than having to wonder about it or waiting too long and then you are embarrassed to ask.

How Rude!

A survey of over 1,000 Americans found the following:

97 percent of people had been bothered by people using cell phones in a loud or annoying way.

44 percent of people were frequently annoyed by children being rude in public.

69 percent of people thought that the main cause of rudeness was parents not teaching good manners to their kids.

Oops, You Forgot Her Name!

Sometimes you'll meet someone and then not run into her again for weeks or years. By then, you've forgotten her name. How embarrassing! If you're *already* with another friend, quietly ask your friend to introduce herself as soon as the person whose name you've forgotten comes closer.

You: Hi! How nice to see you again!

Unknown Person: Hello! How are you?

Your friend: Hi, my name is Jennifer.

Unknown Person: Hi Jennifer, I'm Beyoncé.

You: *Beyoncé*, right! [*To yourself:* Whew!]

If you end up introducing people to each other, the usual rule is that women are introduced before men, and older people are introduced before younger people. If you can give a little information while you introduce others, it helps get a conversation going.

Making Conversation

So you're at a party, and you end up talking to someone you don't really know. Or maybe a relative you don't see much stops by the house and they're sort of quiet or shy or even just *weird*, and you're having one of those uncomfortable moments where neither one of you knows what to say.

So what do you say?

To keep a conversation going, remember this rule: You can learn *something* from *anybody*. But you have to ask questions!

Find out what the person is interested in and then ask them about it. This might be a hobby or job or project or whatever. If the person has kids, ask about them! But the thing is, if you really don't care what the person says, it will show. So at some point, you should realize that it's better *not* to ask about things you really have no interest in.

Here's a good formula to follow when starting a conversation or trying to keep one going: **QCC.** Ask a **Q**uestion, make a **C**omment, give a **C**ompliment. A good listener does more than smiling, nodding, and saying "Uh-huh." If that's not working, bring other people into the conversation. This takes the pressure off you. "I really want you to meet . . ." is a good way to make this transition.

Bored? Find a good strategy for getting away. When there's a pause, say something like "I'm sorry, if you'll excuse me for a moment, I have to ask Melissa about an assignment." (Only use that sentence if someone named Melissa is around.) Another exit line is "It was nice speaking to you. I feel like I've learned so much about loofahs." Smile and walk off with a purpose.

Cell Phone Etiquette

"Remember that as a teenager you are at the last stage of your life when you will be happy to hear that the phone is for you."

~Fran Lebowitz

The average girl with a cell phone texts 60 times a day. Or more! That's why this might be the most important part of this entire book. Knowing good cell phone manners may someday make the difference between LIFE or DEATH for you. READ ON!

The Five Cell Phone Commandments:

1. Don't eat on the phone. (*Use a plate instead!*)

2. Don't get in a car with a driver who talks on the phone or texts while driving. It's danger-ous, and also illegal in many states. (And should be in ALL states!)

3. If you're with other people, it's rude to talk on your cell phone for more than a few moments. (You're ignoring real people because of a voice in a piece of plastic!) And it's also rude to text the whole time. **Also:** If you are paying for something in a store or restau-rant, **NEVER** talk on the cell phone. It is really rude to carry on a conversation while a cashier or clerk rings up your purchases.

4. Don't text and talk. After all, can you text while maintaining eye contact with someone else and having a con-versation? Really? And you're paying attention to what the other person is saying? Look, you may be a good multitasker, but NOBODY'S that good!

5. If you're in an enclosed public place with other people, it is rude to talk on the phone. But if you HAVE

to, at least talk *quietly*. Many people talk twice as loud on cell phones as they do to other people. We call those who talk *really* loudly on the cell phone "stage-phoners." When they unleash their "cell yell," they *must* be doing it for the attention. "Look at me! I'm talking to someone super-fabulous on my phone!"

 A woman named Aimee McPherson had an actual phone line installed inside of her coffin. Can you imagine calling her and getting an *answer*? (That's what is called a "dead ringer.")

Close cousins of stage-phoners are the *cell phonies*. Cell phonies make fake phone calls and then *pretend* to talk to people who aren't there. People sometimes do this to avoid looking like loners or to get out of conversations with other people. (Being a cell phony is a great idea if there are creepy people around, by the way. You can avoid them, and they know you can call for help if they give you trouble.)

 Life's Mysteries: Do you let the phone ring a couple of times before answering it, even if it's right next to you? Us too.

Although it's hard to say, our guess is that over half of us have been cell phonies at one time or another. But to do this job well, you have to be good at faking a conversation.

How to Be a Cell Phony (and Not Get Caught!)

Make Sure the Phone is Actually OFF (or Set to "Silent") When You Speak: Imagine your embarrassment when you're in the middle of a "conversation" and the phone rings!

Avoid the "Uh-Huh" / "Uh-Uh" Trap: A rookie cell phony will be unable to keep a fake phone conversation going because she doesn't know what to say. She often gets trapped into just saying "uh-huh" or "uh-uh" in an unconvincing way. Just remember a conversation you had earlier that day and then try to reenact it.

Use Facial Expressions: Make the little smiles, eye rolls, and hair twirls that you would do if someone were actually on the phone with you.

 A Telephone Tragedy! Alexander Graham Bell (the inventor of the telephone) always answered the phone by saying "Ahoy!" Bell really thought that everyone should use "Ahoy!" It didn't catch on, though, and famous inventor Thomas Edison popularized "Hello" as a telephone greeting instead. (And Edison was no expert in communication; he proposed to his wife in Morse code. **How romantic!**)

Text, IM, and E-Mail Etiquette

The term for using good manners online is *netiquette*. Some netiquette rules are the same ones you'd usually use. For example, *don't talk to strangers*!

If you've been online much, you've probably been "flamed" or seen it happen. (Getting "flamed" is when someone writes a very insulting online message.) For some reason, there are people who will write *much* meaner things online than if they are actually talking to someone. A girl who writes mean things online is a "cyberbully."

It's easy to gossip and say mean things if the other person isn't there, especially if the cyberbully has an online nickname that keeps her anonymous. She thinks she can get away with anything.

So if you ever find yourself about to write something nasty to or about someone on the Internet, STOP. If you really mean it, say it in person or don't say it at all. (And another bonus is that if you *say* it, it can't be forwarded around to unknown people.) Be nice and use proper netiquette! That way you won't have to join the club of girls who write something, hit SEND, and then hit their foreheads with their palms, saying, "What have I done?"

There's a reason not to use ALL CAPS when writing. Yes, it looks like you're shouting. But more importantly, it takes 30 percent longer to read CAPITAL LETTERS than "normal" ones.

Safety Tip

Never leave the room when you're logged into social media. Your little brother may come in and pretend to be you!

Emoticons

As you know, punctuation marks can be used as "emoticons" (*emotion* + *icon*). These can quickly express an idea, facial expression, or emotion. Emoticons have been around for over a hundred years, which is why

they seem so old school. For example, did you know a guy named Scott Fahlman invented :-)
and :-(back in 1982? Here are some of the emoticons that followed:

_/_\o/_	A shark attack!	(=^;^=)	A cat
_/_*\o/*_	A shark attacking a cheerleader!	`~~)_)~~´	A roll of toilet paper
('}{')	Kissing	:@) :8)	A pig piggybacking on another pig
:]~~~*	A frog catching a fly	qo{-<]:	Kid on a skateboard
~)))'>	An armadillo or opossum	% :-(l)	Girl with a trout pout
..._(:)-o	Scuba diver	><((((o*>	A fish
@(*o*)@	Princess Leia or a koala	&:-{}	Girl wearing lipstick
})i({	A butterfly	(__(__)	A butt

Emoji!

An *emoji* is like an electronic emoticon. This is a Japanese word, and the plural is the same as
the singular: one emoji, two emoji. A man named Shigetaka Kurita invented the emoji, and they
began showing up on Japanese cell phones in the late 1990s. Today, emoji are often animated,
and there seems to be one for every emotion and idea. Heck, the classic book *Moby-Dick* was
even translated into emoji. (It was added to the Library of Congress as *Emoji Dick!*)

"2b or Nt2b."—*Hamlet*

Texts can be written using *abbreviations*, for example, **B4** for **before**. Or they might include
acronyms, which are the initials of words, like **TTFN** (*ta-ta for now*). Or the letters may just
"sound out" the word, like **QTE** (*cutie*).

In Japan, typing text messages on cell phones with the thumb has resulted in young people
being called *oyayubi sedai*, or the "thumb generation." And there have even been international competitions for texting speed! A teenaged girl named Ha Mok-min once texted over
seven characters a *second* at one of these events. (And she won $50,000 for her skills!)

Below are a handful of text message abbreviations. *(BTW, dont uz dEz 4 skool asynmnts, cuz ur teacher wll B so grrr!)*

+ly: Positively

4YEO: For your eyes only

aDctd2luv: Addicted to love

AFZ: Acronym-free zone

b3: Blah, blah, blah

DEGT: Don't even go there

DKDC: Don't know, don't care

EOL: End of lecture

IDGI: I don't get it

ILUVUMED: I love you more each day

IRL: In real life

KAMU: Kiss and make up

MITIN: More information than I needed

NME: Enemy

OMSG: Oh my! Sorry, gas.

POAHF: Put on a happy face

ROFLACGU: Rolling on floor laughing and can't get up (for older texters)

S2pid: Stupid

UR O-O: You are cool

WDYMBT?: What do you mean by that?

WOMBAT: Waste of money, brains, and time

XQz: Excuse

YG2BKM: You've got to be kidding me

YYSW: Yeah, yeah, sure, whatever.

Eating Etiquette

It's amazing how many rules about "manners" have to do with food. We don't have room to explain *everything* about food etiquette, but we *will* tell you that if you ever go to a fancy meal and there are 12 different kinds of forks and spoons, and you're not sure which ones are for what, NONE of them are for scratching yourself. (Tell your brother, too!)

You already know to put your napkin on your lap as soon as you sit, but a basic rule that everyone should know is: if you're eating with other people, wait until everyone is seated and served before diving in to your plate.

Another good piece of advice is this: if you're at a nice restaurant or formal meal and you're not sure what to do, you can:

1. ASK! It's not a big deal. If the people you're with are nice, they'll be happy to help.

Do you think this is for the appetizer?

2. If you're too shy to ask, just copy what everyone else does.

If there is more than one piece of silverware (for example, two forks or spoons), begin by using the one on the outside first. With the *next* part of the meal, use the *next* piece of silverware in. (But just to make it confusing, if you have more than one knife, start with the one *closest* to your plate, and then work your way *out*.)

If you have waiters or waitresses, they will serve you food to your left and remove plates from your right. To signal your waiter that you're done eating from a bowl or plate, put your fork or spoon (and sometimes your knife) at a five o'clock position.

Hot Tips! Tipping a person for giving good service is an art form. Did you know that *men* tip *women* waitresses more, and *women* tip *men* waiters more? Interesting! Anyway, the tipping tradition has been around for a long time. For example, it was customary to tip the executioner in England and France in the 1700s. That way, you knew he would grab his *sharp* axe for the job. Nobody wants an executioner with a dull blade. (Actually, nobody wants an executioner at all.)

If you're passing food around the table, it goes from left to right—that's clockwise. (And if you're passing gas around the table, you should probably stop doing that.) Sometimes there will be something on the table you can't reach. It's always more polite to ask the closest person to pass it than to reach over and grab it yourself. Because what if you spill something? Or what if you forgot to use deodorant? Now, here are a few more crucial dining FAQs!

Q. *Can I put my elbows on the table?*
A. If you're not actually eating something, we think it is usually okay to put your elbows on the table. But don't slouch! ☺

Q. *There's something nasty in my mouth. What do I do?*
A. Maybe it tastes bad, or maybe it's a horrible chunk of gristle (yuck!), but whatever it is, you're not going to swallow it. What to do? If you're lucky enough to be standing, walk somewhere private, spit it discreetly into a tissue and throw it away.

It's tougher to pull this off at a table. Get your napkin out and cover your mouth with it, then reach up with your other hand. If you think you can spit the horrible thing onto a fork without spazzing out and dropping it in your lap, do it. Otherwise, it's probably easier and safe to just reach up with your other hand (keep it covered with the napkin) and remove the nastiness. Stick it on your plate and cover it immediately with a chunk of bread.

Q. *If my cell phone rings or I get a text during dinner, can I get it?*
A. No. Turn it off.

Chew This Over

"Chewing gum is really gross, chewing gum I hate the most."
~Willie Wonka

Chewing gum only *becomes* gross when chewed incorrectly. As long as nobody can see it or the inside of your mouth when chewing, you're okay.

Your Parents' Friends

If you've ever babysat a kid with bad manners, or maybe had a dog that jumped on people, you know how embarrassing it is. Believe it or not, you can embarrass your parents, too! Who *you* are is a direct reflection of who *they* are. So when adult visitors come by, be polite and greet them warmly. You don't have to hang around and make small talk, but just a little bit of effort goes a long way.

Saying "Thank You"

Do you like to get gifts? If your answer is "yes" (and we bet it is!), then be sure to write a thank-you note for any present you get. That note is like an *investment* in your gift-receiving future! Write the note and the person will buy you another gift sometime. Skip the note, and the person will think you're ungrateful.

It's easy to *say*, "Thank you," but just saying it isn't enough if you've gotten a gift or personal favor from someone. Timing is everything. The key is to write the thank-you note or card within *five days* of getting the gift. Otherwise, you'll just keep putting it off until it's too late to do it at all!

When thanking someone, be sure to be specific about *what* you're thanking her for, even if you didn't really want it in the first place. ("Dear Aunt Maud, thank you so much for the Princess Fairy Tale Cruiser. I'm sure it will come in handy sometime this year.") If you got money, describe how you plan on spending it. ("Dear Aunt Maud, thank you for your generous gift. I plan on spending it on either a jacket I've had my eye on for a while, or a Princess Fairy Tale Cruiser.")

Saying "I'm Sorry"

"The more we know, the better we forgive. Whoever feels deeply, feels for all who live."
~Madame de Staël

Sometimes your friends can be so sensitive, you have to apologize for silly things just to "keep the peace." You know what we mean! For example, let's say that you didn't see your friend in the hallway as you were walking to class.

Your friend: Okay, BE that way.

You: What? Oh, hi!

Your friend: You think you're too good to say hi to me!

You: What? I didn't even see you there!

Your friend: All I know is that I said "hi" and you didn't say "hi" back.

The World's Biggest Etiquette Mistake!

You: Okay! Fine! I see you now! Hello again!

Your friend: Now it's too late.

You: Arg! Fine, I'm *sorry*. (This is a fake apology!)

Your friend (now happy): Okay, see you later!

What about real apologies? There comes a time in everyone's life when she realizes that she's made a *big mistake*. Dang it! Now she needs to apologize. (Boys never have this problem, because they can never admit when they're wrong.)

In order to apologize in a sincere way that can help everyone feel better, follow this advice:

1. Be specific about what you are apologizing for and the damage it may have done. Example: "I'm sorry I accidentally spilled water all over you. I'm sure that it's pretty wet."

2. **IMPORTANT:** Don't make a "halfway" apology. Accept *full* responsibility. Don't try to explain or justify why you did something.

   Don't do this: "I'm sorry that you were klutzy enough to trip me as I walked by with this pot of water."

3. Come up with a conclusion to your apology that can prevent the mistake from happening again. Example: "I will never carry water again. Now let me get you a washrag, and maybe a loofah."

FAMILY

"Just because your family loves you doesn't mean they understand you."

~**Francesca Shrapnel**

Families rule! When you're in a family, you have built-in relationships with the people in it for the rest of your lives together. So even though your brother might drive you crazy, it's nice to know that he will *always* be your brother. (He doesn't have any choice!)

Parents

We can get so locked into seeing our parents as "Mom" and "Dad," we sometimes forget that they are just *people*. It's always good to be reminded that your parents were once *kids*! Try to imagine your parents when they were *your* age. Would they have been friends with you?

Your parents will probably spend over $250,000 to raise you to the age of 17. (If you're an only child, they will spend even more. See, you ARE spoiled!) And if they help you pay for college, that amount will be a LOT more! So your parents are investing a *lot* of time and money in you. Do you know why they do that? *Because they love you.* Sometimes we forget that fact.

Maybe it's time to give them a return on their investment. The next time your mom or dad comes home from work or seems tired, give her or him a big hug and say, "Thank you." They will think you've lost your mind! If they ask, "What are you thanking me for?" say "Everything." (Now they'll think you want something!)

Think about how hard your parents work to keep your household running. Even though they sometimes embarrass you or make you mad, it's really important for you to love and respect them. Trust us, you'll come to appreciate what they've done for you!

When asked who their biggest role model is, almost half of U.S. teens said their mother or father.

Strategy Tip

When you're trying to get something you really want from your parents, don't say, *If you give me this one thing, I'll love you forever!* Parents know that you'll love them forever anyway, so it doesn't work. Saying, *I'll never ask you for anything again* doesn't work either. Everyone knows it's not true!

Parents don't want to waste money on something that you want today, but might not care about in a week. So if you show your parents that you really do want something by doing chores or trying to earn money for it, they will know you are serious and they'll help a sister out. (Oops, we mean *daughter.*) They'll also think you're responsible!

As you hit middle school and go into high school, you start becoming your own person. Some girls start to resent their parents a little (or a lot!), because this can be a tough process. So if a girl runs into any real trouble, she just might reject the help of the people who love her the most and want to understand: *her parents.*

Your father remembers when you were his little girl running around in pigtails. He might be just as confused as you about who you are now! It's not unusual for a father to stop understanding his daughter as soon as she starts to become a young woman. One thing is for sure: Dad's going to get *more* protective of you as you become a teenager! Keep talking to your father; ask him for advice, and let him know you're still his (not-so-little) girl.

A mother worries that her connection with her daughter will get weaker as she gets older. Help your mom know what's going on in your life by talking with her. Sure, it's annoying that she wants to know **EVERYTHING** that's going on with you, but you'll get out of a lot of nagging if you just talk to her. A great time to do this is when you're being driven around in "Mom's taxi." You have to be in the car anyway and a few minutes of chatting in the car can go a long way. So don't text, TALK.

The reason you should take time to chat with your mom is because it's easy for a girl to make her mom happy, but she sometimes doesn't realize it. And as insane as it sounds, you can even tell your mom about secrets, like who you have a crush on, and *she won't tell anyone else.* YES!

In written Chinese, the character for "trouble" is two women in the same house.

Strategy Tip

You have to give your parents some Bad News. We don't know what you did, but it ain't good. But since you HAVE to tell them, try to pick the right moment. It's all about timing.

Times to Avoid:

- *Don't tell them* bad news when they are leaving for work. (It'll ruin their day.)
- *Don't tell them* right when they get home from work. (They're tired and want to relax a moment.)
- *Don't tell them* on a Friday (ruins the weekend) or a Monday (there's too much stress on Mondays as it is.)
- *Don't tell them* if they already have bad news to deal with.
- *Don't tell them* if you can avoid telling them. (JK)

After you DO tell your parents the bad news, give them a chance to react to it. You've known about this for a while, but it's news to them. Let them process it. They may get angry. Let them! The worst kinds of fights are when you know you're in the wrong, but you argue anyway. It only makes them madder and makes your punishment worse. Say you're sorry. You can have "reasonable discussions" later, when they've cooled down.

At some point, you'll find yourself arguing with your parents about *important things.* Do you want to know the most common argument girls have with their parents? *Half* of all girls say they argue with their parents about cleaning their rooms. Hey, that's not a bad reason to keep your room clean in the first place!

Other common argument topics:

- Not being able to pick out your own outfits.
- Being treated like a little kid.
- Feeling like you don't have any privacy.

- Always having to change the oil in the car.
- Having a curfew that is too early. (If you ARE caught out past curfew, call home, and then when your folks pick up, say *"I've got it!"*)

 Fun Vocabulary! drapetomania: A strong desire to run away from home.

Hey, nobody likes to do chores, but if keeping your room clean is your biggest worry at home **life is good.** Compare yourself instead to the billion girls in the rest of the world who go to bed hungry or who have been working full-time since they were little kids. *Then* clean up your room. (Yes, we know that you're still going to hate cleaning up your room. But we tried!)

If you have a good friend who lives nearby, cleaning rooms (and doing other chores) together can be fun. Put your hair up, turn the music up, and start cleaning and dancing. *Clean it, sister!* If you don't goof off, the job's done twice as quickly, and then you can do *real* fun stuff together. (Plus, the cleaner your room is, the less likely it is that your mom will go through your stuff!)

Helpful Housework Tips!

If you were supposed to be doing housework but it slipped your mind until the last second, these tips might help buy a little time:

1. Sprinkle a little cinnamon on a cookie sheet and put it in the oven at 350 degrees for 10 minutes. Then turn off the oven and open its door a little to let the heat and cinnamon smell get out. When your folks come in, look really tired. Say, "I'm sorry I didn't get to the housework. I baked a bunch of cookies for [insert needy family or charity name here] and I haven't had time to get started yet." Then get started!

2. Quickly spray a little furniture polish on the furniture by the front door. As soon as your parents come in, they will smell it. They will immediately *assume* that you've been working! (This works even better if they find you on the couch looking exhausted.)

Sisters and Brothers

If you're lucky enough to have *sisters* or *brothers*, try to enjoy them! If you fight sometimes, that's normal. If you fight with your brother ALL the time, get an appointment with your family doctor. Once there, request a *brother-ectomy*. (This is the surgical removal of your brother.) That might do the trick!

Strategy Tips

If your brother or sister ever tells you to "shut up," try using this magical spell from ancient times:

I don't shut up, I grow up,
and when I look at you, I throw up.

Problem solved!

But if your older brother or sister is trying to tell you what to do, never say: "You're not the boss of me!" This rarely helps.

The thing is, your siblings are awesome to have around. If you didn't have them, who would you complain about your parents to? If you have *younger* brothers or sisters, try to go out of your way to be nice to them. This might mean something as basic as going to the movies together. It doesn't take much effort on your part, and you will be their hero afterwards. (Given a chance, little kids **LOVE** to idolize their older sisters!)

Girls with siblings will sometimes fantasize about being an only child. Then there would be no more live-in pests to bother with! But an only child dreams about having brothers and sisters. It's natural to wish for what you don't have.

Big Problem: *Mom and Dad (or the rest of the world) always compare me to my older brother/sister.*

"Why can't you be more like your sister?" This has to be the last thing that a girl wants to hear . . . except for maybe, "Why can't you be more like your brother?"

Stay calm. Give a big fake smile and nod silently. Then go to the nearest place where you can be alone and punch the air several times! (Now is also a good time to mutter bad words.) *You* know that you're your own person even if nobody else knows that what you do makes you *you!*

Bigger Problem: *It seems like my parents love my brother/sister more than they love me.*

At some point, everybody with brothers or sisters thinks that their siblings get better treatment. It might even be true! The problem is that parents can't *always* be fair; it's just not possible. If you really think that this is happening, your best move is to *calmly* explain your position to both of your parents. Try to have examples ready.

Do NOT let it turn into an argument. You just want them to see your point of view. Since they are adults, your parents will appreciate your mature outlook, and they may even agree with you! **Stay calm and use examples.**

Why Do Parents Always Say This? ☹

Why didn't you go before we got in the car?

It doesn't look clean to me.

Do as I say, not as I do.

Set a good example for . . .

I'm the parent, that's why.

The world doesn't revolve around you.

You're grounded.

What am I—your maid?

If everyone jumped off a bridge . . .

You're not sick!

When you have kids, they'll be just like you!

I love you, honey! (Loudly in public.)

Go outside and get some exercise.

Do you think I'm made of money?

Some day you will thank me for this.

I love you, but . . .

You did WHAT?

BEAUTY

"Beauty is in the eye of the beholder, and it may be necessary from time to time to give a stupid or misinformed beholder a black eye."
~Miss Piggy

In the animal kingdom, the boys are usually the flashy show-offs; you know, like with lions, peacocks, hamsters, that sort of thing. But we humans reverse this trend, and *girls* tend to be the ones wearing more jewelry, makeup, and more interesting clothing than boys.

But what IS beautiful? If you have ever traveled to another country, you know that what one culture thinks is *beautiful,* another culture might consider just *weird.* Every society has "rules" for what is beautiful. So there has to be more than just ONE way to be beautiful. And what you think is good looking is probably what you have been taught is good looking by our society!

Even more confusing is the fact that the "rules" for beauty **always** change. Back in the 1950s, Miss America was supposed to be the most beautiful woman in the United States. But compared to many women today, she'd be considered short and overweight. So what happened? *The rules changed!*

Of course, having rules for beauty is stupid. Anyone can be beautiful in almost any way that you can imagine. Sometimes the thing that makes a girl beautiful is a strong nose or a slanted smile. Because the girl doesn't look *perfect,* THAT is the interesting thing about her. The French even have a term for this sort of beauty: *jolie laide* (ZJO-lee led). Like the writer Mavis Jukes says, "You don't have to be pretty to be beautiful."

"Energy is more attractive than beauty."
~Louisa May Alcott

An Ohio woman who was caught stealing $1 million in diamonds told police officers she was too "cute" to go to jail. (She was sentenced to three years.)

Here's "Beauty Logic" for you: If there is something about you that you think is beautiful (like your hair!), you can't ever say so. People would think you were *stuck up*! But if there is something about your appearance that you *don't* like, it's perfectly okay to obsess about it and complain about it to your friends. They practically expect it. Weird, huh?

It's all in the way we see ourselves. In France, 80 percent of people look carefully at themselves in a mirror at least once a day. While 88 percent of French men like what they see, only 73 percent of French women think they look good. (And only 1 percent of French women think they are beautiful!) That's odd, because most people think that women are *more* attractive to look at than men. After all, if you look at the covers of women's magazines, *women* are on the covers. And if you look at the covers of a lot of men's magazines, *women* are on the covers too!

GOOD NEWS! Research suggests that most people think that the face of a 12- to 14-year-old girl is one of the most appealing faces around. Whoo-hoo!

The sad fact is that people have always been judged by the way they look. In order to test yourself to see if this beauty peer pressure has gotten to you, try the following activity:

Walk by a Mirror . . . and Don't Look!

This is hard for anyone to do . . . try it for a day and you'll see why!

You will need: Reflective surfaces.

In the course of a day, you will walk by many surfaces that reflect your image . . . mirrors, windows, mirrors, newly washed cars, mirrors, and mirrors. The natural reaction that women and men have is to look at themselves when they get a chance.

Try starting off your day with *one* good look in the mirror as you get ready for school. Then DON'T look at yourself again until noon. (Just check to make sure that there's nothing in your teeth. That's it!) If you can restrain yourself from looking at yourself the rest of the day, you are probably not too self-conscious!

Practice checking yourself in the mirror really fast—check your nose and teeth for trouble and move on.

Boys are as bad about this as girls. Find a spot where there is a big reflective window and watch boys and men walk past it. Although some will walk right by, many will "check themselves out."

Beauty Is Only Skin Deep

"When I was your age . . . I wish I'd known that I already had everything I needed within myself to be happy, instead of looking for happiness at beauty counters."

~Ilene Beckerman

Many children's stories have a moral like "Beauty is only skin deep." We're not so sure about that. How much deeper should it go? Who wants cute *kidneys*? We've also read stories with a moral like "True beauty is on the inside." What good is that? Nobody will ever see it!

It's nice to know that some people think that beauty is as much about *brains* and *personality* as appearances. In Russia, the people once got to vote for their Miss Universe. The winner by a huge margin was a 14-year-old girl named Alyona. She wore a T-shirt and didn't put on any makeup. One of the Russians who voted for her did so because she disliked "unnatural beauties who cannot be distinguished from each other with their fake emotions and smiles." Wow! Unfortunately, Alyona was disqualified because she was too young. *Dang it!*

Okay, it's time to take a special tour of beauty's SECRETS, HISTORIES, and MYSTERIES!

Can You Say "Trout Pout"?

Ever wonder why your lips are a different color than the rest of you? It's because there are a lot more little blood vessels (called *capillaries*) under the skin of your lips than there are underneath your regular skin. (If you've ever cut your lip, that's why it bleeds so much.) You can tell someone is sick if her lips are pale; this shows bad blood circulation!

The most common cosmetics that go on the mouth are lipstick, lip gloss, and lip liner. But adding *color* isn't the only way that women have beautified their lips. They've also done "lip exercises." It was once thought that pronouncing words with a lot of "P"s would give lips a good workout and make them fuller. Girls used to walk around talking about "popcorn and pumpkins" to get puffy lips. Some girls even did lip weightlifting. You've heard of push-ups and pull-ups, but how about lip-ups?

But before you think how weird that is, keep in mind that many girls and women in the United States today buy *lip plumpers,* which irritate and sting lips so that they get puffy. These plumpers use things like cayenne powder or cinnamon oil to do their stinging. Ouch! Girls who lip plump too much suffer from "trout pout." Their lips start looking like a fish face!

 The Japanese thought it was rude to show someone your open mouth, which is why many Japanese women cover their mouths when laughing even today.

The Eyes Have It

Eyes are usually the first thing someone sees when they look at you. But even though we "beautify" our eyelids, eyebrows, and eyelashes, we usually leave our *eyeballs* alone. Most eye makeup makes the eyebrows and eyelashes darker. The ancient Egyptians called eye makeup *kohl,* and it had a practical purpose. *Kohl* was used to protect eyes from the desert sun. You may have seen football players with black streaked beneath their eyes for the same reason. Cleopatra put blue-black kohl on her upper eyelids and green on her *lower* lids.

To get the perfect eye makeup mix, Egyptians mixed either honey, crocodile poop, and onion water OR ground donkey liver, oil, and opium. *Gross!* BTW, nowadays, there is clear mascara, which is terrific for separating lashes. (It can also be used as an "eyebrow gel" to keep your brows looking good!)

As for eyebrows, American girls didn't start tweezing (or even shaving) their eyebrows until the 1920s. Tweezing has continued right up until today. Not only that, but men are getting in on the act as well. Recently, a growing number of men have also begun to have their eyebrows "shaped" with plucking and waxing. (This is called *manscaping.*)

If you're going to tweeze your eyebrows, try to keep them looking **natural!** For some reason, there are girls who get a little crazy with the tweezers and they start pulling everything in sight. This is painful and silly, especially when they end up using eyebrow pencils to fill in the holes where their hair was.

Although it's not such a big deal anymore, pierced eyebrows used to be a real "in your face" way of getting people to pay attention. (Get it? "In your face"?) But eyebrow piercings can be dangerous, because they can damage nerves and leave part of a person's face numb.

"The thing you hate about yourself tends to be the thing that everyone likes about you."

~**Nicole Kidman**

Expressions

Our face can communicate how we are feeling more quickly than words. Our expressions EXPRESS our feelings! And because we are complicated, our expressions can communicate complicated feelings instead of just one at a time. In other words, someone can smile sadly, even though these are two different emotions.

Computers using emotion-recognition software can be used to analyze these feelings. One such computer was used to look at the *Mona Lisa's* famous smile. The computer found that the smile was 83 percent happy, 9 percent disgusted, 6 percent afraid, and 2 percent angry. (And since Leonardo da Vinci painted her, we now know the Da Vinci Code.)

Do You Pick Your Nose?

If you "pick your nose" as the best part of your face, you're not alone. Native Americans like the Nez Perce (which means "Pierced Nose") used piercings to draw attention to the center of the face. Women in Pakistan and India have worn delicate nose ornaments for centuries. Sometimes a fine chain will lead from a woman's nose to a hair ornament or earring. And the ancient Romans believed that a strong, assertive nose was a sign of intelligence and leadership ability.

Do Your Ears Hang Low?

As for ears, they might be the most ignored part of the face. **How unfair!** This isn't a face "rule," but a doctor told us that most people have ears that are about as long as their nose. Check to see if this is true for you!

Do you have earlobes? (This is the lower part of your ear which may hang down a bit.) A traditional Buddhist belief is that long earlobes are a sign of great wisdom. And long earlobes are thought to be beautiful for members of the Kelabit tribe of Borneo. Women there stretch their earlobes so that they hang anywhere from two to eight inches down from their head! At that length, they can tickle your shoulders. (That reminds us of a song: *Do your ears hang low? Do they wobble to and fro? Can you tie 'em in a knot . . .* Okay, we'll stop now.)

Getting pierced ears is pretty common for U.S. girls. You should know that studies show that if the ear piercing goes through cartilage (in the stiffer part of the ear), the chances for infection are greatly increased. One study found an infection rate of almost 30 percent for cartilage piercings. Yikes!

In traditional Japanese culture, pierced ears are considered bad luck.

In Your Face!

"Your brain is the most important part of your body. That's because good looks come and go, but your brain will always be there."

~*Sarah Nader*

In India, the *forehead* is believed to be one of the most important parts of the body. Indian women sometimes have a red or yellow mark in the middle of the forehead called a *tilak* or a *bindi*. The *tilak* is a sign of good fortune; it shows that the person wearing it is pure and thoughtful. The decoration is also supposed to keep the mind calm. Although the *tilak* may show that the woman wearing it is married, it can also be a fashion accessory. (Young girls wearing the *tilak* usually have it done in a light red color.)

The Bigger, the Better!

For originality, you've got to like the standard of beauty that the Massa have. The Massa is a tribe of Africans who live in Chad. For them, the *bigger*, the *better*. The most beautiful feature a woman can have is rolls of fat on her neck!

Fun and Natural Facials

It's time for a guacamole facial! It's fun AND natural! Just cut an avocado in half, remove the pit, and peel. Mash up the avocado. Then smear it on your face! Leave it on for around five minutes and then wash it off with warm water. The natural oils from the avocado will soften and moisturize your face.

The egg white facial is another natural beautifier. You need one egg for this. Crack it, remove the yolk, and whip up the whites in a small bowl. Then spread it on your face. Once you've done so, lie down for awhile and let it dry. Then wash and wipe your face clean.

Trim and Polish

You've probably noticed that your fingernails grow faster than your toenails. Most fingernails grow about an inch and a half a year, while toenails grow just half an inch. (This is because your hands have better blood circulation than your feet, and they get more nutrients.)

 Psychologists believe that fingernail and cuticle biters may be more stubborn than most people.

To decorate their nails, girls in the United States started using nail polish in the 1920s. For a long time, pink was the only color considered "appropriate." If a girl painted her nails red, she was considered a troublemaker!

You might be surprised to learn that "manicures" and "pedicures" don't actually *cure* anything. Nope; this is simply what we call *trimming* and *polishing* fingernails and toenails. They are also a terrific way to "pamper" yourself. It turns out that getting your nails soaked, buffed, polished, finished, filed, decorated, and colored feels pretty good. And it's also a fun thing to do with a friend! Massage her hands with lotion, and to keep her nails soft, wrap them in warm, wet towels. Use a clipper and nail file to shape her nails. **Note:** You may want to take a bath or soak your toes in warm water for five to ten minutes before going through the above steps for a pedicure.

When done, it's time to paint or polish! Clear polish is the most natural look, but if you want to do some color painting, most girls try to match whatever color lipstick they might be wearing. If you're in a creative mood, you could paint each nail in a different color. You can also put clear nail polish on a fingernail and then sprinkle glitter on it. After it's dry, just put one more layer of clear polish on, and you have glitter nails!

 If you ever want to whiten your fingernails, try sticking them into a cut piece of lemon for a while. (Make sure you don't have any fingernail cuts before you do this . . . ouch!)

 Hot Tip! If there is a beauty school near you, they probably offer manicures and pedicures for way cheap.

Fun Nail Trick: Try putting scratch 'n' sniff stickers on your fingernails. They're non-toxic and will make your fingernails smell good all day!

Practical Joke Alert! We encourage you to sneak up on your brother or father while he's asleep and paint as many of his finger and/or toenails as you can reach. Once the painted man wakes up, try to rush him off to work or school as fast as possible so that he doesn't notice!

I'll Never Look Like Her

"Who I am inside determines how I feel about my body, not the other way around."

~Alanis Morissette

In ancient Greece, girls were supposed to be *slim* and *trim*. In order to get their daughters beautiful, Greek mothers sometimes wrapped up their baby daughters tightly with fabric for the first months of their lives to squish and lengthen them. (Sort of a *Play-Doh Not-So-Fun Factory of Beauty* for real girls.)

If that seems weird to you, think about this: The average American woman is about 5' 4" tall and weighs around 160 pounds. The average American fashion model is about 5' 10" tall and weighs around 115 pounds. Wow. There are over 3.5 billion women in the world, and only a few thousand of them are models. And what if you took away the airbrushing, makeup, and expensive clothes? Then even *models* don't look like models!

 In a recent study, 13 percent of men said they wanted to date women shorter than them. But about half of the women only wanted to date men taller than themselves!

Anyway, think about who you are comparing yourself to. And remember that other countries have beliefs about the female body that can be the opposite of U.S. culture. For example, in the United States, girls sometimes get eating disorders trying to keep their weight *down*. In the West African country of Mauritania, *overweight* women have long been thought of as attractive. They have problems with girls eating *too much*! Fortunately, the United States and Mauritania are both trying to educate girls about proper nutrition.

It is possible that times might be slowly changing. Mannequins are sort of like store "models," and lately some of them have been made with 38-inch hips, which is much bigger than they used to be. Storeowners say they now have "butts with attitude" that are easier to model jeans on realistically. ☺

The Belly Button

It's so cute, and so important! In Japan, the belly has long been believed to be a source of a person's warmth and vitality. Traditional Japanese women's clothing has a wide cloth belt around the midsection to protect the belly and keep it warm. The Japanese believe that the perfect belly button (or navel) is narrow, vertical . . . and an "innie"!

As cute as it is, your belly button is also your first *scar*. It is the scar tissue left over from when the doctor cut the umbilical cord that connected you to your mommy. So that means some girls show off their scars with short blouses and tops. It's weird to think about the belly button that way!

 Belly button experts have not been able to figure out why belly button lint is almost always blue, even if it comes from a girl who owns no blue clothing.

In the United States, girls generally have to be 18 to get their belly buttons pierced. (It is one of the slowest-healing piercings there is.) If you want to have a little fun, try the following practical joke.

Fake Belly-Button Piercing

It's time for a fake belly-button piercing. (This trick also works for a fake nose piercing.)

You will need: Beads, glue, a belly button or nose.

Stop by a bead store and look for a bead that you can use to get a "piercing." For a nose piercing, find a small bead with a flat back. If you want a custom belly-button piercing, you may want to get a larger, more impressive bead, maybe even one you could attach a small chain to.

This trick is best done after you have been out of the house for awhile. Wait until it's almost time to return home, and then put a little dab of white Elmer's Glue (not Krazy Glue!) on the back of the bead. Hold it against your nostril or belly. Be patient and keep it there in place until the glue dries.

Then you're ready to parade into the house! Act like you're sort of guilty and trying to hide it, but make sure it's visible, too. Then watch your mom shriek and your dad yell before you tell them, "Just kidding!"

Beautiful Skin

"If you take good care of your skin, you won't need much makeup."
~Brooke Vermillion

Dr. Ellen Gendler is a skin-care expert who was asked the all-important question, "What is the most common skin-care mistake girls make?" Her answer: "Picking at their pimples or using too much moisturizer." Okay, good to know!

Can you believe that *freckles* were once thought to be a sign of disease? Naturally, there were cures for this horrible condition, like having a girl rinse her face with dew and then saying the alphabet backwards.

Getting Soggy in the Tub

Have you ever noticed how your fingers shrivel up when you stay in the bathtub too long? (And then you can pretend you're an old lady!) Guess what? Your fingers don't actually shrivel. The skin just gets BIGGER.

What happens is that the longer you stay in the water, the more water molecules soak into your skin tissue. This stretches the skin out. Basically, you're getting soggy! And the younger you are, the further your skin stretches in the tub.

In India, the people have a cool tradition of skin painting. A plant called "henna" grows in India, the Middle East, and northern Africa. It provides leaves that can be used for a safe dye, usually in some shade of red. The temporary dye can be used for body painting or "mehndi." Women have patterns painted on their hands, feet, or entire bodies, especially for special occasions like marriages. And a new bride didn't have to do any housework until her wedding mehndi wore off. (See pages 70-72 in the "Fun Stuff to Do" chapter to learn how to paint with henna.)

Although almost nobody has pure white skin, this hasn't stopped women from trying to get it with makeup. In the past, Japanese women used face powder made from rice, which was organic and nontoxic. In Europe, some Englishwomen wanted white faces so badly, they put leeches behind their ears to literally suck the blood out of their heads. **Gross!**

In modern times, many people think tans are cool, but of course, tanning can create skin problems. Girls with light skin and light eyes are the most at risk for skin cancer, and should be the most careful about becoming a *tanorexic*. A *tanorexic* is someone who thinks that she's too pale, even when she is *really tan*. The thing is, tans always wear off anyway, but skin cancer can stick around for a long time.

 Unappealing Peeling! When skin peels off after a bad sunburn, it is called *blype*. Now you know.

Goose Bumps!

When you get cold, your skin often gets little bumps on it, which are called goose bumps or goose pimples. How did they get such a weird name?

The little feathers called "goose down" are useful for stuffing pillows and comforters. These obviously came from geese, and some geese get their down feathers plucked as many as five times a year. Once the goose has its feathers plucked, it gets cold, and is covered in goose bumps or goose pimples. What happens is that the goose has small muscles surrounding each feather, which raises the feather up or down depending on the temperature. When it's cold, a goose will "puff up" its feathers to create warmth. Without any feathers, the naked goose just gets covered with little bumps of muscles trying to move feathers that aren't there. Sad!

Humans work under the same system. We don't have feathers, but we do have hair. Even though there isn't much of it, when it's cold, our skin muscles try to raise up our hairs to create warmth for ourselves. We can also get goose bumps when we are frightened. Then it is called *horripilation*. Even though these goose bumps are scary, experts like R. L. Stine agree that *horripilation* is harmless.

Perfume

Smells can have an influence on how we feel. Some people get headaches if they smell something bad, and some people believe that good smells can help us feel better and stay healthy. This is called *aromatherapy*. In aromatherapy, some plant oils, including essential oils, are thought to have the following effects:

- Rose, chamomile, and lavender increase feelings of calmness and well-being.
- Jasmine, orange, and cypress increase feelings of confidence.
- Geranium, grapefruit, and sandalwood are used to treat depression.
- Basil, frankincense, and peppermint are used to help with low energy.
- Black pepper, basil, and rosemary improve memory and concentration.

In traditional Japanese society, women put their clothes in small, enclosed spaces, and burned incense with them so the clothing would smell good.

Nowadays, many perfumes smell somewhat similar because they have an alcohol base. (That's why they evaporate so fast.) If you're looking for a perfume that doesn't smell like everyone else's, keep your nostrils open. For instance, there used to be a store in Williamsburg, Virginia, that specialized in very particular smells, including a ripe tomato, moist earth, fir trees, or roast beef. They even had bottled odors, like Play-Doh and Doll Head (the smell of the vinyl head of a doll!). How *scents-ible* is that?

Sadly, the quest for pricey perfume can have bad impacts on the natural world. For example, the Brazilian rosewood tree once peacefully grew in the wilds of the Amazon. When the perfume called Chanel No. 5 came out in 1921, that all changed. Chanel No. 5 uses rosewood oil, and soon the oil was being used in other perfumes, soaps, and scented candles. Today, the rosewood tree is an endangered species.

Make Your Own Perfumed Body Scrub

You can make your own perfumed scrub without destroying any species.

You will need: A wide-mouthed glass jar with a lid you can clamp or screw down, kosher salt, olive oil, an essential oil you like the smell of (like lemon, eucalyptus, rose, or peppermint), and cinnamon.

Fill your jar a little less than halfway up with kosher salt. Then pour almost as much olive oil into the jar and start mixing until it feels right to you.

Next add in four drops of your essential oils and a tablespoon of cinnamon! Mix it all up completely. (There are no rules, so if you want to throw in some lemon zest, rosemary, or flower petals, go ahead!) Then let it sit for awhile.

When you're ready to use it, just bring the jar with you into the shower. Take a scoop of the scrub out and rub it on your joints and your feet. Be sure to rinse it all off and don't slip on the oily mix while you're in there! (Don't put your *body* scrub on your face, either. It's not designed for it, and it's probably illegal where you live.)

 Hot Tip! Here's our hot tip with perfume: *A little bit goes a long way.* We're sure you've noticed the boy who puts on half a bottle of cologne after PE class at school. He reeks! He thinks that since a little cologne smells good, a *lot* smells great. You know how wrong he is, so don't make the exact same mistake.

MAKEUP

"Beauty, to me, is about being comfortable in your own skin. That, or a kick-ass red lipstick."

~Gwyneth Paltrow

Make up means "to invent." So does that mean if you wear makeup you are trying to invent a new face for yourself, one that isn't yours? Maybe that's why some people call it *fake-up!* Women who always wear makeup sometimes say they feel "naked" without it on. So are women improving their faces with cosmetics or are they using it to hide behind?

Many people have struggled with this question. In Alexandria, Egypt, it was once illegal for unmarried women to wear makeup because the men were worried that they would be tricked into marrying someone who wasn't who she seemed to be. And nowadays, girls often argue with their parents about wearing makeup. Sometimes these arguments go all the way to a court of law. In Los Angeles, a judge once banned a Mexican American girl from using makeup against her parents' wishes.

As far as cosmetics go, listen to your parents and "make up" your own mind. Just don't let yourself become your own favorite hobby or after-school project. Then you really will be stuck on yourself!

Most teenaged girls in the United States do use makeup of some kind. There are bazillions of books and magazines out there with beauty tips about when you can wear purple eye shadow (*never!*) or how to paint your toenails. You probably know more tips, tricks, ideas, and cool stuff than we do, but for those of you just barely getting into makeup, here are some of the basics.

Makeup Basics

"I am not wearing makeup because I need none."

~**Sarah Vowell**

If you are applying makeup to your skin and then cleaning it off again day after day, it's actually pretty hard on your skin. So maybe the most important tip is this: don't use too much makeup! Experts agree that this is the most common mistake that girls make. As a wise woman named Mariam Kanso wrote, "If you put a ton of makeup on everyday, a time will come when you skip it. Then people are going to be shocked by your *actual* appearance and that's *not* a good thing!"

 In France, girls and women try NOT to look as if they are spending hours on their faces. French girls favor makeup that is so natural, you don't notice it's there. The key is not to try too hard. If you *can* see obvious makeup on a woman's face, the French have a word for it: *vulgaire* (vulgar).

Basic Safety! Don't share cosmetics with your friends. Unless you're wearing "natural" makeup, be sure to wash it off before going to sleep at night. Oh, and never keep cosmetics for more than six months. After that, they may have germs living in them. Ick!

Base makeup/foundation: The idea of base makeup (or "foundation") is to make your skin look like it doesn't have any blemishes or look too shiny. So it's important that the base you choose matches your skin type. Experiment with different shades till you get one that's just right. *Tip:* Blend, blend, blend! Your face should not be a different color than your neck. And try not to overdo it. Some people call this "pancake" makeup, and it's not usually a good thing to have your face compared to breakfast food.

Concealer: This is a thick makeup that is good for hiding really bad blemishes . . . okay, pimples. Like your base, make sure it matches your skin. *Tip:* Try dabbing it on, instead of spreading it on. That way, it's less noticeable.

Eyeliner: Your eyelids are one of the most sensitive parts of your body, so be very careful using application wands with eyeliners and mascara. (And never put on eye makeup in a moving car!) Apply the eyeliner outside of the lash line, away from the eye. *Tip:* Don't overdo it, or you'll have raccoon eyes.

Eye shadow: The basic idea of eye shadow is that if you wear lighter shades of it, it will make your eyes appear bigger. Darker shades will make your eyes appear somewhat smaller. *Tip:* Remember, nobody has naturally purple eyelids unless they've been hit in a boxing match!

Mascara: Don't keep mascara for more than three months. If you're going to use an eyelash curler, use it before you put on your mascara! And although waterproof mascara won't "streak," some girls' eyes get irritated by it. Also, water-based mascara is much easier to remove. *Tip:* If your mascara gives you "tarantula eyelashes," you're overdoing it.

Blush: By highlighting cheeks with a rosy color, a girl can look like she just exercised. How healthy! Either that, or like she's blushing from embarrassment. *Tip:* Gel blushes are more difficult to apply than powder or cream blushes.

Lip liner: If you can't really tell where your lips end and your skin begins, then lip liners are handy. They also make a nice outline around your lips so your lipstick doesn't "bleed" out past your lips onto your skin. If you want to use a lip liner, make a border around your lips, and then use lipstick or lip gloss inside the line. Fun!

Lip gloss, lipstick: Do you want your lips to look "wetter" or more colorful? These are the difficult questions. Lipstick can also make lips look a bit bigger than they are, but be sure not to use it beyond the edges of your lips. *Tip:* Don't choose a lipstick color that is so bright, hummingbirds are attracted to your face.

Painting fingernails and toenails: Before painting fingernails or toenails, make sure that you wash them very well. Then trim and file them down. Once you start painting, use short, even strokes going in the same direction. When you're done, dip a cotton swab in polish remover and carefully remove any excess polish around your nails. (Some girls also like to put cotton balls between their toes when painting them, just to be safe.) *Tip:* Both fingernail polish remover and some nail polishes are FLAMMABLE, so be careful. No burning candles when painting nails!

 Petroleum jelly may be the best makeup that isn't makeup. It can be used as a lip gloss or make eyelashes and eyebrows look glossy. A little bit rubbed into each cheek gives the skin moisture and color.

SLEEPOVERS AND SLUMBER PARTIES

"The older you get, the fewer slumber parties there are, and I hate that. I liked slumber parties. What happened to them?"
~Drew Barrymore

When a bunch of girls come over to spend the night, why is that called a "slumber party" or a "sleepover"? Almost no sleeping ever happens! But even if there isn't much shut-eye, a slumber party *is* one of the most incredibly fun things that girls can do. Believe it or not, some girls have had to be hospitalized during them because they started laughing so hard it turned into a medical emergency.

Invitations

When you decide to invite some friends over for the night, it doesn't have to be a fancy affair. But if more than just a friend or two are coming, you may want to send invitations. In addition to the obvious information like the date (duh!), you will want to tell your guests whether they need sleeping bags or pillows. Also remind them that they will need to remember to bring their toothbrush, pajamas, and maybe their favorite blanky. (Okay, maybe not.)

If you put **"RSVP"** on your invitation, that means *Répondez S'il Vous Plaît*. This is French for "please reply and tell me if you're coming or not." To make sure your guests understand this, only invite French girls to your house. ☺

Invitations can be printed on really nice stationery, handwritten on Popsicle sticks, or texted in emoji. It's up to you! But try giving them to your friends privately and one at a time. That way, nobody will feel left out if they don't get one (because naturally **everyone** wants to come to your house!).

There is no perfect number of people to invite to a sleepover. One friend can be a blast, and so can seven! If you end up with a total group bigger than five though, it can get a little crazy. (In other words, you may be asking for trouble!)

 You may want to tell your friends just to wear pajamas over to your house. That way the fun can start right away!

Finally, so your parents don't go insane, you should probably set up a time for everyone to go home the next day. Otherwise, you could end up having two sleepovers in a row—a doubleheader!

Supplies

Your mom will be a huge help here, but in case she needs reminding, sleepovers are all about **unhealthy** food. (That's pizza, popcorn, ice cream, soda, and chips in case you didn't know.)

It's also fun to have on hand some musical instruments that don't require skill to play (like tam-bourines, kazoos, bongo drums, and so forth). Goody bags for girls to take home after the party aren't required, but are nice if you have the time to put them together. These could contain glowsticks, nail polish, hair clips, necklaces, little stuffed animals, bracelets, loofahs, large amounts of cash, whatever you want!

Also, make sure to have plenty of toilet paper on hand. It's amazing how many rolls of it a bunch of girls can go through, especially if they roll someone up in it or go out TPing someone's house.

TIP: Going to someone else's house? Roll your pajamas, pillow, and supplies up in your sleeping bag for convenience. And don't forget a flashlight!

Other Preparations

What room will you be hanging out in the most at your slumber party? Go in there before your guests arrive and move everything breakable *out* of it. Then move everything soft and fun into it. So, big lamps, mirrors, and your mom's china go out, and stuffed animals, bean bag chairs, pillows, and Silly String *in*.

Speaking of rooms, one classic sleepover problem is that while some girls might want to go to bed, others want to stay up late. To solve this, either have an agreed-upon bedtime (*yeah, right*), or have one room for sleeping and a different room for hanging out and being weird.

Whether just one or seventeen of your closest friends are coming over, meet your guests at the door and introduce them to your family (yes, even your brother). A house tour is probably a good idea, too. Ask if your friend wants something to eat or drink, and then get down to having fun!

Party Games and Activities

Depending on how well you know everyone, you might want to plan two or three activities for your group. Although it's not super-imaginative, one thing might be a movie that everyone wants to see. Don't just *assume* it will be fun to get together. It *is* possible for slumber parties to be boring. (But if it's a slumber party, maybe it's not so bad if your guests fall asleep? ☺)

If you have three or more guests, a fun game is Mystery Sleeping Bag. One girl leaves the room, and the other girls zip themselves all the way up in sleeping bags. Then the girl is called back in to figure out *who's* in *which* bag. She can try gently poking or feeling the bags, but the girls inside should try not to talk or laugh!

We have left out a few classic slumber party activities from this chapter on purpose because we figure you already know about them. If you haven't heard of these, ask your mom to explain them to you: "Light as a Feather, Stiff as a Board," "Bloody Mary," "Truth or Dare," and "Who's Got the Hedgehog?" (Also, check other chapters of this book—like "Fun Stuff to Do"— for more ideas for activities.)

Party Themes

As far as party themes, you don't need to have a theme to have a good time, but sometimes a goofy theme can get everyone involved and excited about the party.

There are all sorts of ideas that you've probably heard of, like Movie Parties, Decade Parties (1960s, '70s, '80s), Camping-In Parties, or Treasure Hunts. Naturally, Pajama Parties are an easy type of party to throw. What's more fun than wearing comfy PJs and spazzing out?

Here are a few other theme ideas:

Bead Party

String 'em up! A bead party can be as simple as you and your friends stringing beads together, or as complicated as inviting an expert come to show you and your friends how to make cool stuff with beads. To prepare, you're obviously going to want to get some beads first. ☺ You might want to go with a friend to a bead shop and start loading up, or you may want to shop with your mom online for them. (You can probably get better deals online; just be sure to plan ahead for shipping time.) Be sure to get beads with a good-size hole in them; you want your guests to have fun stringing their beads, not to get frustrated.

Karaoke Party

There's something about putting a microphone in a girl's hand that turns her into an instant ham.

Hand-Painting Party

Follow the directions for henna painting (see pages 70–72) to see if you have the patience and skill to paint each other's hands or feet. Or if you have a budget, have an expert come in and paint for you.

"Come as You Are" Party

Your friends have to be game for this "spur of the moment" party. The idea is that you call them at a weird time (like early morning or

after a soccer game) when the girl might be wearing something out of the ordinary. Whatever the girl is wearing when she is called is what she wears later to the party.

 Sleepover Slang! **Squirreling:** This is what happens when you are eating ice cream (that has chunks of goodies in it) with someone else out of the same container AND the other person keeps digging out the good stuff and eating it. Example: *Hey! You're squirreling all the little brownie pieces!*

Mall Party

A field trip to the mall could be a LOT of fun, if you give it your special flair. As hostess, you split everyone on the field trip into two teams. The teams also need a digital or video camera, and a list of tasks to do.

These tasks are worth "points," and *you* decide how many points they are worth, depending on their difficulty. As the group goes through the mall, they have to record their accomplishments with their camera.

Some ideas of tasks the teams could do for points are:

- Go to a café and order straws.
- Do the splits up the escalator. (See the escalator safety tip on page 272)
- Kiss a mannequin at a certain store.
- Try on a wig.
- Play leapfrog down the hall to the bathrooms.
- Go to a shoe store and try on the biggest pair of boots possible.

You could also give each team a small budget (let's say $15). Give the teams things to buy without going over budget. Examples of things the teams could get might be cheap and flashy earrings, chocolate from See's, wristbands, or a new car.

But remember, you really don't have to have a theme for your slumber party. Since the whole idea of a sleepover is sharing time together, any activity you share will probably be worthwhile. Simple activities like playing board games or making your own pizzas are easy, but you could also have more advanced crafts to try.

Party Favors

BTW, if you have party gifts and you don't want to wait to give them away, try this. Find a hiding place for the gift, and then start unrolling a ball of yarn. Have one end of the yarn start at the front door, and after unrolling it around all the furniture that you can, have the ball eventually lead to the hidden gift. If you want to make it extra challenging, do this with *all* the party gifts and make the balls of yarn all the same color! (Make sure the girls looking for the gifts roll the yarn up as they search.)

Things to Expect

Since everyone gets so excited at slumber parties, it is not unusual for a girl or two (or everybody) to cry during it. This might happen because someone got her feelings hurt, or maybe during Girl Talk time a painful secret or memory came out. If it happens at your sleepover, don't be surprised, and don't let it ruin anything. Have everybody (including you!) get it out of her system, and then get back to having fun.

It's also not impossible that two (or more!) girls might start arguing at *your* party. *The nerve!* Since you're the hostess, you need to take them aside and say, "Look, I invited you here to have fun. Right now, you're ruining the party. Stop it." That should be enough to wise them up!

How to Have a Pillow Fight!

Finally, it's hard to beat the excitement of a good old-fashioned *pillow fight!*

Rules:

- All pillow fighters must have at least one, *large, fluffy pillow.*
- All pillow fighters must hit their opponents ONLY with their *large, fluffy pillow.*
- A pillow fighter can use one or both hands to swing the pillow. However, if one opponent is 25 or more pounds heavier than the other, she can only use *one* hand to swing with. (And she has to put her other hand behind her back.)
- A pillow fighter can try to *block* her opponent's pillow, but she can't *grab* her opponent's pillow.
- The pillow fight ends when anyone wants it to end!

Troublemakers

For some reason, pranks are extremely fun to play at slumber parties. (See the "Practical Jokes" chapter for fabulous ideas.) Perhaps the all-time classic trick is to wait for someone to fall asleep and then to gently spray whipped cream or shaving cream onto her hand. Then take a feather and tickle her nose. She will still be half asleep, and she'll reach her hand up to scratch her nose and get cream all over her face. Ha! (Oh yeah, and don't forget to throw someone's bra in the freezer.)

Getting Ready for Bed

Between finding the right spot to sleep, brushing teeth, putting on pajamas, and pillow fights, this getting ready for bed thing could take an hour.

But when the lights finally do go out, that's when some of the best conversations happen: *Girl Talk!* Secrets can come out under the cloak of darkness. By morning, you and your guests will feel as if a special bond has strengthened your friendships. (And if that doesn't happen, you can always just tell a scary story lying there in the dark.)

Sleepover Survival Tip

Try not to be the first person to fall asleep at the sleepover. This will prevent you from waking up with toothpaste in your hair or a secret message on your face.

The Morning After

Whew. Nobody is going to be bright and chipper if they stayed up till 3 a.m. the night before! But there are still fun things left to do the morning after your sleepover. It might be fun to find out what everyone dreamed about. Then try to figure out what the dreams meant! (Go to page 256 to find out.) Maybe you'll want to whip up a batch of chocolate chip pancakes. Be sure to make some for Mom and Dad, too, to thank them for letting you have friends over.

When your guests get picked up, walk them to the door so that the last thing they see is you waving good-bye!

HAIR

"Wow, Blossom, it's amazing how silky your hair is, considering it smells so funky."

~The Powerpuff Girls

There are *four* parts of your body that are not actually alive. See if you can guess what one of them is! (Are you guessing? This is a pretty hard one!)

That's right, your *hair* is not alive!* Your hair is made up of the same stuff that makes fingernails, feathers, and hooves. It's a protein called *keratin*. But you sure can do a LOT with it. A little rearranging with a hair clip, or a lot of styling with a haircut and dye can change a girl's look dramatically. And it's so easy! All you have to do is shampoo, condition, rinse, dry, pluck, shave, cut, dye, perm, style, bleach, curl or relax, crimp, braid, comb, and brush your hair and it's good to go!

Hair has long been thought to have special powers. People in many cultures saved and destroyed their hair clippings so that their enemies couldn't use their hair to cast spells against them. Julius Caesar shaved the heads of his enemies to teach them the power of ancient Rome. And today, some Jews and Muslims feel that for a woman to be properly modest, her hair should be covered when she is out in public.

 Two thousand years ago, Jewish law allowed a man to divorce his wife by uncovering her hair.

We humans have the longest hair of all the animals. Without haircuts, the hairs on your

I have more keRatin!

Why do you get to go fiRst?

---

* If we count your hair and nails as one category (they're both made of keratin), the other nonliving parts of your body are your cartilage, tendons, and the solid part of your bones.

head could get up to four feet long or more. Guinness World Records says the longest hair in the world belongs to a woman named Xie Qiuping. Her locks measure over 18 feet long. Also, a man named Tray Van Hay reportedly didn't get a haircut for over 30 years, and his hair was supposedly even longer. The *good news* is that if there were a fire on the second floor of a building, you could use his hair to escape. The *bad news*? Tray Van Hay once skipped washing his hair for six years! Talk about oily . . .

 If you added up the hair growth of ALL of your hair over your lifetime, it comes to about 590 miles.

If you've ever had a haircut and then noticed that your hair took *forever* to grow out, it was probably taking a *growing break*. Hair grows in a cycle of anywhere between two to seven years, and then it takes it easy for a few months before kicking in again with more growth. And the average human hair lives between six to 10 years, and then it goes dormant and falls out. You lose 50 to 100 hairs a day because of this, but new hairs grow in their place.

 If your dad doesn't have any hair, tell him he's not bald, he's *glabrous*. That should make him feel better!

The Ups and Downs of Having . . .

Red Hair: Because only 2 percent of people in the United States have *naturally* red hair, redheads probably get more attention. That's nice if you *like* attention, and redheads have been getting more than their fair share for a long time. Many ancient Romans thought that red hair on a woman was the most attractive color there was. It's so special, fairies and pixies in stories and art are usually depicted with red hair.

 In the United Kingdom (where 10 percent of people have red hair), redheads are called "coppertops" and red hair is often called "ginger hair."

The downside of being a redhead is that red is a symbol of fire, blood, passion, and anger. This has created a stereotype that redheads are hot tempered and out of control. Ancient Egyptians considered redheads to be so "special" they were treated as foreigners. Modern people will ask redheads if their hair color is real and kids may call them "carrot top." (And don't forget the annoying boy who whispers, "I see RED people!")

 Interesting Fact! Studies show that redheads, especially women, may not be as sensitive to pain as other people.

Really Curly Hair: Really curly hair can be any color, but it is often black. Girls with really curly hair can wear it in an *afro*, a *semi-fro* (almost an afro) or a *low-fro* (a really short afro). Interestingly, girls with *straight* hair often want *curly* hair, while girls with *curly* hair sometimes wish their hair were straight. So if a curly-haired girl gets a "permanent," she has her hair "relaxed," or "conked" (straightened), and if a girl with straight hair gets a "permanent," she gets her hair all curly. Funny, huh?

Really curly hair has unique style possibilities. For instance, it is perfect to braid with. Curly hair can be turned into a tight *cornrow* (braided close to the scalp.) In Nigeria, members of the Igbo tribe braid their hair tight to the head and end up with geometric patterns laid out on their heads. Curly hair can also be grown into dreadlocks more easily than any other hair type. *Dreadlocks* are what happen when you don't comb long curly hair; it can then be easily twisted into "natural"-looking braids.

Many African American women (and men) grew their afros out in the 1960s to show their African roots. Today, it is estimated that about 70 percent of black women have their hair straightened, or "conked."

Blonde Hair: There are more clichés about girls with blonde hair than any other hair color. Because many babies are born blonde (and then their hair darkens as they get older), blonde hair is associated with *innocence,* but not *intelligence.* Our culture says that *Blondes have more fun,* but women with this hair color are also sometimes referred to as *dumb blondes.* (Just so you know, scientists agree that hair color has nothing to do with intelligence!)

Marilyn Monroe was an actress from the twentieth century. She was famous for being the source of the stereotype of the dumb blonde. But guess what? She was a brunette!

Blonde hair was thought of as "good" in places like Greece and Italy. After all, Aphrodite (a.k.a. Venus), the goddess of love, was a blonde. Also, because most Greek and Italian women have dark hair, blondes were rare and considered special. Black-haired women sometimes rubbed yellow mud and saffron (an orange-yellow dye) into their scalps to look blonde. (If you've ever wondered how many women in the United States are natural blondes, the answer is only about 5 to 15 percent of them.)

 Blondes sometimes get a rare condition called *loose anagen syndrome.* This means they have hair that can be pulled out very easily; just combing it is enough to pull the hair out. Luckily, the hairs usually toughen up as the girl gets older.

Brown Hair: *Brunettes Are Number One!* Brown is the most common hair color for humans. And there are probably more variations of brown hair than any other color. For example, girls can have brown hair that is so dark it looks black. Or a brunette can have auburn or mahogany hair, which is brown hair with red highlights.

Brown hair is thought of as being natural and earthy, and it looks great in the sunlight. Brunettes may also be taken more seriously by other people. If a brunette has light brown hair that is almost blonde in color, some people call this "dishwater blonde," "dirty blonde," or "swamp-water blonde." (Some people are apparently messed up!)

 Bad Hair Joke Alert:
Q. What do you call a brunette in a roomful of blondes?
A. Invisible.

Black Hair: Dark hair is beautiful; it has a mystery and magic all its own. It can be anything from a very dark brown to jet black, like many Asian, Latin, and black women have. Cleopatra, one of the world's most famous enchantresses, almost certainly had black hair. In Mexico, the women of the Tzotzil people pull black hair from their combs and save it. They believe that after death they can climb to paradise on a rope of their own hair. And *Chicanas* in the Mexican American community have a hair fashion that involves really long hair with lots of body, curls, and flips.

BONUS! Black hair has the best words to describe it. For example: *ebony, inky, glossy, sable, lustrous, jet,* or *blue-black.*

Long Hair: Long hair looks cool, and it's good for getting attention. When a long-haired girl swings her mane around or runs her hands through her hair, people can't help but notice. (And from Samson to the kings of France, men have thought that long hair gave them strength.) Although it's a lot of work to take care of, long hair can also symbolize freedom. In many traditional societies, a girl would wear her hair in a long braid. Once she was married, she would wind the braid into a bun at the back of her neck.

Short Hair: We'll keep this short. ☺ There are three important things to say about short hair:

1. It's usually easier to take care of than long hair.

2. People tend to take women with short hair more seriously.

3. It's still feminine!

Hair Weaves: Braiding, extending, or weaving with colored silk, thread, or another person's hairs can really change a girl's look. The women of the Hmong tribe of Southeast Asia may take the prize for most variety with their hair extensions. They use cotton, hemp, and black wool and weave it into huge combs stuck into their hair. **Note:** Women with thin or "weak" hair shouldn't use extensions. They can lead to bald spots. (Really!)

 About one-quarter of black women use weaves, extensions, or "additions."

Bleached Hair: Oh no! You were the victim of a horrible laundry accident. ☺

Uncombable Hair: *Uncombable hair syndrome* is a medical condition where a girl (or boy) has hair that literally CANNOT BE COMBED! (Don't worry, if you don't have this condition by now, you never will.) People with this condition (also called *cheveux incoiffables*) have hair that stands *straight up*. You can gel it all you want, and it won't matter. This hair is literally *impossible* to work with.

Bad Hair: If you suffer from "bad hair," or even just a "bad hair day," we can suggest a discipline program for it that might work. The key is to be tough, but fair to the hair. (*That rhymes!*) One way to solve the "bad hair" problem is just to stuff it all in a headband or hat. Another solution for bad hair is to put your hair up in a loose or "messy" bun with a hair band. But don't be tempted to cut it all off . . . you may regret that decision later!

Mythical Bad Hair: Medusa (the character from Greek mythology) had snakes for hair, so imagine what her hair looked like when they were digesting mice! And when it came time for the snakes to shed their skin, well . . . that was "hat day."

Hair FAQs

Why are some hairs straight, while others are curly?
A hair grows out of a root in your skin called a *follicle*. If the shape of the hair shaft at its root is *round*, the hair is *straight*. If the shaft is *flattened*, the hair will be *curly*. And if the shaft is *oval*, the hair will be *wavy*.

What decides the color of my hair?

You have a color or "pigment" in your body called *melanin*. This coloring is in your eyes, your skin, and in your hair follicles. Whatever color melanin you inherited from your parents is what you get for your hair color. (Unless you use dye!)

Why does hair turn gray or white as a person get older?

Your body makes less melanin as you get older. So where there used to be a *color* in the hair, an older hair has *air bubbles* instead. Strange, huh? Air bubbles *in* the hair. These air bubbles are what make an older person's hair look gray and white!

Is it bad for my hair if I pull on it?

Yes. This nervous habit can damage your hair roots, and lead to hair loss. The compulsion to pull on hair is called *trichotillomania*, and nine times as many women as men have it.

Why don't girls get beards?

Because that would look bad.

Washing Your Hair

Hair experts agree that you don't need to automatically shampoo your hair every day! It sounds weird, but your hair looks healthier if there's a little natural oil in it, so why waste all that water?

 Some of the strangest hair care products we've heard of include goat milk shampoo, carrot oil conditioner, and garlic shampoo (it'll keep vampires—and everyone else!—away).

Before going much further, just remember that your hair is *dead*. So if a hair product advertises how it's full of the vitamins or protein that your hair needs, remember that's lame. Anyway, if you want your hair shiny and aromatic, eucalyptus trees make an oil that can give your scalp a nice tingle and a fresh forest smell. After washing your hair, get some eucalyptus oil and rub it into your hair to see if you like it.

 A salon in England once used "caviar conditioner." (Caviar is a food made from fish eggs.) For about $350, a person gets to have fish eggs stuck in their hair. The fish oil is supposed to be good for it. (Right!)

Speaking of organic hair treatments, here are two that you may want to try.

Go Heavy on the Mayo!

Your own all-natural conditioner!

You will need: Mayonnaise, a plastic bag or towel.

If you're trying to give your hair some life, there are girls who swear by their mayonnaise bottles. Just go ahead and shampoo your hair like normal, then fill your palms with globs of mayonnaise and work it into your hair!

Once you have it pretty well mayo'ed, cover your hair with a plastic bag or towel for about 15 minutes. Then wash it out. We can *almost* guarantee that your hair won't be dull after doing this.

 Note: Mustard doesn't work as a conditioner. (You'll end up smelling like *Grey Poupon*.)

Split End Serum

If your hair's too dry, olives are the answer!

You will need: Olive oil, a damp towel or shower cap.

Warm up ¼ cup of olive oil a little bit in the microwave and then work it into your hair. Once it's been massaged in, wrap a warm, damp towel around your head (or use a shower cap) and leave it on for 15 minutes or so. Then take off the towel or cap and shampoo.

Then shampoo again! If your hair doesn't come out moisturized and luxuriant, you can have your money back. If you do this once a week, it will really start to show.

A Little Syrup on the Side ☺

A sweet shampoo prank for a loved one near you!

You will need: Pancake syrup.

What with all the organic shampoos available, why not treat a family member to a shampoo of your own invention? Once a shampoo bottle has been finished, snag it from the recycling and fill it up partway with pancake syrup. If you think your potential victim will be fairly clueless, put the old bottle (with the syrup) back in the shower and remove the new bottle. If your victim is more observant, wait until their "real" shampoo bottle reaches the level of your syrup bottle . . . then switch them.

We're not waffling when we say that there will be loads of laughs from this one! (And don't worry, the pancake syrup washes right out.)

Drying Your Hair

Ready to dry your hair? Use a towel! Either that or set your blow-dryer to a low setting. That's because Dr. Janet Roberts (professor of dermatology and hair loss expert) says, "Blow-drying with a hot hair dryer is the most damaging thing that women do on a daily basis [to their hair]."

Hair Styling

Like we said, your hair goes up and stays in place better if it isn't *perfectly clean.* Your hair's natural oils are sort of your own styling gel. You've seen women (and men) with hair that is "grungy" or messed up on purpose. How stylish! The thing is, you just know that these people didn't actually stop washing their hair. Maybe they use a product like "Rusk." Rusk was a hair-styling product that gave clean hair "the look and feel of hair that hadn't been washed for days." Really!

If you ever want to really spike your hair up, use the punk rock recipe: *egg whites!* Crack a bunch of eggs, separate the yolks from the whites, and start working the egg whites into your hair. What a mess! But it will dry and stiffen into beautiful spikes.

💬 **Curling Iron Justice!** In Shreveport, Louisiana, a man entered a beauty college to rob it. The store's manager yelled, "Get that sucker!" as the man tried to leave. Then the students and teachers attacked the robber with curling irons. (He was later arrested and given a bad perm.)

Maybe now you're ready to do some braiding! The "rule of thumb" to do this is that your hair be long enough to fall past your shoulders. And it's easier and more fun to braid your friend's hair and then have her braid yours.

We're sure you've done this before, but . . . all you have to do is get your hair into a ponytail and then put a tie around it. Separate the hair into three parts. Then start braiding by bringing the right part over the center part. Then bring the left part over the new center. Keep doing that! Tie it off at the end with elastic.

Hey, besides braids, do you already use one of these hairstyles?

BRaid   FRench bRaid   twists   buns

ponYtail   CORnRows   pigtails

These are all styles that can *pull* on your hair for long periods of time. Believe it or not, over time, these can all lead to some form of *baldness*. If there is too much tension on your hair, you will start noticing broken strands. From there, your hair may start getting shorter and thinner. The scientific term for this is *traction alopecia*. What it means is that the hair falls out and doesn't come back. (So be sure to give your hair a rest from these styles sometimes.)

Nurses, people from India, and African Americans are *most* likely to get this condition. The same thing can happen when tight curlers are being used. Hot combing, chemical straighteners, and "hair relaxing" have also been found to sometimes cause thin hair.

 About 20 percent of women will experience some hair loss in their lives. Men suffer from a 50 percent baldness rate.

To take care of your hair, avoid using harsh chemicals on it. Be sure to eat some protein during the day (since that's what your hair is made of), use gentle shampoos, and don't brush too much. A pick or comb with wide teeth does the least amount of damage to hair.

Haircuts and Coloring

"Read lots of books so you don't end up with a $100 haircut sitting on a $10 brain."

~Rose Leaf

No matter how much you love your hairstyle now, in 10 years you will look at pictures of yourself and be embarrassed. *It's the law of fashion.* Then 10 years after that, your pictures will look good again! Anyway, you've probably had your hair cut in a salon. The average cost for a "salon" haircut is around $45. If the salon has more than 13 chairs, it will run you closer to $65. And big-shot hairdressers in New York can charge as much as $800 for a haircut! Let's see, assuming that the haircut takes 80 minutes that would be $10 a minute . . . Heck, just to have the hairdresser look at your hair for a *second* would cost a dollar!

If your haircutter is someone you trust, and she wants to try something a little different with your hair, that's okay. But be stern with your haircutter if she just wants to do *"her*

How to Deal with a Bad Haircut

Rearrange it with barrettes!

Hide it with a cute hat!

OR try to grow it out fast!

205

thing" with *your* hair. If you do ever get a bad haircut, the last thing you want to hear is, "Don't worry, it'll grow out." You want it to look better *now*!

 Think of the Money They Save! There is a tribe of people who live on Madagascar named the Tsimihety. Their name translates to "the people who don't cut their hair."

Natural Auburn Highlights

"Auburn" is a brownish red color that looks good in almost everyone's hair!

You will need: Henna powder (henna is a plant with leaves that are perfect for skin and hair dyes).

Put ¼ cup of henna in a plastic cup and bring it in the shower with you. Get your hair wet, and then divert some hot water into the cup of henna. Mix it around with your finger. Once it's well mixed, pour it on your head.

Work the henna around in your hair and then go about your usual shower routine, keeping your head away from the water. When you're ready to condition and/or shampoo, just wash out the henna and do your regular thing. You will have lovely auburn highlights when you get out of the shower.

Natural Blonde Highlights

How to get natural highlights that aren't naturally yours!

You will need: A lemon, some salt, a sunny day.

If you want to keep it organic, here's the way to highlight your hair. Squeeze a lemon into a bowl until all the juice is gone. Add a teaspoon of salt and stir it up.

Then lean your head over a sink and work the concoction into your hair. Rub it in well; then go outside. Let your hair sit in full sunlight for a couple of hours. Then go back inside, rinse your hair with some water, and dry it. *Ta-dah!*

Celtic Fashion! You'd probably rather not style your hair the way the ancient Celts of Europe did. They soaked their hair with a mixture of water and crushed chalk, which made the hairs stick up in pale, stiff clumps. The hair spikes were so stiff that you could impale an apple on one!

Body Hair

Not all women shave. As a matter of fact, the whole *idea* of shaving body hair is a very recent development. Most cultures haven't worried much about hair on a girl's body. And in the United States, women never showed their armpits or bare legs in public, so some hair in the armpits or on the legs was no big deal.

 There are even places in Asia where a slight mustache on a woman was seen as attractive!

So why the change? *Fashion.* Blouses without sleeves became popular in 1915, and dresses that showed a woman's legs soon followed. **How shocking!** The old rule of "If you don't show it, don't worry about it" had to be changed. And then nylons came out, and they are uncomfortable to wear with hairy legs. Razor companies saw their chance to advertise to women for the first time, and nothing's been the same since.

These days, some girls shave because they've seen their mothers shave and it seems "adult." Girls with light skin and dark body hair might shave because body hair can be seen more easily on them. Many black girls (and of course, many women of all races) don't shave at all.

 Thirty percent of men between the ages of 18 to 34 shave their chests.

Good Shaving Tips

1. Check with your mom before shaving. Once you *start* shaving, you *can* stop anytime, but you probably won't!

2. Bathing beforehand will prepare your skin and soften the hairs. And use shaving cream!

3. Don't push the razor down hard. Razors are *razor*-sharp, and they don't need much pressure to work!

4. Try to shave without turning the razor sideways. (Nothing is worse than getting a nick in the underarm or on your ankle!)

5. Don't use a dull razor!

6. Be careful!

There are other ways to deal with unwanted hair. For instance, *electrolysis* involves electro-cuting the root of a hair to kill it. (It hurts.) *Laser hair removal* is a more recent version of the same idea. It costs about $1,200 for a full treatment. (It hurts, too.) A famous hair removal technique is the *hot wax treatment*. The idea of this is to pour hot lava—we mean, hot *wax*—onto an area where hair is not wanted. The wax then cools, and is then pulled off, sort of like a big Band-Aid. *Wax on, wax off!* Does it hurt? Of course it hurts!

HUMOR

"I'm not funny. What I am is brave."

~Lucille Ball

As a girl becomes a teenager, she might act less goofy and silly. This could be because she's more *mature* OR because she is more *self-conscious*. It takes some courage to be funny, and a self-conscious girl could be afraid to crack a joke. So remember that the one thing *all* people in the world share is laughter. Whether you're in Timbuktu or English class, laughter means something is funny. Don't be afraid of it!

It's very healthy to laugh. Scientific research shows that although laughter isn't "the best medicine," it's still pretty good for you. Unless you have a bad skin rash, and then laughing actually doesn't help very much. But at least the laughter will put you in a better mood!

Scientists love to research humor and try to figure out what makes us laugh. In one study, they watched people in shopping centers and carefully took notes. They found that fewer than one laugh out of five was because of a joke or funny story. Most of the laughter happened when people said "hello" or "good-bye" to each other! (That must mean it's really good to see your friends . . . and to get away from them!)

Another study tried to find out what happens with our brains when we laugh. The research showed that when something funny happens, your brain has to go through all of its memories to compare what you just saw to everything else you have ever seen. Then the brain makes comparisons and tries to solve the problem of whether what it saw was funny. Then the emotions have to kick in and help create laughter.

And that all happens in a *microsecond*. So humor is great exercise for your brain!

Next time you're having fortune cookies with your friends, add two words to the end of your fortunes: *with [the name of the boy that girl likes]*. So a fortune like *You will have good luck* becomes *You will have good luck with Timmy*. And *Trust your intuition* becomes *Trust your intuition with Timmy*. There will be laughter. (See how to make fortune cupcakes below.*)

---

* Take a piece of a cupcake paper liner and write a fortune on it. Then fold the paper and put it at the bottom of the tin just before you pour batter into it. When you unwrap the cupcake, you will find the fortune at the bottom! Make up fortunes like: "Anything worth doing can be done" and "Check your shoes—you may have stepped in something."

Obviously, different people laugh at different things. Little kids like very simple types of humor, which is called "slapstick" humor. Slapstick revolves around people falling down, telling poo-poo jokes, or making weird faces. It turns out that boys and men also prefer this same sort of humor. Surprise!

Girls, and especially women, prefer humor that comes from memories, personal information, relationships, and stories. In short, women like complicated humor. Why? Because they're smart!

The Most Ticklish Spot on Your Body! Scottish scientists have figured out the most ticklish spot on the body. It doesn't matter if a person is right- or left-footed, a small area in the middle of the right foot is the most ticklish spot for most people. BTW, right-handed people *are* more ticklish than left-handed people. (This really is true!)

Think about the last slumber party you attended. You probably took part in what the French call *fou rire* (FOO rear). This means "insane laughter." In the United States we call them "giggle attacks." Sometimes two girls can just look at each other and start laughing. (There's something about seeing a good friend laugh that makes you want to laugh too.) This can lead to trouble if you're in a library or a classroom!

In the early 1960s, there was an epidemic of uncontrollable laughter in East Africa. It started with some schoolgirls getting hysterical, and their laughter was so out of control, schools had to be closed down to prevent the "laughing disease" from spreading. Nobody knows for sure what caused it, but it may have been started by a really good knock-knock joke.

As we said before, many women remember their girlhood as a time when they were embarrassed about who they were. They felt awkward or self-conscious or confused. But humor can really help with those feelings; it puts things in perspective! Humor is also good for your social life: girls who laugh a lot also talk more and make more eye contact than others. These girls also tend to be more relaxed and less stressed than *really serious people.*

Looking for a funny gesture? Try the *fingernail buff*. This is where a girl rubs her fingernails against the clothing of her shirt, as if to polish them. It's a good thing to do when you're doing some "pretend bragging." For example, "Hey, I got my science test back today . . . C+!" and then a fingernail buff.

Hey, I got my science test back today. C+.

Oh Yeah

Here are a few jokes and funny stories. They are arranged from the easiest to understand to the most incredibly complex jokes of all time. You may have to read them over and over for weeks before you see the humor hidden in them. Good luck!

Jokes and Funny Stories

The only knock-knock joke you need to know.

Knock knock.

Who's there?

Panther.

Panther who?

Panther no panth, I'm going thwimming.

> **Girl:** Mom! There's an invisible woman at the door who wants to talk to you!
> **Mom:** Tell her I can't see her now.

Q. How is a duck like a pickle?
A. Neither one can ride a bike.

Q. What are twin babies called before they are born?
A. Womb-mates.

Q. What did the female seagull say to her buddy when she flew off?
A. *You go, gullfriend.*

Q. How many boys does it take to change a roll of toilet paper?
A. Who knows? It hasn't ever happened.

Nurse: How is the little girl that swallowed ten nickels and five dimes doing?
Doctor: No change yet.

A true story that is funny in a horrible way!
In Broward County, Florida, a school district failed 6,559 public middle school students due to a computer error. Try explaining that one to your folks!

Q. What do you call a polite, funny, sensitive, good-looking boy?
A. A rumor.

One hot summer's day, a woman took her daughter to a clothing store.
"Can I get a swimsuit for my daughter?" she asked a salesperson.
"No," the salesperson said. "We don't do trades."

Historians believe that this may be the world's oldest joke:

The ancient Greeks believed that their gods were immortal. That means that they never died. They were eternal.

A Greek girl was praying to Zeus, the king of the gods. She was trying to understand his *eternal* nature.

"Zeus," she asked, "what's a million years to you?"

"A million *years* is like a *second* to me," Zeus explained.

"And a million dollars?"

"A million dollars is like a *penny* to me," Zeus replied.

The girl felt daring, and she asked, "Zeus, would you give me one of your pennies?"

"Sure," Zeus replied. "Just a second."

A ventriloquist who used a puppet was doing his act in Los Angeles. The show was going well until the man had his dummy do a "dumb blonde" joke.

Suddenly, a woman with blonde hair stood up in the audience. She pointed at the man and said loudly, "That isn't funny! What does the color of a person's *hair* have to do with her *intelligence*?

The ventriloquist realized she was right. He started to apologize, but the blonde woman interrupted him.

"You stay out of this, mister. I'm talking to that little jerk on your knee!"

"I'm not offended by 'dumb blonde' jokes because I know I'm not dumb. I also know I'm not blonde."

~*Dolly Parton*

A girl was walking home from school when she saw a cute brown dog tied up in a front yard. The dog had a sign around his neck that read, "Take me home: $10."

The girl stopped and looked at the dog. It was watching her and wagging its tail. "I wonder if you're friendly?" the girl asked aloud.

"You bet I am!" said the dog.

The girl was amazed. "You can talk?" she exclaimed.

"Yes," the dog said. "I can actually speak TWO languages because I was born in Germany. English is my second language. I trained as a Seeing Eye dog AND a special police dog over there. I also used to do some mountain rescue work."

Since she had $10 and knew this was a great opportunity, the girl knocked on the door of the house. A woman answered the door.

"I'd like to buy your dog," she said. "But before I do, I have to ask, why is he so cheap?" The woman looked at the dog and shook her head. She leaned toward the little girl and whispered. "That dog is *such* a liar. He hasn't done *half* the things he says he has."

A little girl named Katya (who always wore skirts) went to school for the first day of kindergarten. A little boy named Timmy asked her to climb on the jungle gym, so Katya did.

When she went home, Katya told her mother about her day. When she got to the part about the jungle gym, her mom said, "Don't do that. He might just be trying to look at your underwear." Why this was such a big deal, Katya didn't understand, but she didn't say anything.

The next day, Timmy asked Katya to climb the jungle gym again, and she did. When she got home, Katya told her mom about her day, including the jungle gym.

Katya's mom was angry. "What did I say, young lady? How do you know he wasn't just trying to look at your underwear?"

Katya said, "But I tricked him, Mommy. Today I didn't wear any underwear!"

Some of the jokes in this section were in bad taste, and to offset them, please read this story. It teaches us about the beautiful things that can happen if we just pay attention to little children. They are our most precious gift.

A five-year-old girl named Maria noticed that a construction crew had started work on the vacant lot next door to her house. Maria watched the men talking and moving their heavy equipment around with great interest.

The next day, Maria asked her mom if she could go over and get a closer look at the construction. Her mom was reluctant; not only was it possibly dangerous, but she knew that construction workers sometimes cursed. Maria really wanted to go though, so the mom allowed it.

It turned out that the workers had hearts of gold. They showed her around the site, and because she seemed so interested and willing to help, they gave her a hard hat and let her do some little jobs. She also got to listen to their conversations.

Maria loved it! She came home and told her mom she wanted to be a construction worker when she grew up. Maria went back the next couple of days to "work" and at the end of the week, the foreman gave her an envelope with her week's pay: five one-dollar bills.

Maria's mother decided it was time for her to start her own bank account, since she had a job. They both went to the bank and Maria proudly presented the teller with her money.

He was *very* impressed when he found out that Maria worked in construction.

"Will you keep building the house next week?" the teller asked her.

Little Maria frowned and said loudly, "We will if those *idiots* at Home Depot deliver the $!#@!%*?& lumber on time!"

FASHION

A "fashion" is the latest trend that is popular at the moment. The only problem is that as soon as any fashion becomes *really* popular, it's suddenly out of date! Plus, it's hard to be unique when somebody else "invented" the fashion, and everybody else is wearing it.

But you don't have to wear the latest fashions to have *style*! You can create your own style by picking outfits that YOU think look good because they have that certain "flair." Maybe your style is elegant or creative or goofy. Hey, it's your style, so express yourself with it! Add a trippy new accessory. Put on a man's hat. Mix stripes with plaid. (Or not.) That's turning *fashion* into your *style*!

Although generally women are more interested in fashion than men, way back in the twentieth century, 65 percent of the top fashion designers were males. Jacques Fath, a famous French designer, even said, "Women are bad fashion designers. The only role a woman should have in fashion is wearing clothes." That jerk! The good news is that nowadays, female fashion designers rake in over 60 percent of the total fashion sales to women. Sisterhood!

Did you know girls get twice as many fashion possibilities as boys? That's because a girl can dress like a boy and look normal, but boys can't do the same with girls' clothes!

Today there is a trend for young women and girls to get involved in fashion. Many teenagers have started selling their clothes to local stores and friends. Fashion websites and magazines highlight do-it-yourself youngsters who have good taste. And fashion schools are getting record enrollments.

You shouldn't take this stuff too seriously. For some girls, fashion can turn into a dead-end alley, and they become *slaves to fashion.* A fashion slave notices that there is always another girl with more expensive and more up-to-date clothes, and she spends a lot of money and energy on the latest trends to keep up.

But since people are more important than clothes, maybe the best clothes are the ones that make you notice the *person* wearing them. Anyway, try making fashion *your* slave . . . or at least your servant!

Fashion Model Secrets!

For laughs, take some pictures of your friends in silly, fake-serious fashion model poses. The key? Models usually look over the photographer's shoulder (lifting their chin so they look posed), almost always put one foot in front of the other, and love to pull their shoulders slightly back. And don't forget to slightly purse your lips and look oh so *serious*!

Your Personal Fashion

There are places out there that can give you advice on the "fashion of the month." But if you're looking for some different ideas for an outfit to wear to school, here are some to get you thinking!

Go Through Your Parents' Closet (with Their Permission, of Course!)

If you're looking for some old-school, retro clothes, hit up your parents! They will be stunned, and then flattered, when you take an interest in the Pearl Jam or Backstreet Boys T-shirt that's been hidden away for so many moons. Old jeans, cowboy boots, and T-shirts are instantly cool again. Other finds might include flares, biker boots, glitter tops, velvet jackets, hip belts, and leather wristbands. Rock on!

Clothes

East Indian skirt
caftan (a long, loose shirt or top; can be a dress, Middle Eastern style)
poodle skirts
Fair Isle sweaters
tutu
pantsuits
polo shirts
khaki pants
ruffled blouses
halter tops
cardigan sweaters
cashmere sweaters
paisley prints and tie-dye
bell-bottoms
pedal pushers
denim jackets
pleated skirts

Accessories

colored or patterned scarves
shawls
pearl chokers
long bead necklaces
hemp purse
anklets
bangle bracelets
big sunglasses
ties
decorated hairpins or barrettes
(glue cool beads on them!)
beaded handbags OR handbags
made out of old jeans
brooches
knee socks
bunny slippers

Hats

fedora (a felt hat with a brim)
floppy-brimmed hat
beret
cloche (a close-fitting hat from the 1920s)
feathered hat
newsboy cap (watch the movie Newsies to see how cool they are)

Shoes

loafers
T-strap shoes
combat boots
lace-up or zippered boots
saddle shoes
ballerina flats
cowgirl boots
"go-go" boots
patent leather shoes

Clothing

"Some people don't think that women in the military can kill if they get into a fight. I think we can. All the general has to do is walk over to the women and say, 'You see the enemy over there? They say you look fat in those uniforms.'"

~Elayne Boosler

The Outfit Switch!

See if anyone is noticing what you wear!

You will need: A friend who's about your size.

Have you ever gone to school and discovered that two of your friends are wearing matching outfits, by accident or on purpose? Try this twist on that situation.

You'll have to make arrangements with a friend who's about your size to do this before school. Go to school and about halfway through the day (maybe at lunch) go to the restroom together and quickly trade outfits. Then come out and act casual, like nothing is different.

If NOBODY notices that you changed, that will be a little scary. But if someone does notice and she asks you if you were wearing something different earlier, act like you don't know what she's talking about.

An Important Question! When a girl comes out of her bedroom wearing an outfit, why do parents sometimes ask: "You're not planning on wearing that, are you?" Duh!

"Eventually, I managed to cheer Mum up by allowing her to go through my wardrobe and criticize all my clothes . . ."

~Helen Fielding

One obvious part of putting together a good outfit has to do with matching colors. Before 1920, pink was considered a BOY'S color in the United States. Times sure do change! Dark blue is associated with loyalty (*true blue!*), which is why many police officers wear it. Purple is still considered to be the "royal" color because it was an expensive dye in the olden days. (In England during Shakespeare's time, it was illegal for most people to wear purple because it was saved for royalty.) Yellow was considered to be a wedding day color by the ancient Romans. And in China, white is considered to be the color of sadness and mourning, not black.

Black has become the most fashionable of colors. The beauty of black is that it can make a person appear slimmer. It also seems serious, and that makes people take notice.

 New Vocabulary! A Crayola storm is a girl who wears as many bright colors as she can, ALL the time. Crayola Storm also kind of sounds like the name of a female weather forecaster, huh? (Which reminds us, if you watch weather reports carefully, it will help you choose comfortable outfits for the day.)

"Fashions go out of style, but style never goes out of fashion."
~Constance Noring

T-Shirts

One of the most important items a girl can own are nice cotton T-shirts. If you want to wear them long or short, it doesn't matter, but a white T-shirt is the most multipurpose piece of clothing there is. That is, unless you want to wear a *black* cotton T-shirt!

Have a long-sleeved sweater or shirt, but want something under it? T-shirt. Just wearing a skirt or shorts on a nice day? T-shirt. Going to a formal event? T-shirt. (Oops, okay, we're getting a little carried away.)

Tank Tops: These always look cool if you wear two of them, with one being a different color. It gives extra support and also gives you style points.

Blouses

The blouse used to be the part of a woman's dress that was above the waist; it was a detachable vest. Now a nice white blouse or crisp white shirt can be worn with skirts, pants, suits, shorts, and under vests and jackets.

BTW, buttons have been around for 5,000 years . . . but button HOLES were only invented about 800 years ago! What gives? You see, buttons were originally invented just for decoration on clothing. It took a while for some genius (probably a girl) to see that they could be useful!

Blazers

Blazers got their name in the late 1800s, when light jackets with shining bright colors were all the rage. Nowadays, you can blaze a fashion trail with a blazer that goes well with jeans or a skirt.

A New Wrinkle: Ever hear of *extreme ironing*? In this sport, athletes set up ironing boards and then iron clothes in very difficult situations. For example, they might iron while rock climbing, sailboarding, or bouncing on a trampoline.

Pants

Although pants and trousers have been around for a long time, the first real pants actually made for girls were called *bloomers.* In 1851, an American woman named Amelia Bloomer had seen women wearing trousers, and she marketed her own version of them. Women in the United States wore these bloomers for about eight years, but then they went out of fashion. Men had a lot to do with this, because they wanted to keep pants for themselves. (Keep in mind that women couldn't vote back then and slavery was still legal!)

When asked if she felt like a man when she wore pants, Amelia Bloomer answered, "I feel no more like a man now than I did in long skirts, unless . . . enjoying more freedom . . . is to be like a man."

Wow, times have changed! Now, girls can wear blue jeans or "denims," which are probably the most basic sort of pants there are. Although there is nothing expensive about denim, if you want it prewashed, preshrunk, aged, styled, distressed, or customized, it's possible to spend as much as $400 on a pair. That's kind of a *rip-off* for pants that might become *cutoffs*!

Dresses and Skirts

"Some women hold up dresses that are so ugly and they always say the same thing: 'This looks much better on.' On what? On fire?"
~Rita Rudner

Long skirts are cool—pick a soft fabric and enjoy. But if you're going to be doing a fair amount of walking, don't wear dresses or skirts that go below your ankle. As for skirts, they can be casual or dressy depending on your top and accessories. Denim skirts seem to survive most fashion changes.

As for miniskirts, they can be a challenge. As you sit down, it can be tough to smooth the fabric of the mini down so that it doesn't hike up *too* high. There is sort of an art to it, as you keep your back straight, bend at the knees, smooth the skirt, and sit.

Cotton skirts are easy to smooth down, but they also hike up worse than, say, denim. Many girls agree that corduroy smoothes down and stays put the best of all the fabrics.

Stockings and Tights

Stockings were made out of thick wool cloth for many years. Talk about itchy! In the 1800s, a French acrobat named Jules Leotard got tired of his baggy pants and came up with a new type of legging. What name do you think Mr. Leotard came up with for his invention?

Scarves

Scarves are *very* cool accessories. They come in such a wide variety of sizes, patterns, and colors, and they can go with almost any outfit. Also, if you ever want to stand out from the girl crowd, a scarf is the ticket.

A scarf can cover up a "bad hair day," and it can also cover your hair when it's windy and you don't want to wear a cap. Want to look *trés* French? Take a scarf and fold it in a triangle. Then take the long side (where the tip of the triangle is) and roll it toward the crease. Once you have a scarf-rope, wrap it around your neck, tie a knot on the side, walk around with a croissant and a beret, and act *trés chic*! (BTW, how did an elegant word like *scarf* ever get the meaning "to gobble up," as in "My brother scarfed the waffles"?)

Remember, a scarf doesn't have to go around your head or neck. You can run a long scarf through the belt loops of a pair of pants and tie it off in the front. For an exotic look, make a scarf sarong. Take a long scarf and fold it corner to corner (for a triangle) or in half; wrap it around your waist and knot it up. It can go over pants or a skirt, or if it's warm enough out, your swimsuit.

If a scarf is too bold a statement for you, try some brightly colored ribbons (the thicker the better). Tie ribbons off around your wrists or ankles. *Ninja style!*

Swimsuits

Women used to wear pretty gigantic swimsuits until World War II. The government required swimsuit makers to use 10 percent less fabric for swimsuits to save resources for the war effort. Then, in 1946, a French designer came up with a small two-piece bathing suit called the "bikini." As far as most people could tell, the bikini reduced fabric use by about 95 percent! No model would wear the bikini for fashion shows. It would take more than a decade for swimmers to feel comfortable wearing so little.

After you buy a swimsuit, you probably should wear it in the shower first and then run the water. That way you'll know how it fits and what it looks like when it's wet.

Shoes

"Life is short. Buy the shoes."

~*Samantha Crouton*

Remember how none of Cinderella's stepsisters could get their feet into her dainty glass slippers? The fairy tale seems to have a moral that says, "Bad people have big feet." That's not a very good message for a children's story! (Even worse, in older versions of the story, the stepsisters cut off their toes trying to fit into the slipper. *Yech.*)

Besides, even though glass slippers may be every girl's dream, they are very dangerous. If you step on a rock with glass slippers on, you can get a nasty cut on the heel. Today's safety-minded fairy godmothers recommend a nice pair of clogs, or maybe some hiking boots.

If you think that *your* feet are too big, look at a puppy. Dogs are like humans when they're growing up: their feet grow first. Puppies have pretty big paws for their size, and so do lots of girls and boys. Don't worry, you'll grow into your feet; just give it time.

The reason we mention this is because many women *never* get over worrying about having big feet. They have their toes straightened, shortened (and even removed!) so that they can fit their feet into high-heeled pumps. These women don't need plastic surgery on their feet. They need a new attitude and different shoes!

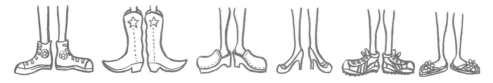

The Statue of Liberty wears size 879 shoes!

A comfortable pair of shoes is one of the most important things to keep you feeling good. You take about 15,000 steps a day, and if your shoes don't fit right, it can affect your mood and how your day goes. If you've ever had sore feet or a blister, you know what we mean.

The Meaning of Shoes

Shoes have special meanings for different cultures. Take a look!

Southeast Asia: Showing someone the sole of your shoe is a horrible insult.

Mongolia: Removing shoes after a meal is believed to help digestion. (Unless everyone's feet stink!)

Oz: Apparently, some girl named Dorothy can travel there in special shoes.

Japan: Shoes are removed before entering a building.

Holland: To fool the police, Dutch criminals have invented shoes that leave footprints going in the opposite direction.

Muslims: Before taking part in their daily prayers, Muslims often remove their shoes.

Good Luck! Shoes symbolize good luck in many places, which is one reason they are sometimes tied to the back of a car belonging to newlyweds. In case you've wondered what leprechauns do all day, they make *shoes*, the lucky little fellows. (BTW, how come you never see *girl* leprechauns?)

High heels are often considered stylish, but they are not very comfortable shoes. They squinch the toes together and then put 85 percent of the body's weight right on them. But those little piggies are the part of the foot least able to handle that kind of pressure. The heel itself is designed for that kind of pressure, but it sits up high, doing nothing. It's unnatural!

As a result, women who wear high heels a lot often get back problems, corns, bunions, and sprained ankles. Spiked heels or "stilettos" are especially harmful. If high heels are shoes you'd like to try, you might want to start with a low pair of heels until you feel comfortable walking around in them.

Stupid Joke!
Question: What do you say when you tickle a rich girl?
Answer: *Gucci, Gucci, Gucci!**

---

* If you don't get it, Gucci shoes are an expensive brand of shoes made in Italy.

Cool Flip-Flops!

If you have any fake flowers around, use them to spruce up your flip-flops. Just cut the flower from its stem and glue it to the strap of your flip-flops. Styling!

Jewelry

Most jewelry doesn't have any useful purpose. So what? It looks good! Wearing these decorations dates way, way back to prehistory. One of the oldest types of jewelry ever found was a cowry shell necklace from 20,000 years ago. Here's a cool bracelet you can make yourself:

Toothbrush Bracelet

This fun homemade jewelry is a good reminder for dental care too!

You will need: One old (or new!) plastic toothbrush in a color you like (Barbie or Little Mermaid toothbrushes are perfect), a pot, two pliers, a parent helper, small bowl of cold water, oven mitts.

1. Fill the pot with water and bring it to a boil.

2. While the water is heating, pull out any bristles you can from the toothbrush with your pliers.

3. When the water is boiling, put the toothbrush into it for 45 to 60 seconds. (Put on your oven mitts while the toothbrush boils.)

4. Grab the pliers and pull the toothbrush out of the water. Now take the other pair of pliers and hold onto the two ends of the toothbrush. Turn the ends to bend the toothbrush into a horseshoe shape that will fit around your wrist!

5. Once the bracelet is the right size, put it into the bowl of cold water to cool it off. It will harden quickly and you'll be ready to show it off right away!

Another reason girls like to wear jewelry is because an item has personal meaning or a special power. *Charm bracelets* are like this. "Charms" are also sometimes called *talismans*. Originally, these charms didn't have to be on a bracelet; they could be pinned to clothing, the hair, or attached to your backpack, handbag, or belt. Charms like these have been found that are 30,000 years old!

Some charms, like stars, hearts, horseshoes, and four-leaf clovers have become worldwide symbols. If you start your own charm bracelet, you can use the ideas above, or come up with charms that reflect your own interests. Once you get a few charms, it's hard to stop collecting until your bracelet is full of symbols that tell a story about who you are.

Charm Meanings

Egypt: *Scarab* (beetle) = life; *Cobra* = protection

Judaism: *Star of David* = protection from misfortune

Hinduism: *Ganesha* (a god with an elephant's head and human body) = luck, protection

East Asia: *Turtle* (tortoise) = wisdom, long life, strength

Buddhism: *Buddha* = happiness and wisdom

Medieval Europe: *Ladybugs* = wealth, success, health; *Heart* = love

Mediterranean cultures: *Shark teeth* = protection from evil and poison

Christianity: Crosses are popular, as are medals that show saints on them

Cool Anklet

Here's a simple anklet idea: You just need a thin strip of leather cord and some beads. Cut a cord long enough to go around your ankle twice and tie a knot at one end. Then put beads on the cord until you're almost at the point where the cord goes around your ankle once. After your last bead is in place, tie a knot after it and then tie the anklet off. Cut off any leftover cord.

Rings

The most well-known rings are probably wedding rings. Have you ever wondered why married people wear their wedding ring on the third finger of their left hand? It's because the ancient Romans thought that there was a special nerve that ran from that finger to the heart.

Although we think of diamond rings as traditional for weddings, that's only been the case for a short time. Up until the twentieth century, diamond wedding rings were not that popular. Most wedding rings had colorful stones on them: emeralds, opals, sapphires, and rubies were some favorites. (For tips on making the famous "Dollar Ring," see page 66.)

But in 1947, a big diamond producer came up with an ad slogan to sell their gems: *Diamonds Are Forever.* The ads stressed that of all the gems, only a diamond could express love and eternity. People bought it! And they bought diamond wedding rings and engagement rings too. And people STILL do this (often just because everyone else does) because of an ad long ago.

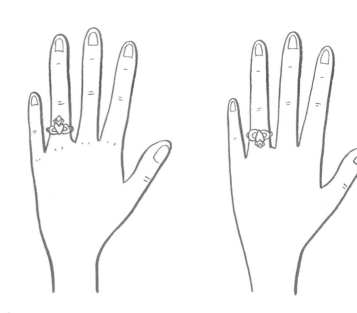

The Irish claddagh ring has the design of a heart held by two hands. You can wear it two ways: If the heart points *out* (away from you), that means you're available. If it points *in* (toward you), it means you have a boyfriend.

Final Fashion Tip: Smile a lot. And always wear clean underwear.

"Oh, never mind the fashion. When one has a style of one's own, it is always 20 times better."

~**Margaret Oliphant**

HOW IMPORTANT ARE LOOKS?

"Dolphins. They think they're so cute. Oh, look at me, I'm a flippy little dolphin, let me flip for you."

~Chum in Finding Nemo

Have you ever wondered about what makes one thing "cute" and another thing "icky"? Why are panda bears and penguins cute, while warthogs and vultures aren't? Researchers have figured out some of the things that people consider "cute" on animals (or stuffed animals) and humans (or stuffed humans).

It turns out that any harmless or babylike quality can make something seem cute. For example, anything that is a bit like a human baby is cute. So a baby monkey is cute, but so are baby birds and puppies. If an animal or young child walks slowly with a little teeter-totter from side to side, we find that adorable—floppy arms and legs and a bit of fuzz are also a plus. Other cute markers include:

Head: Round

Eyes: The bigger and brighter, the cuter! (They should of course be set on the *front* of the face.)

Nose: Small and flat

Ears: Big and round

Skin: Loose

Want to learn more about this amazing topic? Take a look at *Cute! A Guide to All Things Adorable.* As to the traits above, no animal (or person) has all of these traits, but two or three may be enough to make it cute. But this kind of "cuteness" is different from "beauty." (A girl might want big eyes, but she probably doesn't want big ears and loose skin!) So how does beauty affect how we think?

"Women must suffer to be beautiful."

~Dumb saying

Whatever! We all wonder how we might look if we changed something about ourselves. For some people, a change in exercise, diet, fashion, or a haircut is enough. Others think that "cosmetic surgery" is the answer. (This is plastic surgery that a person chooses to have done to make themselves look better.)

Cosmetic surgery is far more popular now than it ever has been. In recent years, it's had a 700 *percent* increase in the United States, with about 15 million surgeries annually. And approximately 90 percent of all plastic surgeries are done on *women*.

And it's not just in the United States that it's in demand. For instance, Brazil has more plastic surgeries than any other country. The Brazilian culture prizes beauty so much, they even have beauty contests for women in prison! In nearby Venezuela, it's not unusual for teenagers and tweens to have plastic surgery as well.

In 2005, the people of Iraq were trying to rebuild their country after many years of war. And yet there was a 100 percent boom in the popularity of plastic surgery for Iraqi women! Why? With more TV sets, they could see music videos from other countries, and many women felt their noses were the wrong size or shape. And one of the most popular plastic surgeries in China and Japan is to have the eye "widened" by removing part of its eyelid. This makes the person's eyes look less Asian and more "Western." Is this a sensible decision?

What about you? The way to look your natural best is with exercise, a good diet, and getting enough sleep. But there is a chance that at some point in your life, you will think YOU need plastic surgery. We won't try to talk you out of it, but think about this: Don't be afraid to *be yourself*!

(Okay, we lied. We tried to talk you out of it!)

Liposuction!

Liposuction sucks! No, really. It is a surgery where the doctor sticks a hollow metal rod into a fatty area of a person's body and vacuums out the fat. If this sounds gross to you, it should. It is also the most popular form of plastic surgery, with about 200,000 people in the United States getting their fat sucked out each year. Liposuction is also one of the few plastic surgeries that men have as often as women.

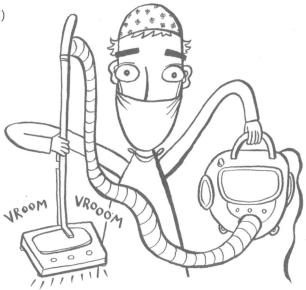

VROOM VROOM

Most Popular Female Liposuctions

thighs
buttocks
abdomen

Most Popular Male Liposuctions

love handles
neck
head

Botox

Botox is a brand name for something that is sometimes injected into a woman's face. The Botox paralyzes any face muscles around the area where it is administered, which smoothes out the skin and gets rid of some wrinkles. It also gets rid of the woman's ability to have any facial expression. (Doctors also sometimes inject Botox into armpits to prevent medical problems like sweating too much.) Many actresses have Botox injected into their faces to look good . . . but of course, it's kind of hard to "act" when your face can't move! (If you're wondering if a celebrity uses Botox, just look at her forehead. Can she raise her eyebrows in surprise? If not, Botox!)

Botox is short for "botulinum toxin" a dangerous poison. A little Botox paralyzes muscles for about four months. A lot of Botox can give a person botulism, which paralyzes a person all the way, forever.

Try It Yourself!

Don't worry, you're not going to inject any toxin into your face. The forehead is one of the more popular spots to get a Botox injection, which is why it's sometimes called Forehead Freezing. To understand what it feels like, try sticking a piece of duct tape to your forehead, with another little piece of tape between your eyebrows. Now, almost any time you make a facial expression, the tape will crinkle and feel tight against your skin. That's exactly the kind of expression that Botox prevents—the NORMAL kind!

Smile, Smile, Smile! It takes over 200,000 frowns to make a permanent wrinkle in your forehead.

The Fashion and Beauty Hall of Shame

Join us in this tribute to the bottom seven worst fashion ideas of all time!

7. The Fake Butt

The *bustle* (or, as we like to call it, the "fake butt") was a round wire attachment that a woman wore under her skirt and over her rear end. You could come up behind a girl wearing one and set a plate of doughnuts on her bustle without her knowing it. Thankfully, by 1900, the bustle had gone extinct . . . or is it just waiting for a comeback?

6. Hobble Skirts

One male designer invented something called the *hobble skirt*. The hemline of these long skirts was so tight that a girl wearing it had to *hobble* along in it with tiny little steps. (No woman could come up with an idea that lame!)

5. Head Squishing

It's not usually a good idea to mess with the brain. But that hasn't stopped people from changing the shape of their skulls because it "looked better." In Central Africa, the Mangbetu people used to wrap up the heads of female infants in pieces of giraffe hide to give the girls cone-shaped heads (a sign of beauty and intelligence.) And the Chinook Native Americans used to flatten the noggins of babies by attaching vices to their skulls for over a year. Their foreheads would end up being no more than two inches above their eyebrows. **Dang!**

4. The Fake Tummy

Hundreds of years ago in England, men exaggerated certain parts of their body. One example of this was the *peascod-belly*. This was a *false belly* that a man wore underneath his clothing. (That's right, he TRIED to look like he had a potbelly!) The peascod-belly was usually a wooden frame stuffed with rags or sawdust. An English noble with a fake belly once approached Queen Elizabeth in her court, and when it split open, the embarrassed noble spilled his "guts" all over the floor!

 In the 1700s, European men often wore "hose." If they didn't like the shape of their legs, the men would strap on fake calf muscles underneath the hose to make themselves look more buff.

3. The Power of Television

Fiji is a beautiful island in the South Pacific. The people of Fiji have always valued big, full-figured women. In 1995, American television came to Fiji, and many teenaged girls reported feeling "fat." Since then, almost 20 percent of Fijian girls have become *bulimic* (purposefully throwing up after eating) to control their weight. Harvard Professor Anne Becker said, "I never expected 2,000 years of tradition to be washed away by a couple of years of [television]."

2. Gone with the Wind! (Thank Goodness!)

The movie *Gone with the Wind* has a scene where Scarlett O'Hara tries her hardest to get into a tight vest laced in the back called a *corset*. The corset was kept *really* tight by being tied off with long laces that squeezed a girl's upper body. (If someone described a woman as "strait-laced," it meant that they were very strict.) The corset was supposed to give the figure support, but they were worn so tight that girls often fainted in them. This is why women got the reputation of fainting a lot; a man would faint too if he were wearing a vest that cut off all his circulation!

1. Foot Binding

About one thousand years ago, wealthy Chinese families began the tradition of foot binding. Really tiny feet were once considered a sign of beauty for women in China. When a girl was five, her feet were wrapped up so tightly in bandages that they almost folded in half. Naturally, this hurt. It also prevented the feet from growing properly.

The best kind of foot was called the "golden lily," which was a three-inch foot. **THREE INCHES!** Your middle finger might be longer than that. Next best was the "golden lotus," which was a bit larger. To get to these tiny sizes, the girl's feet were squeezed into a smaller set of shoes every two weeks. One Chinese woman recalled the torture she went through as being so bad she couldn't eat or sleep. But she was willing to live with it, because, in her words, "no one wanted to marry a woman with big feet." Fortunately, it has been illegal to bind a girl's feet in China since 1912.

During the time of foot binding, the worst insult a girl could hear was to be called "large-footed."

FOOD AND DIETING

"Food is an important part of a balanced diet."

~*Fran Lebowitz*

After a lot of research on flavors and nutritional content, scientists have come up with the proper name for good food: NUM-NUMS.

Just kidding! Speaking of scientists, as you may know, *The Five-Second Rule* states that any food dropped on the floor can still be picked up and safely eaten if it doesn't sit for more than *five* seconds.

Jillian Clarke, a high school student from Illinois, did a scientific study of this rule. She found that:

- Food dropped on the floor can get germs in LESS than five seconds. *Dang!*

- Women were more likely to pick up and eat dropped food than men. Go *figure!*

- Different versions of *The Five Second Rule* have been around for more than 600 years. For example, in Mongolia during the rule of Genghis Khan, there was a similar custom called *The 12-Hour Rule.*

- Candy or cookies are far more likely to be picked up than vegetables. *Surprise!*

Anyway, this chapter is devoted to food! Knowing how to make your own meals will help you avoid fast food, which can be dangerous. For example, what if you dropped some french fries on your sofa? They would become *couch potatoes,* and then you'd never be able to get rid of them!

Taste Buds

Have you ever wondered why some people REALLY hate broccoli or can't handle hot sauce? It's because no two tongues taste things alike! Even though you might think that the same foods will taste the same to people, they don't. We're all different.

For example, one out of four people is a "super-taster." These amazing folks can have up to one *hundred times* more taste buds than other people. What that means is that food can taste much more powerful to super-tasters than it does the rest of the population. If the food has a strong flavor—like onions or grapefruit—it can really do a number on their mouths.

 The hottest taste in the world comes from the *habanero pepper* in Mexico. It is hundreds of times hotter than the jalapeño pepper and will leave your mouth burning for hours afterwards.

Test Your Taste Buds

Can you deactivate your tongue?

You will need: A tongue, dark chocolate, tonic or mineral water.

Your tongue only has a few taste buds that can detect *bitter* flavors. These taste buds can be easily overloaded using this easy experiment. (**Note:** Dark chocolate is sometimes called *bitter* chocolate because there is very little sugar added.) Take a swig of the tonic water and let it swish around in your mouth for a moment. Then swallow it. Now take a bite of the chocolate. *You can't taste it!* It just feels like a load of wax in your mouth. Weird!

 Cool black coffee will also work with this experiment.

Now here is another kind of taste test: Do you know what the five main flavors are? Let's see, there's *sweet, salty, sour . . .* and, uh, *bitter.* That's four. What's the fifth one? Check the bottom of the page if you give up.*

It's fun to try to figure out what category different flavors fall under. For example, if you eat chili peppers, you may *think* they taste hot. But you're actually not "tasting" them at all. You have a type of cell in your mouth (and throat and nose) called *trigeminal* (try-JEM-in-el) cells. The job of these cells is to report PAIN to the brain. When you eat hot chilis, these cells are tricked into going on red alert, and they begin sending their pain

---

* The last taste is called **umami.** *Really!* This is the name of the flavor of meat and savory flavors. It can be enhanced by steak sauce or soy sauce. (Now see if the other people in your family know the fifth flavor.)

message, even though there is no real damage to the mouth. That's why the pain goes away pretty quickly.

Seasoning food with spices to add to its flavor is pretty standard. But be careful . . . there might be *poison* in your spice drawer. Nutmeg is poisonous unless eaten in small amounts. One whole nutmeg is enough to do some real damage. And if you know any girls named *Nutmeg*, avoid them just to be safe. (Heck, we even know some *Megans* who are troublemakers!)

 Garlic Breath! Garlic adds a terrific taste to food, but it gives people horrible breath! Alfonso the Wise (1221–1284) was a Spanish king who hated garlic breath so much, he outlawed anyone who had eaten garlic in the last month from visiting his court.

Your nose is just as important as your mouth when tasting food. Like taste, food aromas also *smell* very different to different people. Scientists now believe that there are some smells that only about 10 percent of people can detect.

Just as there are super-tasters, there are also "super-smellers." (They smell super!) If you think *you* are a super-smeller, there are careers to be found in your nose. You could be an "odor judge." That's a super-smeller who works for a deodorant or perfume company.

A lot of a food's taste comes from its *smell*. The importance of smelling is revealed when you eat food when you have a stuffy nose. When you can't smell very well the food seems to have hardly any taste either! Even super-smellers have this problem. Don't believe us? Try this:

Test Your Nose

What's the difference between an apple and an onion?

You will need: A nose, an onion, an apple, a friend.

Cut up an onion and an apple into identically sized cubes. (Cut the skin off the apple and peel the onion first.) Then wash your hands and go into another room. Blindfold yourself and pinch your nose closed perfectly tight. Have a friend come in with the cubes on a plate and quickly pop a cube of either the onion or the apple into your mouth. *As you chew, keep your nose sealed so that you can't smell.*

Amazingly, most people can't tell the difference between an apple and an onion this way, unless they are guessing based on the food's texture in their mouth. Behold the power of your nose!

So now we know that what food *tastes* like is only part of its appeal. Not only is the *smell* of food important, so is the *look* and even the *sound* of food. Hey, if it wasn't for *Snap, Crackle,* and *Pop*, Rice Krispies might have gone out of business a long time ago!

If you are hungry and you can smell good food, you are already anticipating something great. Who you eat with, what the lighting and surroundings are like, what kind of a mood you are in, even the silverware can affect how much you enjoy a meal. Experiments have been done where food is served under puke-green lighting. Even though the meals were delicious and prepared by expert chefs, people just could not stomach eating the food.

 "It rocks my face!" This is what you can say for food that tastes so good, calling it "good" or "delicious" doesn't really cut it.

Gum

Yeah, we *know* that gum isn't food. Even if you swallow it, your body can't digest it. But humans have enjoyed chewing on things like tree resin since the ancient days. While parents may think gum unladylike, and teachers may hate to find it under desks, gum is hard to resist.

The "chicle" tree has resin (or sap) that is good for making chewing gum. (You've heard of *Chiclets*, right?) But these days, most gums are made with something that's listed on your gum pack as "PVA," or polyvinyl acetate. What is PVA? It's plastic!

But that plastic just might make you smarter! In 2004, a dentistry professor at New York University did a study comparing test scores between gum-chewing students and those who did without. The gum-chewers averaged a "B" on their tests, and the nonchewers only got a "C."

The world record for biggest bubblegum bubble was once held by teenager Susan Williams. She blew a bubble bigger than a basketball to become a famous bubble-head. To blow big bubbles like Susan, chew until the flavor is gone from the gum. You may also want to consider taking a swig of cold water. As you may know, cold gum is stiffer and keeps its bubble longer!

Recipes

Although this isn't a cookbook, we've included some tasty snacks that we like.

Frouta kè Yaoùrti

This traditional Greek snack is really good . . . and really good for you!

You will need: Four cups of any sliced fresh fruit or fresh fruit mix, plain yogurt (Greek style if possible), almonds, honey. *Optional:* Grated lemon rind.

Combine 1 cup of plain yogurt and 3 tablespoons of honey in a bowl. Add lemon rind, if you are using it.

Mix your fruit and almonds in another bowl. (Berries, grapes, melons, bananas, apples, peaches, nectarines, and oranges are some possibilities.) Then pour the yogurt over the fruit.

Really Bad Candy Ideas

There are some candy ideas that should never have been made.

The Exploding Candy Bar! During World War II, Germany designed an exploding chocolate bar. The explosive was surrounded by a thin layer of chocolate. As soon as someone broke a piece of the bar off, *kaboom!* That's one way to keep Halloween candy safe.

Animal Gland Life Savers! Musk is a liquid from the gland of an animal. (Ever see a cat spray a wall? *Musky.*) Did you know there are musk-flavored Life Savers? This is not a good candy idea. And if you have ever had a Necco, you may have wondered what the *purple* Necco flavor is supposed to be. It's *clove.* Since some people smoke cloves in cigarettes, maybe tobacco-flavored candy is next?

Chocolate-Covered Vegetable Sandwich! But the All-Time Worst Idea for candy was the "Vegetable Sandwich." It was a candy made from dried-out vegetables (like peas, cabbage, and celery) that were then covered in chocolate. It is such a horrible idea, we are getting goose bumps right now just thinking about it. *Dried cabbage covered in chocolate.* Blech!

Ice Cream Sandwich

If you like sweet stuff stuffed between something, these are for you!

You will need: At least 2 cookies (anything will work, but homemade chocolate chip, oatmeal, or snickerdoodles are our favorites), your favorite ice cream or frozen yogurt, miniature chocolate chips.

The average girl eats almost 15 quarts of ice cream a year. (We don't recommend trying to keep up with her!)

For this tasty treat, scoop about ½ cup of ice cream onto 1 cookie. Then make a sandwich by pressing the other cookie on top, so that the ice cream comes to the edges of the sandwich. Turn the cookie on its side and roll the ice cream edge in miniature chocolate chips so they stick to the ice cream. Then eat it!

ech h

A Japanese ice cream business named Ice Cream City has a number of strange flavors available. These include spinach, garlic, tomato, seaweed, oyster, chicken, and wheat.

Do you like peanut butter? How about hot peppers? If so, then you'll love *Jalapeño Kick*. This is peanut butter that is flavored with *hot peppers*. It comes in a tube! Offer to make your friends a sandwich and enjoy the fireworks. (Extra credit for hiding the milk!)

Demon Corn! Historians believe that popcorn is native to North America. Europeans had never heard of it until a Native American named Quadequina showed popcorn to the Pilgrims. Quadequina explained that the reason the kernels "popped" when they got hot was because a little demon lived inside them. If it got too hot, the demon had to angrily leave the kernel and find a new home.

Cool Slang! **Food coma:** Being so full after a good meal, all you can do is sit in a daze. You might be able to mutter, "I'm SO full."

Homer Goes "Mmmm"!

Even though there is a whole channel devoted to food (*The Food Channel*), nobody on television is more devoted to eating food than Homer Simpson. His "*Mmmm . . . donuts*" is world famous. Here are some of the other things that have made Homer go "*Mmmm*."

"*Mmmm . . . unprocessed fishsticks.*"

"*Mmmm . . . 64 slices of American Cheese.*"

"*Mmmm . . . historically inaccurate.*"

"*Mmmm . . . free goo.*"

"*Mmmm . . . purple.*"

"*Mmmm . . . money.*"

"*Mmmm . . . me.*"

"*Mmmm . . . something.*"

"*Mmmm . . . forbidden donut.*"

Special Vegetarian Section

Many girls think about becoming vegetarians. It might be because they believe it's a healthier lifestyle or because they support an animal's right to live. In other words, they are *thinking* about what they eat and they are trying to do the right thing. So good for them! But there are also less good reasons to be a vegetarian. These include trying to lose weight, doing it because all your friends are, or wanting to say "rutabaga" as often as possible.

 Lisa Simpson is a vegetarian, so she doesn't eat cartoon animals.

The key thing for a vegetarian girl to know is that she needs *protein*. Meat and dairy products are great sources of protein, so if they are eliminated or reduced, there may be a protein problem. Soybeans are a good source of protein—so we hope you like *tofu*! (It's made of soybeans.) Or you could try this:

Edamame (*ed-uh-MOM-ay*) Mama

A tasty snack and a great source of protein!

You will need: Soybeans (a.k.a. edamame), salt, a pot of water, a colander.

Natural soybeans still in the pod are delicious. You can buy them fresh or frozen; supermarkets often stock them in the frozen vegetables section under their Japanese name, *edamame*.

Fresh soybeans are usually steamed for around 5 minutes (or until they're bright green), while the frozen ones can be boiled for 2 to 3 minutes. Then they are drained and put into a bowl. We like to lightly salt them, too.

You don't eat the shell, just the soybeans. Bring the pod to your mouth and pop them out with your teeth; that way you can enjoy the salt, and it makes this a food that keeps you busy, like unshelled sunflower seeds. This is the perfect food to snack on during a movie or between meals, and it's also a great appetizer.

There are other ways to get protein without meat by combining foods. For example, rice and beans or nuts and beans together can create proteins. Also, many vegetarians eat dairy products, eggs, and even fish. So a glass of milk or a piece of cheese can be very important for a vegetarian girl.

Vegetarian or not, taking a multivitamin every day is a good idea, especially if a girl has started her period. Among other things, it helps keep enough iron in her system. That's iron, like the *metal*.

There should be enough iron in your body to make one nail.

Here are some of the different vegetarian types:

Vegans won't eat any food from any animal; no meat, dairy, honey, or eggs.

Raw Foodists are kind of like vegans who don't cook.

Fruitarians will only eat fruits, nuts, and any vegetables that can be eaten without killing the plant. (So cucumbers would be okay, but not carrots.)

Pizza-Cheater Vegetarians pick the meat off their pizza and may even try to soak up the pepperoni oil with a napkin.

Pesceterians will eat fish, because everyone knows that fish are swimming vegetables. ☺

Lacto-Ovo Vegetarians will eat dairy products and eggs. (They also need to get a less silly name!) **Nachoarians** claim to be vegetarians, but only as an excuse to subsist solely on nacho chips and Velveeta cheese.

The Master of Cheese! One of the most specialized jobs in the world is being a *Maître Fromager* (MATE-trah fro-MAJ). That's French for "Cheese Master." The *Maître Fromager* is in charge of tasting and testing different cheeses to judge their quality. But it's a dangerous job. "Cheese elbow" is a common injury you can get from cutting different cheeses over and over again every day. (Hey, if you had to cut the cheese for a living, you'd be in pain too!)

Sev Mamra!

What is it? A delicious snack mix from India!

You will need: Cayenne pepper, onion powder, ground turmeric, ground cumin, sugar, garlic powder, salt, packaged chow mein noodles, Rice Krispies (or other puffed rice cereal), mixed nuts or salted peanuts or cashews, cooking oil. *Optional:* Raisins.

If you like to try new things, this is a really tasty recipe. Put ¼ cup of cooking oil on the bottom of a large frying pan and heat it on *low*. Once it gets warm, add all your spices:

¼ *teaspoon cayenne pepper*

¼ *teaspoon onion powder*

½ *teaspoon ground turmeric*

½ *teaspoon ground cumin*

½ *teaspoon sugar*

¼ *teaspoon garlic powder*

¼ *teaspoon salt*

Stir them in while the oil gets hot. You may need to turn the heat up a tiny bit, but you will smell the spices cooking in the air. Once they're blended in, take the pan off the heat and mix in 1 cup of chow mein noodles and 3 cups of Rice Krispies. Get everything coated in the spices. When the mixture is cooled, add 1 cup of nuts (and 1 cup of raisins if you want to try them). Mix them in and enjoy!

This recipe makes about 6 cups of snack mix.

Crème Brûlée (*krem brool-LAY*)

This is French for "burnt cream," but don't let that stop you!

You will need: Sliced pieces of fresh fruit, plain yogurt, brown sugar, small bowls that can go in the oven (ramekins are good), a cookie sheet.

Is this a dessert or a healthy snack? Answer: **Both!**

First, turn your broiler on high. Then wash your fruit and slice it up; fill the bowls or ramekins you're using about halfway up with them. Spoon yogurt into the bowl, filling it almost the rest of the way up. Finally, sprinkle a thick layer of brown sugar on top of the yogurt to cover the bowl.

You're almost done! Put the bowls on a cookie sheet and stick them into the oven for a little while. Keep an eye on them; once the brown sugar is all melted and caramelized, it's time to pull the cookie sheet out. Turn off the oven and let the little crème brûlées cool. (We usually put them in the fridge for a while.) Then enjoy breaking through the caramel topping to the creamy goodness beneath.

Special Cookie Section

"I make the best oatmeal-raisin cookies in the world. Well, I don't make them a lot because I don't think it's fair to the other cookies."
~**Phoebe, from Friends**

The most famous cookies in the nation are probably Girl Scout cookies. There are about four million girls and adults in the Girl Scouts, and you've probably bought cookies from one of them. But do you know which Girl Scout cookie is their bestseller? (Make your guess and then check the bottom of the page.*)

Some places in the United States have laws that forbid selling food in public places without a license. So there have been times when Girl Scouts have been told to *stop selling* cookies. An Atlanta newspaper reported a case of eight-year-old Girl Scouts who were *arrested* for selling their cookies. Now that's one tough arrest! (Or should we say, one tough cookie?)

Chocolate chip cookies are probably the all-time favorite cookies. And they were only invented because of a happy accident! In 1930, a woman named Ruth Wakefield was working at the lodge she owned in Massachusetts called the Toll House Inn. One day she was making cookies and needed some baker's chocolate. (Baker's chocolate is unsweetened chocolate that completely melts when baked.)

Ruth didn't have any baker's chocolate, so she experimented with a Nestle chocolate bar. She noticed that the chocolate didn't melt all the way in the cookie; as a matter of fact, it held its shape pretty well! Although this wasn't what she was shooting for, Ruth shared the "accident" with her guests. Toll House chocolate chip cookies were born!

---

* Thin Mints make up a quarter of all Girl Scout cookie sales.

The chocolate chip cookie is the "official state cookie" of Massachusetts and Pennsylvania.

Strategy Tip: When you're dunking your cookie in milk, one cookie in five will get too soggy and fall in! ☺ If you are dunking your cookie in something warm, like tea, coffee, or hot chocolate, the odds are even worse. To avoid this horrible disaster, research shows you should not put your cookie *straight* into the liquid you are dunking it in. Instead, tilt it at an *angle*, so that the cookie doesn't get soggy at the same "break-off" point all the way across.

Dieting

"How long does getting thin take?" Pooh asked anxiously.

~*A. A. Milne,* **Winnie-the-Pooh**

Some adults believe that girls are always *starting* a diet, already *on* a diet, *finishing* a diet, or *wondering* if they should go on a diet. We don't believe that, but surveys do show that about 50 percent of all girls think they are overweight. (BTW, *overweight* means a person is carrying a few more pounds than she should. *Obese* means that someone is *really overweight*.)

Should that many girls be worried about their weight? Well, 70 percent of adult Americans are *overweight* or obese. (They're the ones who should be dieting!) As for the younger generation, almost 20 percent of kids in the United States are obese. That's . . . not good. The state with the lowest percentage of overweight girls is Utah; the state with the highest percentage of overweight girls is Mississippi.

 Prejudice! Studies show that kids between the ages of five and nine have very negative attitudes toward overweight people. These kids dislike chubby people even more than they dislike bullies.

So this is tricky. We now know that girls obsess about their weight, and we know that some of them are actually overweight. And yet lots of girls think they're overweight even though they're not! Rats. And it doesn't do any good to tell someone she's not fat. Girls never listen to that sort of thing.

You have to decide for yourself. But whether you think you're fat or thin, we hope that you will love the skin you're in. Take care of yourself! If you are overweight, don't let your body image ruin your life. Writer Wendy Shanker points out that when people someday go to your funeral, they won't say, "She was a good person. Too bad she couldn't lose 15 pounds."

> *"[When I was 19] I'd wake up in the morning [and] look in the mirror: 'Oh, my bum looks big. Oh, my face is fat.' And I just felt, 'What am I doing to my life? I can't even think about others.' . . . [But now] I'm just happy being me."*
> **~Kate Winslet**

Besides, it's not like being skinny solves problems or makes you a better person. There are plenty of mean skinny girls! One theory about why some girls worry so much about their weight is that the girls think there is an "imaginary audience" of people who notice every little thing about their bodies. This is "skinny paranoia."

We hope you don't get hung up on worrying about an "imaginary audience." It is just imaginary! Be confident in yourself and you will *always* be attractive. If other people don't see it, that is their problem. (Besides, if true beauty is on the inside, nobody is ever going to see it anyway!)

 Want to Lose Weight? Eat Something! A study that tracked thousands of girls for 10 years found that girls who ate breakfast were slimmer than girls who skipped breakfast. The girls who skipped breakfast tended to eat high-fat items (and a lot of them) later in the day. One of the study's authors said that the message for girls was that "not eating breakfast was the worst thing you can do."

Now watch this amazing magic trick. You will never need to bother with a diet plan again once you know this VALUABLE SECRET:

The Greatest, Super-Duper, Amazing Diet of All Time!

If you ever REALLY want to lose weight, *exercise more* and *eat less*. It's that simple. (And don't skip breakfast.)

THE MIND, EMOTIONS, AND DREAMS

"Women are like teabags. We don't know our true strength until we are in hot water!"

~*Eleanor Roosevelt*

Being a girl means that sometimes you want to be the most beautiful and most brilliant girl in the world. But at other times, you wish you could be just like everyone else. (And it's possible to have both of these feelings in the same day!) This is a good example of how amazing a person's mind is. The ways that people think may not always be logical, but they are really interesting.

Most of the people who study *psychology* (the study of the mind) and *therapy* (helping people with mental or emotional issues) are women. That's because women are good at really listening to other people, and they are also smart enough to help them deal with their problems.

Intuition

Intuition is that special feeling that tells you when something is right or wrong. Call it a hunch if you want, but if you can see a problem or opportunity before anyone else does, you've got intuition. Girls and women are famous for their intuition. Is it a sixth sense? A superpower? Part of your imagination? We're not sure, but sometimes when we are lost or confused, if we listen to that small voice inside of us, it might be able to lead the way.

The brain has two sides, called *hemispheres*. It used to be believed that each side of the brain was responsible for certain abilities, and that many people relied more on one side than the other. For instance, a girl might be called "right-brained" if she were creative and imaginative.

Scientists now believe that *both* sides of your brain are involved in most of your mental activities. For example, there is a band of nerves that connects your two hemispheres together. Called the *corpus callosum*, this is where a lot of your creative and problem-solving abilities come from.

In the course of growing up, we all develop our own thinking styles. These seem to happen pretty naturally, and they influence our personalities. You may know someone who loves change and is super-creative. We bet she is also often running late! Or maybe you have a friend who is very practical, makes lists, and doesn't make decisions until thinking about them.

Mind Games

Have you ever had a feeling that you have experienced something before? This unusual sensation is called *déjà vu,* which is French for "already seen."

About 66 percent of people report having *déjà vu* at one time or another. It seems to be most common in people with good imaginations. People who travel a lot and people who are tired also report more *déjà vu* than others.

The "thing" that seems so familiar is usually nothing very dramatic. It might be anything from a conversation at the breakfast table to unwrapping a Popsicle. And nobody knows exactly where *déjà vu* comes from. Maybe the person had a dream that is really similar to what happened to them in real life. (Or perhaps it's a message *from beyond!*)

The opposite of *déjà vu* is *jamais vu* ("never seen"). This is when a person sees or hears things that *should* be familiar, but seem totally strange. You can give yourself *jamais vu.* Just take a piece of paper and write a word on it. The word doesn't matter, so let's say you pick "SUGAR."

Find a quiet spot and stare hard at the word. Now say it. Keep staring at the word, and say it over and over again. At some point (and it may take a few minutes), you will probably feel *jamais vu.* The word (and sound) SUGAR will seem totally meaningless to you. *Jamais vu.* Get yours today!

It seems like I've been here before.

Another Amazing Term!
Déjà moo: The feeling that you have seen a cow somewhere before.

Fears and Doubts and Phobias (*Oh My!*)

"Courage does not always roar. Sometimes courage is the quiet voice at the end of the day saying, 'I will try again tomorrow.'"
~*Mary Ann Radmacher*

The most common "mental health issue" among people of ALL ages is a fear, or *phobia*, about a particular thing. Some adults say that you can't run away from your fears, and that you have to face them. *This is nonsense.* You can always run away from a spider or snake if you're afraid of it!

Phobias are sometimes "learned" during childhood. If a dog snarls at a young girl, she might be afraid of some dogs. This doesn't mean that the girl has a phobia, though, unless she's afraid of *all* dogs. (Even the stuffed ones!) It's all a matter of degree.

Common Phobias

aichmophobia: Fear of sharp objects, like needles or boys with too much mousse in their hair.

arachibutrophobia: Fear of peanut butter sticking to the roof of your mouth.

ergasiophobia: Fear of work.

blennophobia: Fear of slime.

lachanophobia: Fear of vegetables.

peladophobia: Fear of bald people.

phobophobia: The fear of being afraid.

scolionophobia: Fear of school.

xerophobia: Fear of dryness. Break out the hand lotion!

aughhhh!!!

Unusual Phobias

ambulophobia: Fear of walking.

catoptrophobia: Fear of mirrors.

chorophobia: Fear of dancing.

chrometophobia: Fear of money.

euphobia: Fear of hearing good news.

geniophobia: Fear of chins.

metrophobia: Fear of poetry.

panophobia: Fear of everything.

parthenophobia: Fear of girls.

pediophobia: Fear of dolls.

scopophobia: Fear of being seen.

telephonophobia: Fear of phones.

Here's our phobia: *We are afraid that many girls lose their self-esteem between the ages of 12 and 15.* Research shows that girls start out in school feeling good about themselves. They also usually get better grades than boys. But as girls hit middle school and become teenagers, their self-esteem scores often go way down, and so do their grades!

What happens? One theory is that some girls want to be popular so badly, they spend all their time socializing. Other girls are self-conscious and might be *afraid* they will be called "brains" or "nerds" if they study. Because they're *afraid* of what other people think, they stop doing what they're good at. Either way, it's not a good phobia to have!

Emotions

"If you're never scared or embarrassed or hurt, it means you never take any chances."

~Julia Sorel

Emotions might be the best and worst things about being human. Because they can change, they can put us on a roller coaster of feelings. When emotions do change, people call them "mood swings." A study done in Chicago found that some teens have a mood swing every 15 minutes. *Wow!* Sometimes your mood will depend on random factors like the weather, or if you are having a good hair day.

Sometimes you'll have a crummy day, but won't want to talk about it. If so, when someone asks how you are, just say, "FINE" This stands for *Fed up, Insecure, Neurotic,* and *Emotional.* That way you're being honest and you don't have to talk about it!

Strong emotions can get the better of us. A woman named Ruth Bell compares strong emotions to smoke alarms. Both of them alert you to important situations, and if you ignore them, you can get burned. So if you need to cry, don't try to hold it in all the time. Let it go.

If you have issues, get out the tissues!

Up until they're 12, boys and girls cry the same amount. But by the time they're 18, girls will be crying *four times* more than boys. A girl can cry because she's happy, afraid, angry, or excited. But men are discouraged from doing this, so they have a hard time crying. They spend years bottling up their feelings until they either lose all feeling entirely or they are incredibly tense. No wonder they're so uptight!

Some girls have the ability to cry almost instantly. That is like a superpower! Those girls can fully experience their emotions right away. Plus, they don't retain as much water. ☺ You know what we mean when we say that you can feel a lot better after a good cry. All that tension is gone.

Deep Question: Why does releasing water from our eyes help us? No other animals do this!

"Laugh and the world laughs with you. Cry and you cry with your girlfriends."

~Laurie Kylansky

Is it a *mood* swing or a *food* swing? If you're hungry, you're more likely to be sad (or crabby or homicidal). Take a bite out of depression. Eat something!

Even though there's no quick way out of depression (besides chocolate), wise women have come up with many ways to deal with it. Writing or doing anything creative, spending time with an animal (dogs always cheer us up), enjoying a good movie or book, listening to your favorite music, getting some exercise, or putting on your favorite outfit are a few ways to get out of a funk. Sadness experts also recommend taking a hot bath. And speaking of baths, here's a good . . .

Crying Tip! If you want to have a good cry without your family wondering WHAT'S WRONG, try this. *Cry in the shower!* It's the perfect private place to let it all out. The noise of the water pressure camouflages the sobs, and you're getting wet anyway. If you come out with a red or puffy face, that's pretty normal for a hot shower. Plus, you can cleanse your emotions and body at the same time. Now that's efficient!

One wise girl also suggests crying while you are in bed. Since everyone thinks that you are asleep, you have a little privacy. And if you have a good cry, you will be so worn out that you can feel relaxed and sleep like a baby!

How did you sleep? I slept like a baby. I woke up and cried every hour.

Do you have a hysterically *funny memory*? *This would involve something that happened that never fails to crack you up.* If you DON'T want to cry, try thinking of this memory. You'll laugh instead (or laugh and cry) and everyone will be tricked!

Moodiness and Tantrums

"I would say, express your feelings at all times. Unless you're trying to hide something."

~**Miss Piggy**

When someone is described as "moody," it's a polite way of saying the person is always in a BAD mood. How come a moody person is never a person who's always in a GOOD mood?

Let's say you are in the worst mood possible. Everything and everyone is bothering you; it's like people are *trying to make you go nuclear*. Sometimes (but not very often) you may want to give in to the temptation to just have a TANTRUM!

Little kids get to have them, so why not you? We're talking about a raging, yelling tantrum, not some little tizzy or junior conniption fit! Tantrums can be fun in a drama queen sort of way, and they can help to clear out some of those bad emotions. Tantrums also usually get sort of boring after a while, and then it's time to move on with your life.

Tantrum Tips! It's usually more considerate to throw a tantrum when you have a little privacy. That way you won't scare anybody when you slam a door or stomp your feet. If you *really* need to get some anger out of your system but there are people in the house, try screaming into a pillow. You know, just lie down on your bed face-first onto your pillow and HOWL. It's great therapy.

Don't throw things while having a tantrum. They tend to break.

"The glass is always half empty. And cracked. And I just cut my lip on the edge of it. And chipped a tooth."

~**Janeane Garofalo**

You Have a Right to Feel Crummy! In a study of kids' moods, seventh- through ninth-graders were found to have the most "negative life episodes" and depressed feelings. ("Negative events" were defined as boyfriend problems, family trouble, low grades, and so on.) So if you're in that age range, just remember: things *will* get better!

Happiness

We don't want to dwell just on the negative emotions, so let's talk about feeling good. When things are going well and everything seems all right, enjoy the moment. Go outside and let the sun shine on you. Look at a tree. Take advantage of your happy times to spread the joy. Give a smile to others, play with a little kid, or donate $50,000 to charity.

 Studies show that in public, women smile and laugh much more than men.

When you're feeling happy it's a great time to get some exercise! Many girl athletes report that when the mood is right, their basketball or volleyball or chess skills just can't be beat; they're in the zone. It's also an opportunity to get creative. Whether you write something down, work on a painting, or play a musical instrument, you can accomplish amazing things when your attitude is right.

Dreams

"No wonder Sleeping Beauty looked good . . . she took long naps, never got old, and didn't have to do anything but snore to get her Prince Charming."

~Olive Green

Before YOU can get your beauty sleep, you have to *fall* asleep, and this might be a problem for some girls. Most people fall asleep within ten minutes of going to bed. But a study of *insomnia* (not being able to fall asleep) involving 40,000 people found that women are *twice as likely* to have trouble drifting off compared to men. Why? Women and girls probably think too much! (It's also been found that girls typically wake up earlier than boys. Dang it!)

Dream Stages and Brain Waves

How does falling asleep work? Sleep studies have found that your mind goes into different levels of slumber.

Level 1: You're pretty much awake, though you can daydream here.

Level 2: Now you are starting to nod off . . . won't that teacher EVER stop talking? *Zzzzz . . .* In this stage, you might do one of those weird full body jerks and wake up, embarrassed.

Level 3: So peaceful . . . *Deep sleep . . .*

Level 4: You are now drooling on your pillow.

REM: This is **R**apid **E**ye **M**ovement sleep, when really intense dreams happen. Have you ever seen a sleeping dog twitching and barking? The dog's eyes are usually bobbling around a lot, and the eyelids may actually be wide open. So why are the eyes moving? It's because they are trying to see the dream images that are in the dog's *mind*. And the same thing happens when *you* sleep! Weird, huh?

Level 1

Level 2

Toward the morning hours, you have more deep sleep and your body really relaxes. Usually, the big muscles of your body, like your arms and legs, don't move too much when you are in REM, but your face and hands might.

Level 3

Level 4

Most girls really do hit the snooze button. What a great invention! It allows you to get another few precious moments of sleep. But not all sleep is equal! The kind of sleep you get *after* you hit the snooze button will almost never be as restful as the kind you were having *before* the alarm went off.

Typical Pattern of Sleep Stages for a Girl in the Morning

REM, alarm goes off, push snooze button.

REM, alarm goes off, push snooze button.

Repeat!

But what *is* a dream? Good question! Nobody knows for sure, but we do know they're important. According to sleep specialists, even unborn babies have dreams. (What do they dream about? They're not talking!) We do know that the number one thing that little kids dream about is *animals*. And the most popular story line for a little kid's dream is being chased by something (usually an animal).

But starting at about the age of nine, your dreams get a whole lot more complicated. As your body and mind change, your dreams reflect this. Also, you start sleeping more. By the time girls become teens, they *should* sleep more because their bodies are growing, and they need more rest.

But just because you NEED more sleep doesn't mean you GET it. The average sixth-grade girl averages 8 hours of sleep a night. The average eighth-grade girl gets 7 hours, 17 minutes of sleep. This trend of getting less sleep continues throughout high school. Students who get less sleep report feeling grumpy and getting worse grades. In the worst cases, people not getting enough sleep get headaches, forget things, and even gain weight. So take care of yourself and try to get to bed at a reasonable hour.

 The same study found that people who exercise regularly also sleep the best.

You don't dream the whole time you're asleep. In fact, some adults only dream about 25 percent of their sleep time. Research also shows that people who fall asleep staring at a television, cell phone, or computer don't have as much REM sleep as normal. In other words, their sleep is like junk food; not very healthy.

You usually learn by an early age that what you're dreaming about isn't real, so you don't act out dream movements in "real life." (This is one reason why you don't have to wear diapers anymore!) But some people do things like talking or walking in their sleep. The strangest case of sleepwalking happened to a girl in Connecticut named Felicia Gonzalez. She apparently *cleaned her room* while asleep. Unbelievable!

Boys sleepwalk more than girls, but they never clean their rooms while doing so. (Of course, boys don't clean their rooms while awake, either.)

Sleepwalking happens during the deepest stages of sleep. Sleepwalkers are often confused when they wake up outside of their bed, but it is okay to wake them. Just gently take them by the arm and guide them back to bed. Other sleep disorders can sometimes combine with eating. The girl will be asleep, get out of bed, go into the kitchen, and start eating. She may eat odd things: spaghetti sauce, dog biscuits, frozen peas, and so forth.

Where Do Dreams Come From?

"Dreams come a size too big so that we can grow into them."
~Josie Bissett

Are they messages from the future? Could be! Are they messages from a hamster? Probably not! Here are some of the places where dreams can come from:

Your Body. If you are hungry, but you're asleep, you may have dreams of eating food . . . lots of food! It never seems to fill you up, though. Dream food is famous for being low in calories. **WARNING:** If you have to pee while you're asleep, you may find yourself looking for a restroom in your dream. It's usually better if you *don't* find one. That's because if you do find a dream restroom and you use it, you might use it while you're dreaming . . . and then wake up with wet sheets! Talk about *nightmares!*

Your Surroundings. Where you sleep can change your dreams. For example, if you are dreaming about being really hot in the middle of the desert, you may wake up later and find that you are all tangled up in your blankets and you're sweating. Or if there's a dog barking next door, you may dream about a barking dog. You can hear it in "real" life, but since it isn't loud enough to wake you up, your mind uses the material for a dream.

Recent Memories. When you fall asleep, the memories of the day will stick with you. So if you went to school, you might have school dreams. The most common school dreams involve forgetting your locker combination, finding out that there is a *huge* test that you didn't study for, not being able to find the right classroom, and being a teacher's pet.

Sometimes, what you saw (or were thinking about) just *before* you go to sleep is what your mind uses for dream stories. So if there is an important drama or conflict going on in your life, it will probably show up in a dream.

Wish Fulfillment. *Anything* can happen in a dream. That means that you may have a dream where you are holding hands with that cute somebody you have a crush on. This is called *wish fulfillment;* you are fulfilling your own wish! Because you get to be your own genie, these dreams can be about anything you want. It might be raining money, or you might be shopping for expensive clothes, or maybe you found a really great loofah.

Random Shuffle. Your mind sometimes ransacks your old memories for ideas. That's why you might dream about that time in kindergarten when you dressed like a ballerina and brought a penguin for show-and-tell.

Meaningful Dreams. You can learn interesting things about yourself by thinking about your dreams. Dreams can teach us about our "real" feelings that we sometimes hide from ourselves when we are awake. Try keeping a dream journal by your bed. When you wake up, write down whatever you can remember from your dreams. But be quick: if you don't write them down quickly, you will forget these dreams fast! Your "waking" mind wants to clean up and get the day started, and all those dream memories get swept up and put in the trash. If you do write the dreams down promptly, you will notice certain patterns. (*Why is the Popsicle always lime-flavored?*) Also, it may help you to understand yourself a lot better than you do.

 Funny Thought! Have you ever had a friend say something mean to you in a dream? And then the next day you're mad at her in real life?

Nightmares

The thing about nightmares is that even though they're scary, it's YOU who is scaring yourself in them. That's right! *Who* do you think is writing the story for the nightmare? *You* are! Once you see nightmares that way, they don't have quite as much power anymore.

The next time you're in a nightmare, think: *What is the worst thing that could happen?* For example, a boy once said that if you are falling in a dream and you land, "You will wake up dead." We think you'll agree that that is just silly. If you are falling in a dream, just let yourself land. You'll bounce! If a monster is chasing you, *stop running.* Turn around and make friends with it. Or go for a pony ride together!

If you can change your dream while you are having it, it is called *lucid dreaming.* It means that you are in control. (Some people even think it's a sign of good mental health.) But nobody can stop the *night terrors.* These are nightmares so horrible, the girl having them can only scream and scream and SCREAM! Once the girl is finally awake, she usually can't remember anything about her dream. (Night terrors are rare in older kids, so you've probably outgrown them.)

 If you are still worried about nightmares, get a *dream catcher.* These were used by Native Americans to catch nightmares before they could get to the dreamer.

Dream Symbols and What They Might Mean

A *symbol* is just something that can stand for something else. For example, a happy face emoticon **:)** is just two dots and a curve, but it symbolizes laughter and humor. While an emoticon means just one thing, dream symbols can mean different things for different people. A dream about a poodle might be good for one girl (*Here pretty doggie!*) but bad for another (*A poodle bit off my spleen two years ago!*).

It is fun to try to figure out what *your* dream symbols may mean. For example, let's say you dream you're at the mall, but it's deserted and all the stores are closed. If the mall is a place where you normally hang out, this dream may mean that you are feeling lonely or unpopular. But if you don't like crowds or shopping, this could be a good dream.

Keep in mind that a lot of dreams don't mean anything at all. They are just random stories with weird details, such as "I was playing catch with an armadillo." Other symbols in dreams are pretty obvious. And there are certain things that girls dream about that can have the same meanings for lots of people. Here are a few of them.

Baths and Water: Water usually is pure, cleansing, and soothing. But if the water is really *warm*, you may be in hot water! Or if it's deep, you may be "in over your head."

Naked: There are *no secrets* when you have *no clothes*. You feel exposed and embarrassed! If you're just a *little* embarrassed, you might be in your pajamas.

Driving in Cars: *Who* is driving? If you're a passenger, this may show you feel you don't have control over your life. *Good sign:* You are driving, and you are driving well. *Bad sign:* You are driving and you go over a cliff! *Worst sign:* Nobody is driving. Talk about no control! Common dream-driving problems include disappearing steering wheels, the brakes in the car going out, and no turn signals. See your dream auto mechanic to solve these.

Falling: Everyone gets these dreams, especially when they're insecure or afraid. Maybe you feel that you have let yourself *down* or have *fallen below* the expectations that you have for yourself. Maybe you're afraid of something that has happened or something you think will happen.

Flying: Flying is usually a good sign! It shows that life is going well for you.

Phone Calls: This may be a sign that you are trying to give yourself an important message. Pick up the phone and listen! And keep in mind that you have unlimited texting. (**WARNING:** Caller ID is not always accurate in dreams.)

Someone Is Chasing You: *Who* is chasing you? In about 10 percent of "getting chased" dreams, the person chasing you is just sort of a general "villain." If it is someone you know, guess what? You feel *threatened* by that person. (We hope it isn't your best friend!)

Kissing: What can we tell you? If you find yourself kissing someone that you really like, this is a *wish fulfillment* dream! If it's someone you dislike, it's a nightmare . . . or a message that maybe you don't *dislike* that person as much as you thought! ☺

Scientists still have not figured out why you always run in slow motion when you are being chased in a dream. They have a theory that there is too much quicksand in Dreamland. Another theory is that since you can't move your big muscles (like your legs) when you are asleep, you feel paralyzed in your dream. Luckily, this prevents you from running with scissors in your dreams, thus preventing serious accidents.

PRACTICAL JOKES

"The best tasting foods are fattening. The best clothes are overpriced. My best friend likes the same boy who I like. Is someone playing a joke on me?"

~*Sandy Beech*

Complimenting your best friend is a good thing. But one special compliment you may not have realized you can pay your friend is playing a practical joke on her! That's because a practical joke says, *I cared about you enough to play this joke. You have a great sense of humor.* But it is important to use good judgment if you give this kind of compliment. The person you play the joke on almost has to be a friend or family member. Otherwise a practical joke is not funny, it's just *mean*.

 There Are Exceptions! Very rarely, a joke played upon strangers *is* funny. For instance, a practical joker posted a huge sign in front of a runway at Los Angeles International Airport that said "Welcome to CHICAGO." And incoming passengers freaked out! Now *that's* funny.

The best way to test a practical joke is to imagine if it were played on YOU. Would *you* think it was funny? If the answer to that question is "No," then do not play the joke on someone else. The best joke is the one where everyone laughs, especially the person upon whom the joke is played.

Practical jokes don't have to make sense to be funny. For example, let's say that you're at a friend's house. You say you're leaving, and then you sneak back inside, maybe into your friend's bedroom. If your friend is busy or in another part of the house, go in her bedroom and turn all the furniture upside down or rearrange it so that the room is reversed. Then you really do leave. This is really stupid *and* it's really funny!

Quick Prank

Hide in a friend's or sibling's closet until they open it and then jump out! If you're an overachiever, try crawling under their bed and waiting for them to sit on it or lie down. Then reach out with a hand to grab their ankle and listen to the screams!

Another fun prank is to gently pull the labels off of a few cans in the pantry and then reglue them onto different cans. At some point your dad will open a can of "beans" and instead get a can of sliced peaches. "Why would someone do this?" he will ask. Your answer: "Because it's funny!" This is called "TP logic." It doesn't make any sense to TP (toilet paper) a friend's house, yet it's fun to do!

But sometimes a joke makes perfect sense. Depending on your neighbors, going trick-or-treating on October 30 (the night *before* Halloween) can be a good laugh. On one hand, you may get some very surprised people who give you candy because they think they read their calendars wrong. On the other hand, some neighbors will tell *you* that it's the wrong night. In that case, just say, "Oops! We wondered where everyone was! Can we have some candy anyway?"

If you're looking for ideas, the tricks below are arranged in order, from the simplest to the more complicated.

The "No Joke" Joke

The easiest joke to play is the joke that is never played!

You will need: Nothing!
This trick works best if you already have a reputation as a joker. During the last couple of days of March, start making little warnings to your victim that she better be on her toes on April Fools' Day.

"Yep, it's going to be pretty incredible," you say, with an evil gleam in your eye. Naturally, she'll want to know what the joke is, or even try to talk you out of it. "I couldn't call it off even if I wanted to," is a statement guaranteed to get her even more worried.

As you've already figured out, there *is* no big joke, which IS the joke. If you've prepared your victim properly, she will be looking over her shoulder all day. Nice work!

Quick Prank

If you don't see your friends for a winter's weekend, try getting a spray-on tan. Then tell your friends that you went to Hawaii or Florida for the weekend! (**Note:** If you already live in Hawaii or Florida, this trick will be less impressive.)

You're Going on a Trip

This is really immature.

You will need: A friend who wears shoes.

Remind your friend that some people think it is possible to tell a person's fortune by reading her palms. Then tell her that you've been doing some research, and you've found that it really *is* possible to tell a fortune by reading a person's shoes. Show her the "Shoes" section of the "Fashion" chapter on pages 223–225 to impress her with your knowledge if necessary.

Anyway, you want to convince your friend to take off at least one of her shoes so that you can tell her fortune. Once you have your friend's shoe in hand, look it over very seriously and make some meaningful utterances. *Wow . . . Uh huh . . . Just as I suspected.* When the timing is right, tell your friend that her fortune has been read. Say, "I can tell from this shoe that you will soon be going on a trip."

Then throw the shoe as far as you can and run away!

Quick Prank

After someone opens up a package of Oreos, remove a couple of the cookies. Carefully open the Oreos and use a butter knife to scrape the filling out. (Don't waste it! *Mmmm . . . Oreo filling.*) Then take white-colored toothpaste and spread it on the inside of the cookie wafers. Spread it around a bit till it looks right, put the cookies back together, and be patient!

Big Wheels Keep on Turning

Round and round and round it goes . . . where it opens, she doesn't know!

You will need: A bathroom, a glue stick.

Go into any bathroom that has rolls of toilet paper. Take out your glue stick and find the opening square that you would usually start unrolling from. Run the glue stick across the inner edge of the square and neatly press it against the roll. It's sort of hard to see where the roll begins now, isn't it?

If you've ever heard a hamster running on its wheel, that's the sound the next person to sit down after you will be making as she looks for the opening square!

Quick Prank

Between classes, fill up one of your friend's lockers or closets with lots of wadded-up pages from the newspaper, balloons, Ping-Pong balls, or stuffed animals.

Trapped

How to trap your friend in one easy lesson.

You will need: A full glass of water, a kitchen table.

Start up a conversation with your friend, and while you're talking, innocently go into the kitchen and fill up your glass of water nearly all the way. As you raise the water to your lips, say (as if you just thought of it), "Hey, you have to see this." Have your friend put her two index fingers (those are the nose-picking fingers) next to each other on the top of the table, as if she were pointing to something on the table itself.

Once she's in position, put your glass of water on top of her fingers, balancing it there. Guess what? Now she's trapped! It's almost impossible to escape from this situation without spilling the water, unless someone helps. (And you're not going to do that, right?)

FINGERS are TRAPPED!

Quick Prank

The next time a friend spends the night, try this one. After you're pretty sure that your friend is asleep, get out the baby powder. Sprinkle it lightly but generously over her hair. Try not to laugh or you'll wake her up! In the morning, your friend may make it to the mirror without noticing anything wrong. But when she sees her white hair, she'll realize that she's been "antiqued"!

 Amazing Riddle!
Q. What's white, green, blue, purple, black, red, brown, and yellow?
A. A box of crayons.

Fake Cereal

A good way to get rid of the breakfast "blahs"!

You will need: Crayons or other harmless small items, cereal boxes.

Because people are often bleary and "out of it" in the morning, they fall easy prey to practical jokes. For this one, just save an empty bag that holds the cereal inside a cereal box. Fill the bag with crayons, kitty litter, or any other innocent item that doesn't weigh too much. Then switch it with a cereal bag inside a box and put the box back on the shelf!

At some point, an innocent person will pull the box out and pour herself a bowl of crayons and kitty litter. And it will be funny! (And it'll be even funnier if you forget what you did because you're bleary in the morning, and you pour *yourself* a bowl of crayons and kitty litter. The joke will be on you!)

Raccoon Eyes

Turning friends into raccoons is fun!

You will need: Shoeblack or marker, binoculars or telescope.

Secret preparation: Run a black magic marker or some shoeblack along the edge of the eyepiece(s) of a telescope or binoculars. (If you use the magic marker, you'll want to play the joke before the ink dries.)

After secretly preparing the binoculars, you need some (any!) excuse to get your friend to look through them. The best way to do this is to look through them yourself, while exclaiming, "Look at the size of that bird!" or "That man's not wearing any pants!" BE CAREFUL not to let the blackened eyepieces touch your face, or the joke will really be on *you*.

Your friend will then want to look. Let her! And try not to laugh when she gets her raccoon eyes. See how long it takes for her to notice!

The Talking Appliance

Take advantage of the nice people who invite you into their home!

You will need: A neighbor who likes you, a pair of walkie-talkies.

Although this trick can work in your house, the odds of it working are improved with a neighbor or friend. Smuggle one of your walkie-talkies into your neighbor's house, maybe during one of the times they've foolishly invited you over. When it's safe, turn the walkie-talkie on and set its volume on "high."

Where you put the walkie-talkie is up to you. It could be in the back of the refrigerator or inside the laundry hamper. After you leave, get the other walkie-talkie and speak into it. What you say depends on where you left the device.

Refrigerator: Help me! I'm freezing in here! So cold . . . can't feel my control knobs!

Laundry hamper: I don't mean to complain, but it smells like an outhouse in here.

Oven: I'm burning up in here!

Be sure to use your common sense with this. Don't put the walkie-talkie in the oven unless you're sure you can get it back out before someone starts baking!

The Princess and the Pea

How sensitive is your victim?

You will need: A variety of balls, patience.

In case you've never heard the story of the "Princess and the Pea," a pea is put under the mattress of a girl to test whether she actually *is* a princess. Since she is a princess, the girl feels it, because everyone knows that princesses are very sensitive! (Even though peas play a role in it, the story has a happy ending.)

For this joke, first, pick a victim who is a sibling. (It doesn't have to be a girl.) Take a small ball (smaller than a tennis ball but bigger than a marble) and set it under the mattress, not necessarily right in the middle though. Drop the mattress back down and practice your innocent expression.

Unless the ball is pretty big (or the mattress is thin), the odds are that the first ball won't be noticed. For the second night, put a second ball under the mattress in a different spot. It can be the same size or slightly bigger than the first ball.

Depending on how sensitive your victim is, this can go on for some time. But at SOME point, your victim will notice the bumps in the mattress and look underneath it. When that happens, remember what your line is:

Victim: What the heck! Mom! Dad! There's a bunch of balls under my bed!

You: Hurray! You're a princess! You're a princess!

Here's an INSTANT prank

You will need: A box or two of instant potatoes.

In the evening, pour the flaked potatoes onto your friend's lawn, spelling out a message. The dew will make the potatoes expand. In the morning, your friend will see big, puffed-up, huge letters conveying your message. **Jessica Loves Timmy!**

Want even more innocent yet mischievous pranks? Take a spin through *The Pocket Guide to Mischief*!

GIRL SECRETS
No Boys Allowed!

"I can keep secrets. It's the girls I tell them to who can't keep a secret at all."

~**Brooke Vermillion**

WARNING: This book has a *gender sensor* that will give a mild electric shock to any *boy* trying to read this section. So if you're a boy, put the book down now. (Go to a chapter you can learn from, like "Boys" or "Dolls and Stuffed Animals.")

Hiking in the Flowers

This chapter is about hiking and flowers. Yes, there is nothing a girl likes more than hiking

and picking flowers. So if you like flowers and the great outdoors, you've come to the right place. Because that's all that this chapter is about! Okay, we're pretty sure no boys would read this far, so it's probably safe to admit that this chapter isn't *really* about flowers. It's really about topics that are good for a girl to know about.

The Joys of Childhood

Childhood is great, and one reason for that is because you don't have to be self-conscious about your body. When you were in nursery school and your dad put you up on his shoulders, you didn't worry about being too heavy for him. It was fun! And if there was a pool nearby, you and the other kids just put on your swimsuits and jumped in. There just aren't many five-year-olds who worry about their thighs looking fat.

So it seems like we start off in life with our eyes wide open to the world around us. It's awesome! We take everything in and enjoy most of it. But as we get older, we go into a "tunnel of self-consciousness." This is a place where we worry much more about ourselves and our appearances. This often happens when a girl's clothes aren't fitting the same way that they used to because her body is changing.

As you hit puberty, you're going to put on weight. A girl can expect to add anywhere from 10 to 30 pounds to her overall weight as she matures. Your hips will widen and your butt will be bigger. That's when it's even more important to keep a healthy lifestyle by eating right and getting exercise.

And of course, your breasts will change. If you don't have breasts yet, don't worry about it. If you are starting to get them (or already have them), don't be embarrassed. You're a *girl*, not a woman, so enjoy it! Some people make such a big deal about this, it is easy to forget that breasts exist to *feed babies*. That's it!

In Chinese, the character for mother is drawn with two square breasts. 母

Babies couldn't safely drink animal milk from a bottle until the late 1800s. (That was when a process called *pasteurization* made drinking cow's milk safe.) So back in the day, if a baby couldn't breast-feed from her mother, she might have a "wet nurse." A wet nurse was a woman who had also recently given birth. She was hired to breast-feed other people's babies.

As you know, cultures all have fads and fashions for beauty, which *always* change over time. Because of this, breasts have been thought of in many different ways. At certain times, a very flat chest or small breasts have been highly prized, while at other times, large breasts have been esteemed. As an example, Helen of Troy was one of history's most beautiful women. Her breasts were used as a model for how large a wine cup should be. (And those old Greek wine cups weren't that big.)

Speaking of classical figures, the Department of Justice in Washington, D.C., has a statue of a woman wearing a toga. She is called the Spirit of Justice and she was created in a classical style that leaves one of her breasts exposed. An official once spent over $8,000 covering this statue (and her male partner) with drapes because the nudity was "inappropriate." (The drapes have since been removed.)

 Look carefully at movies and advertisements and look at how women's bodies are shown. The message seems to be *You can sell anything you want with breasts.* If you dislike this message, write to the companies that advertise this way and tell them how you feel.

There are over 100,000 breast *reduction* surgeries in the United States each year. (From 18,000 to 20,000 U.S. men have this same surgery annually.) That's because large breasts can cause neck and back pain, and they also can make it hard to exercise. Speaking of breast reduction, you've probably heard of the Amazons. This is the Greek name for a mythical tribe of warrior women who cut off their right breasts so that they could shoot arrows more accurately. (In Greek, the prefix *a-* means "without" and *mazos* means "breast.")

Medical Breakthrough!

About 200 years ago, a young lady in France visited her doctor because she thought she might have heart problems. The doctor wanted to help, but he was too shy to put his ear on the woman's chest to listen to her heart. So he tried putting a tube on her chest with his ear on the other end. Amazing! He could hear her heart better than he could have dreamed. Eventually, the tube became the stethoscope (Greek for "chest watcher") we have today.

Bras

"Friends are like bras: close to your heart and there for your support!"
~*Emily Glitter*

The word *bra* comes from the old French word *brassiere* which means "upper arm." This was a word originally used 400 years ago to describe *arm armor* (you know, like armor for the arms?). Armor exists to provide support and protection, which are also things that a good bra can provide. At some point, you're going to think you're ready for a bra. If your parents agree, then it's time to go bra shopping.

Bra sizes come with a NUMBER and LETTER value. The NUMBER is the number of inches it is around your chest under your breasts. The LETTER is your breast size. (Letters start at AAA, then go to AA, then A, and so forth.)

To get an idea what size you are, take a soft measuring tape and measure around your chest just *below* your breasts. (By the way, you can do this with your shirt on!) If you measure your chest and get an *even* number of inches, add 4 to the number. If you get an *odd* number of inches, add 5. So if you measured 30 inches around your chest, your chest size is 34; if you measured 25 inches, then your chest size is 30. Write your number down. (This is called your *band* size.)

 The word *bra* means "good" or "excellent" in Swedish.

The ancient Greeks invented the bra with the scariest name: the *mastodeton*. Eek!

The next thing to figure out is *cup* size, which is labeled in letters. Measure again around your chest, but this time, have the tape go right across the center of your breasts. If the number you come up with is the SAME as the number you wrote down earlier, your cup size is probably what is called AA. If the measurement is one inch bigger, you're an A cup. Two inches bigger is a B cup, three inches is a C cup, four is a D cup, five is a DD, and six is a DDD. (These are just educated guesses, though. To get the right bra, you really need to go in for a fitting.)

Useless Fact: The average bra size of a full-grown woman is 34B.

Bra Shopping Tips

Shopping Tip #1: Always shop with your mom or a girlfriend so that they can help you with fitting and finding bras.

Shopping Tip #2: Make sure the back strap is at or above the bottom of your breasts. If the strap in the back isn't comfortable, or if the cups look wrinkled, you're wearing the wrong size.

Shopping Tip #3: Department stores often have "Bra Fitting Specialists" who can help find the right brand and size for you. There are a lot of factors to consider, so when you go shopping see if there is someone who can help you with a fitting.

A French woman named Herminie Cadolle is usually given credit for being the true inventor of the bra in 1889. She was a busy woman who was tired of having to wear uncomfortable corsets. So Herminie came up with the idea of "sustaining the bosom and [supporting it] by the shoulders." No more squeezing up!

Even though they're just pieces of clothing, bras have been controversial. In 1968, some women protesting the 1968 Miss America pageant threw bras, high heel shoes, cosmetics, and other symbols of what they considered sexism into a trash can. At that time, "bra burnings" were thought of as a symbolic way for women to protest sexist treatment and create their own identities. But many feminists today embrace bras and other symbols of the female body, emphasizing that women do not have to be *the same* as men to be *equal*.

A lot of girls like to wear tank tops and camisoles with built-in bras. Other girls like to collect fun bras. You can find anything from plain white to lace to polka dot to your favorite cartoon character patterns. Some girls wear special holiday bras, like ones with a jingle bell in the center for Christmas. Whether you have fun with them or they are just another piece of clothing like socks, bras are nothing to be stressed out about.

See page 91 for tips on buying a sports bra.

A Scary Word

Why does *puberty* have to be such an uncute word? It sounds so scary. How about just "becoming a teenager" or "growing up"?

As a girl goes into puberty, a *lot* of things are happening in her body. Acne shows up, and, oh joy, body odor can be smelled! 🙁 You'll want to start using soap on all parts of your parts every time that you shower. And you definitely need to shower every day. Once puberty hits, it's all about deodorant, breath mints, and *loofah, loofah, loofah*! (Washcloths work too, but they don't sound as cool.)

Maturing like this is also one of the most important things in the world. For example, if women didn't menstruate (a.k.a. "get their period"), they wouldn't be able to have babies later in life, and the human race would become *extinct*! Different families treat the topic of menstruation in different ways. Sometimes it's a big secret that only a girl and her mother know about. And in places as far apart as Japan, Africa, and Sri Lanka, a girl's first period is a reason to throw a big party.

Back in the old days, girls often didn't menstruate until they were 17 years old. Now, with better nutrition, the average age has dropped down to 12 years old, although a girl can be younger or older than that when she first gets her period. Anyway, if you're 10 or 11 years old, you should know something about this topic.

Because we don't know WHO is reading this book, we're not going to go into more details here. If you are curious or are unclear about what menstruation is, we suggest talking to your mom, your older sister, or another trusted adult about it.

You will probably also learn about this in school, either in a health class or in a workshop with other girls your age.

If you want to, you can also talk with other women relatives and friends about this part of growing up. They'll have their own wisdom to share with you. Sharing personal information like this can be a great way to strengthen a relationship with someone. It will also help you gain more understanding about what you are going through yourself.

GIRL EMERGENCIES

"Your seat cushions can be used for flotation, and in the event of an emergency water landing, please take them with our compliments."
~Label on the bottom of airline seat cushion

Dangerous situations can occur **ANYTIME, ANYWHERE**. You may not realize it, but you might be in danger right now. Just being in your bedroom can create problems. That's because every year in the United States, almost 500,000 people have to go to the hospital because of injuries from *mattresses* and *pillows*. (We aren't kidding!) Pillows are very dangerous, you see, because they are so soft and . . . uh . . . cushy?

It's amazing and it's true! Chairs and sofas will also injure hundreds of thousands of people this year. Vacuum cleaners will claim over 10,000 victims (which is a good reason to avoid them) and pens and pencils will get even more of us. But worst of all, many girls will be injured by their own clothing. Yep, we can expect over 100,000 victims of bloodthirsty blouses, pugnacious pajamas, and homicidal halter tops this coming year.

But how is this possible? Well, the truth is that almost anything can be dangerous. You just have to be careful! But we do have some good news for you: 85 percent of all people hit by lightning are men. So that's one less thing to worry about. ☺

Personal Emergencies

Here are some personal emergencies you might run across and how to deal with them:

You're Wearing High Heels and You Have to Walk on a Stairway or Escalator

Heck, if a pillow can send someone to the hospital, then escalators should be outlawed! Any time you are wearing high heels and have to take the stairs or an escalator, *put one hand on the railing*! Many, many girls and women have fallen down stairs because they tripped on their high heels.

Our Escalator Safety Tip

Don't go down an "up" escalator. Even though it's fun, if you fall down, you may fall *forever*, because you'll never reach the bottom. *Ouch! Oof! Ag! Urk! Oogie!*

You Have to Go to the Bathroom in a Dirty Place

If it's your bathroom, CLEAN IT!

1. If it's a really dirty public restroom (and you can't "hold it"), wash your hands with soap and water when you go in. That way you can feel a little better about touching anything. Once inside the stall, put the toilet seat liner (also called the "toilet halo") on like usual, and then put toilet paper on top of that if it makes you feel better.

2. If the seat is *still* too horrible to sit on (and your legs are strong enough), straddle the toilet without touching it or just "squat" over it. You may be able to steady yourself with your hands against the walls of the stall, but then you're still touching something dirty!

 Porta-Potty Tip: Breathe through your mouth. **AND DON'T LOOK DOWN.** The horror!

You Have to Go to the Bathroom in the Great Outdoors

So you're on a hike or camping and you need "to go." Pick your spot wisely and try to find a little privacy. Out in the open or on the edge of a cliff are obviously bad spots. You should also be careful *not* to pee within 200 feet of any water. If you're on a slope, face downhill or you'll get your shoes wet. And you should avoid big rocks or shrubs with leaves because these will create more splashes. Sand, soil, dead leaves, pine needles, or grassy areas are all good surfaces to pee on.

If you're with someone (and you should be) post a lookout! Your friend can wait on the trail and make certain no one heads near your peeing site. If you have a backpack on, you'll probably want to take it off. (You could leave it on and lean against a tree, though.) If you have on shorts that fit loosely, or are stretchy, it will be a big help. (A skirt is handy too, but not everyone hikes in those.) Now, *be calm!* If you're worried about someone seeing you, or if you are in a hurry, you're going to spatter.

Once you're done peeing, you can "drip dry" or wipe, but don't use moss or poison oak leaves! Sanitary wipes or toilet paper can both be used, but remember to "pack out" anything you use. Don't leave anything in the wilderness that you brought into it. Seal any paper in a ziplock bag. If you have something to dig with, you can bury used paper at least six inches down in the soil. (Only do this in areas with growing plants.)

What if other hikers show up while you're peeing? First of all, it's not the end of the world. They will probably look quickly away, especially if they're not morons. But just in case, we recommend this strategy: point in the other direction and yell "Bear!"

You Are Pulling on Jeans (or a Dress) and They Get Stuck Halfway

There's always the "ripping and tearing" option, but since you don't want to ruin the clothing, you need help. In a perfect world, your trusted friend or family member will help you wiggle your way out of it. (This is handy when you're trying the wrong size on in a store!)

But what if you're flying solo? If the floor is clean, you may want to lie down and squirm around to pull it on. Sure, you could try the bed, but then there's the possibility of falling onto the floor, so if you start on the floor, it's less dangerous!

BTW, if your jeans are too tight and you can't button the top button, you can run a hair tie or hair band through the buttonhole and around the button to keep them together. (Although if they're *that* tight, do you really want to wear them?)

You Lost Something and You Need It Right Now

Few things are more maddening than losing something in your own house. You know the shirt or keys or backpack is around here somewhere! Luckily for you, your mom has a superpower you may not know about. It's called *Mom Radar*.

Your mother has a nearly magical ability to find things if you give her a chance. Get her *Mom Radar* working for you. This may involve having to answer some silly questions, like "When did you have it last?" As if you hadn't thought of that already! (Uh, you *did* think of that already, right?)

If your mom's not around, think of the *last* place you would look for the missing item. Then look there. That's where it is!

You Got Gum in Your Hair or on Your Clothes

Don't panic, and especially don't just start pulling on the gum if it's in your hair! It will get all tangled up . . . *Blech.* The key is to get the gum COLD. Gum stiffens up when it gets cold; the colder it is, the harder it gets. If you put ice on any gum stuck to you, it is much easier to get it out.

If that isn't a possibility, try working some vegetable oil into the gum. This will soften and dissolve it. (It will also get your hair oily!) No vegetable oil? Try peanut butter. It works pretty well, but stick with creamy, not chunky.

You Have the Hiccups and They Won't Stop

A bad case of hiccups can be pretty embarrassing. What if you met the president of the United States and you got the hiccups!

The President of the United States: Hello! Good to meet you.

You: Hic!

Actually, we bet she would be pretty cool about it.

There are many remedies for the hiccups, like holding your breath until you turn blue, drinking out of a glass backwards, holding your breath until you turn green, being really frightened by someone, holding your breath until you turn purple, and so on. None of these solutions work reliably.

The real solution? SUGAR! Sugar has a relaxing effect on the muscles of your throat and chest, and this allows the hiccups to go away. You can suck on a cube of sugar or mix some sugar into a glass of water and then drink it. Delicious sugar has saved many girls from the hiccups!

Static Electricity Is Driving You Crazy

Especially if you ever wear a skirt with leggings or tights, the odds are this will eventually happen. Here are two different solutions.

1. Take a dryer sheet and rub it against your skirt and/or tights. It works!
2. Go to the bathroom and get your hands wet. Then get some liquid soap and rub it between your palms. Put your hands under the water again to rinse off most of the soap.

Then fling your hands around to get the excess water off them. Finally, run your hands down any parts of your clothes that have static. It will magically disappear!

Social Emergencies

Social emergencies happen around other people. Prepare to learn more!

Dealing with Embarrassment

Okay, you said something silly or got klutzy and broke a vase. It's not the end of the world, but you *are* embarrassed. What's a good general response?

Turn Back Time. Be like Hermione and just magically set the clock back to undo your embarrassment!

Laugh at Yourself. If you can't laugh at yourself, pretend that you're laughing at someone else. When you do something stupid, just say, "I'm SO embarrassed!" The key is to fess up and laugh. (But don't laugh too hard, or people will think you're insane.)

Forget About It. As soon as you can, *just get over it*. Embarrassing things happen to *everyone*, even though it feels like these things only happen to *you*!

 Remember: Clumsiness Brings People Together! Your most embarrassing moments will make great stories for you to tell in the future. These tales of your own klutziness will inspire others to share their tales with you, and you'll bond with new best friends.

 Blushing is a reflex (you can't help it!) where all the blood rushes to the small blood vessels in your face. It's called *vasodilation* (vay-so-dye-LAY-shun), not that that helps any.

You're at a Party and You Don't Know Anyone

It can be tough finding yourself alone in a crowd of people. If there is a hostess, she may notice your problem and help you out, but don't count on it. If you're not going to pretend to be the hostess yourself, some possible solutions include:

1. Go to the bathroom and never come out.

2. Buy yourself some time by being a cell phony (see page 161 for tips).

3. Make a friend. Your best bet for a new friend is the person who also seems to be alone.

Good conversation starters are "I love your skirt!" (only say this if the person is a girl AND she is wearing a skirt) OR "I love your hair!" (only say this if he or she has hair).

You Think You See Someone You Know and Wave to Her (or Him!) and It Turns Out to Be a Total Stranger

This can be REALLY embarrassing! But the key is to bluff your way through it. If the other person is looking at you like you're nuts, just wave again, smile, and say something like, "How ARE you?" Then keep moving! Don't stick around; let her wonder where she knows *you* from!

Optional Embarrassment: A nice person smiles and waves at you, so you smile and wave back, and then maybe say, "Hello!" The only problem: he's not talking to you!

As far as we know, there is no solution to this. You will be embarrassed!

You Don't Know How to Dance Very Well

See the "Dance and Cheerleading" chapter on page 98.

Your Friend Just Got Dumped by Her Boyfriend

This often happens at big social events. One of your friends gets dumped by a boy. You can bet that her self-esteem is pretty low, so what can you do to cheer her up?

First, Rally the Troops! Surround her with her friends and let her know how fabulous she is. Try to avoid questions like "What happened?" and focus on "You're a great person and we love you." Check the Compliment Kit on page 41 for ideas.

Later, Do a Dozen Sweet Things! Try to do a number of small, different things for your friend to keep her mind off her problems. What would make her smile through her tears? Put a handmade card in her locker, take her to a comedy, or give her a loofah.

You Go Out in Public Not Looking Your Best, and You See a Bunch of Cute Guys from School

Luckily for you, boys are not very observant. Sure, if you stare at them in terror and freeze, they will see you with your greasy hair and mismatched sweats. But if you walk quickly and look away from them or act casual, they probably won't even see you.

WRONG! RIGHT!

News flash! Even if the boys do see you, they won't care! Guys never notice new haircuts or stylish outfits anyway, so what makes you think they'll notice the bad stuff?

You Tear the Seat of Your Pants While Out in Public

If you have torn pants in public, wrap a sweatshirt or something around your waist or loosen your backpack straps so it hangs lower than usual. Or find your Nurturing Friend (see page 47) from whom you can hopefully borrow a safety pin, quick iron patch, or new pants. And of course, there's always a fallback: your PE shorts!

School Emergencies

These are not the kind of school emergencies where the fire alarm is going off . . . these are way more important!

People Are Blocking Your Locker

Maybe a girl who has a locker near yours always has her friends grouped around her. Or even worse, a couple is making out in front of your locker. They are so wrapped up in each other, they don't even know you exist!

Aside from the usual "excuse me" comments, one stink bomb might make all of them go away and *stay* away. Of course, setting off stink bombs is usually against school rules, so you might just act like a spazz and elbow your way into their group. Then say, "Really? Wow, really?" to everything the girls say until they are annoyed and leave.

As for the kissing couple, just tap the girl on the shoulder and say, "When you're done, can I try?" That should do the trick!

It's Lunchtime and You Have Nowhere to Sit

This might be the world's most horrible feeling. Maybe you came to lunch late, or you're the new kid at school, or you just had a fight with your friends . . . we don't know! But anyway, there you are in line at the cafeteria, and as you wait to pay for your food, you realize that there is nowhere for you to sit!

Believe it or not, teachers have the same problem in their staff lunchroom. So we suggest you go in there and brainstorm solutions with the teachers. We're sure they'll appreciate it!

You Forgot to Finish the Very Important Assignment That's Due

Sounds like it's time to budget your time better. In the meantime, you need an excuse, pronto! Whatever you do, when your teacher asks for your homework, don't say, "My dog ate it." You can be much more creative than that!

- If it's English or language arts, try: "My dog ate it last night after I put it in her dog dish in the pale moonlight."
- In science, "I was conducting an experiment with dog food and paper when my dog ate my homework."
- If it's PE, say something like, "After I did my five-minute warm-up and ran a mile, my dog ate it."

Something Happens Unexpectedly

Once you've hit puberty (see the "Girl Secrets" chapter), you should start carrying a couple of pads with you in your purse or backpack, and know how to use them. That way, you can't be caught *entirely* by surprise by your period. You could even keep an extra pair of underwear and/or pants at school.

But let's say that you do get caught unprepared. Feel free to ask other girls or women to borrow a pad. They will be more than happy to help! (BTW, even *mean girls* will be helpful in this situation. Sisterhood is powerful!)

If your period comes near the end of a class, wait until everyone leaves and let a trusted friend or the teacher know about the situation. It's perfectly okay to tell a teacher, the office secretary, or the school nurse. You might feel embarrassed, but they won't be. They deal with this situation ALL of the time. If you are worried about a stain showing and don't have a change of clothes, try tying a shirt or sweater around your waist.

HOT TIP! If clothing gets stained, don't soak or wash it in warm or hot water. This will "set" the stain. Use cold water, and if you do so soon enough, the stain will wash out.

You Have to Get a Ride from Your Teenaged Sister

Yeah, we know you're probably not old enough to drive. So you're probably getting rides from your parents or an older sibling. But you should know that females between the ages of 15 to 20 have had a 30 percent increase in fatal crashes over the past few years! It looks like cell phones, makeup, music, friends, and even hot beverages in the car may be distracting young female drivers from watching the road. So help your sister stay focused on her driving, and when you're driving *yourself* in the not-so-distant future, be careful and pay attention!

Keep Your Sister's Eyes on the Road!

PETS AND ANIMALS

"I think animal testing should be stopped. They always get all nervous and give the wrong answers."

~Rhoda Ponee

Girls love animals. That's why most veterinarians in the United States are women! Getting a pet (*any* pet) can make a girl a better person. Loving and caring for the animal enriches her life, and the responsibility of taking care of a pet makes her more aware of how important all life is. So having a pet is sort of like being a parent, but in some ways, it is even *better*. As you can see, there are many advantages to having a pet.

Kids	Pets
Will talk back.	Can't talk back. (Unless it's a parrot.)
Want an allowance.	Don't seem to know what money is.
Poop their pants for the first two years (and for some boys, even longer!)	No pants!
Might try to run away. If that doesn't work, will eventually move out.	Will always be with you.
Are picky eaters.	Eat whatever you drop on the floor.
Have gas.	Have gas.
Require long and expensive educations.	Can be homeschooled.

If you're not sure you are up to the responsibility of taking care of an animal, try taking care of a stuffed animal first. If that works out well, babysit someone else's pet for a few days and see if you enjoy it. Of course, it is also possible to enjoy wild animals (not counting your brother). For example, a bird feeder can bring you hundreds of outdoor birds, as opposed to just one bird sitting alone in a cage.

If you decide to get a pet, *please* go to your local animal shelter (or other animal rescue organization) to find one. There are A LOT of animals there that already need a home. *And you will be saving an animal's life.* About 60 percent of the dogs at your local animal shelter eventually end up being "put to sleep." This happens because new animals come in all the time, and there just isn't room for them all. That is, there's no room unless you help them out.

In this chapter, we won't mention *all* the cool animals that can make fun pets, just some classics.

Names for Your Pet

Whatever pet you get, please give it an *original* name! No more dogs want to be named Molly, Max, or Bailey, and cats have been known to attack their owners when given boring names like Tigger, Socks, Princess, and Kitty. Look in a name book, visit a good website for creative names, or make up your own.

 Baby Talk Your Pet. Try combining a silly name with a title, like *Cap'n Doodles* or *Dr. Chumples*. These names are excellent to use when baby talking to your pet.

Horsies

"I have never heard anyone say, 'Oh, ick! A horse!'"

~*Elinor Goulding Smith*

Someone once said "Girls fall in love with horses first and boys later." Why is this? Is it because horses are beautiful animals, and it's fun to groom their long flowing manes? Maybe. Is it because riding on such a big animal makes a girl feel like a princess? Maybe. Or is it because horse manure smells good? Maybe not!

Horses have been symbols of wealth and good fortune for a long time; even their shoes are famous signs of good luck.

Although lots of girls would like to have a horse, they aren't the most practical pets for most families. As a matter of fact, a horse is somehow more than just a pet. It's a *lifestyle*! Buying a horse can run between $2,500 and $5,000, and you could spend a lot more than that. It's too bad there isn't an animal shelter where you can pick up cheap horses that have run away from home! And getting a saddle, bridle, and other supplies (called *tack*) can run about $1,000 or more. Horses need open pastures, exercise, shelter, good food, good schooling, and grooming. Just like girls! So as you can see, the money for all this can really add up.

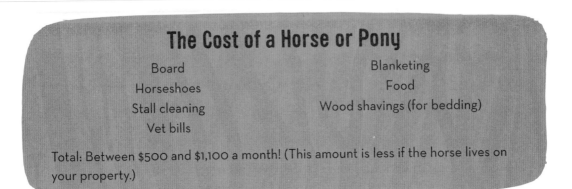

The Cost of a Horse or Pony

Board

Horseshoes

Stall cleaning

Vet bills

Blanketing

Food

Wood shavings (for bedding)

Total: Between $500 and $1,100 a month! (This amount is less if the horse lives on your property.)

But you don't have to OWN a horse to RIDE one. If you're interested, try renting (or leasing) a horse from a good stable or trainer. This might cost around $100 each month. You also could work around the barn or ranch where your horse is kept to help pay for your own horseback riding. Cowgirl up!

The people at your local stable will make sure that you ride horses that are safe and trained, and they can teach you how to act around horses, put on their tack properly, and how to ride. This will help you find out whether it's something you like. (We bet you will!)

As for ponies, they really are very cute. The problem with ponies is that they stay small, while girls grow up. A full-grown girl is too big for a pony, so if you get one to ride, the day will come when that is no longer possible.

Bad News! Horse trainers have found that even with hours of practice, My Little Pony cannot be taught to trot.

Horses don't use facial expressions to show their feelings. Instead, they let their ears do the work!

| Interest | Uncertainty | Anger | Fear |

Look, we may as well admit that one of the cool things about a horse is how fashionable they are. What a great accessory! They are such strong and graceful animals, they make their riders look good. The clothes that go with horse riding can appeal to both the rough-and-ready girl as well as the more dainty ones.

For example, English and Western are two of the primary styles associated with horses. Western is very rodeo style. It's flashy and bright, with lots of silver and color, and big hats. English style is more refined. This is the traditional clothing of equestrian events, with the rider wearing jodhpurs and a hard hat for protection from falls. Riders often dress in tan breeches and white shirts for competitive events.

Hello, Kitty!*

"Dogs come when they're called. Cats take a message and get back to you later."

~*Mary Bly*

Cats are special animals, and they have a special place in many girls' lives. If you have a rough day, your cat can take your mind off of it by curling up in your lap and purring like a little chainsaw. And if you're having a good day, your cat can make it even better by doing silly things like chasing balls of yarn or stealing the family's car keys and disappearing for the weekend.

 Cat Training Tip: The reason that cats love to jump on couches is a case of a simple misunderstanding. Cats hear humans talk about "FURniture," and the cat assumes it is okay to get its FUR all over the sofa. If you explain this miscommunication to your cat, it should solve the problem.

Although cats need love, food, and care, they are pretty good at taking care of themselves. Just be sure to take care of other animals around them! A cat is a predator, so any animal its size or smaller may look like fair game to the cat. Protect other household pets like gerbils or parakeets from your cat, and put a bell on its collar if it goes outdoors.

 If you have birds, small mammals, or fish in the house, they will be constantly terrified if you get a cat, even if they're safe in a cage. Don't stress them out!

---

* If you're a dog person, we're afraid you need to check *The Big Book of Boy Stuff*; that's where all our good dog info is.

The fact that cats are predators can be used to your advantage. If your cat is a picky eater, try warming its food up a little. This will make it seem like "fresh game" and will probably make the cat happy to eat it.

You may know that the word *catty* means "hurtful" or "mean." Our theory is that cats are catty because they can't taste sweets. Cats (and all members of the cat family, including lions, tigers, leopards, etc.) do not have the ability to taste sugar or any sweet flavors. So after a cat has its kitty-kibble (or a cheetah or jaguar eats its prey) there is never any dessert. **How sad!**

One of the most horrible things to deal with when you have a cat is cat litter. **Ick!** Once a boy told his little sister that the kitty litter box had Tootsie Rolls in it. *That was mean!* Cats bury their poop because they want to hide the evidence that they were there. Predatory animals that hunt (like cats) don't want other animals to know that they're around, so they will go to great lengths to cover their tracks—and their poop!

One neat thing about cats is their whiskers; these long, thick hairs have roots going through the cat's skin and into its muscles. **Super-hairs!** They help the cat sense its surroundings. For example, the cheek whiskers allow the cat to know if it can fit into a tight spot or not. They're sort of like antenna or even fingers. Try touching your cat's whiskers. It will blink! This reflex is so that if the cat is sneaking through a hedge, it won't get poked in the eye.

Fun Slang! Flurfled: When a cat's whiskers are in the forward position, showing excitement or playfulness. Example: "Beware of Fluffy when she is flurfled!"

The greatest thing in the world to give a cat is *catnip*. **They go crazy!** It's like the cat's addicted and allergic to it at the same time. Scientists say that catnip stimulates the pleasure center of a cat's brain and makes it act strangely. No kidding! (BTW, the cat has to be 12 weeks old to have this reaction, and 20 percent of cats have no reaction to catnip at all.)

Cat Types

Cats come in different sizes, colors, and personalities. Here are a few of them.

Stray Cat: Although strays can be nice, don't try to pick one up. Things might go badly, and you could end up with a nasty scratch or no purse.

Feral Cat (a.k.a. wildcat): Hey, if a cat is wild, it's *wild*. Don't mess with it.

Scaredy-Cat: Like his relative the 'Fraidy-Cat, the Scaredy-Cat will suddenly run away from odd things like shadows, its own tail, and lint.

Copycat: Ha!

Catloaf: This is any cat that tucks its feet and tail in close to its body, making a round shape like a loaf of catbread.

Polecat: This is actually a ferret.

Flumpus: Any cat who sprawls around while looking cuddly and cute is a Flumpus.

The Hacker: Not only is this cat good with the computer, it's always hacking up a hairball. Long-haired cats are often Hackers.

Hairless Cat: If you don't like hairballs, this might be a good cat to get.

Magic Trick! Sometime when your cat is purring loudly, have someone run water from the tap. The purring instantly stops! Just the *sound* of water is enough to turn off the motor. That's because cats were originally desert animals, and they are uncomfortable around water. Cats don't need much water to survive. Watch your cat drink water sometime; its tongue curls inward toward the body, and picks up, like, a *drop* of water.

Lucky Kitty! A cat in a restaurant's window is a sign of good luck in Japan. And everyone knows a black cat is considered bad luck, but on board a ship, a black cat is *good* luck! You see, cats don't *like* water, and the ship is floating *on* water, so no matter what, the cat will not allow the ship to sink.

Bunnies

Sure, there are plenty of other rodents that are also cool, like the guinea pig, hamster, rat, and mouse. But is there ANY animal that is as cute and cuddly as a *widdle bunny wabbit*? (Okay, that was sickening. ☺)

Rabbits are also pretty awesome pets! They can be house-trained and they become very affectionate, especially if you handle them a lot or get them young. Rabbits are also quiet, and they are clean. We hate to jump to conclusions, but what's not to like?

But you do have to be careful with rabbits, because they are fairly fragile. Their skin is sensitive and big animals (like us!) can hurt them if we're not careful. Rabbits shouldn't roughhouse with the dog, and little kids can freak them out. (Cats are also sometimes mean to rabbits.) But if you take good care of your rabbit, it should live from six to ten years.

Keeping your bunny in a cage or hutch and then letting it out to exercise (indoors or outside) is a pretty good system. If you live in a warm enough area and your rabbit sleeps outdoors, be sure to get a strong hutch so that nighttime predators like raccoons don't get at your bunny. (Rappers also try to steal rabbits because of that whole *hip-hop* thing.)

Some rabbit owners give the bunny the run of the house, which is fine as long as nobody steps on it. Make sure the rabbit is also house-trained before doing this. Your average bunny can poop almost 4,000 of those little rabbit pellets in a week, and we're guessing you don't want them rolling all over the house, although they are pretty easy to clean up.

 We know it sounds sick, but if your rabbit eats its own poop pellets, that's actually normal. (Some rabbit food has to be digested twice to give nourishment.)

Picking Up Bunny!

Grab the scruff of the rabbit's neck (just behind its ears) and scoop its rear end up with your other hand. (It will freak out the bunny if you pick it up like a cat or small dog.) *And don't lift it up by its ears!*

SPECIAL WARNING: Like other rodents, a rabbit's teeth will keep growing unless it chews on wood (or another hard substance). Keep wood chew sticks in its hutch or cage so

it doesn't go after your furniture. And don't leave it in an area with wood furniture or electric wires by itself. It will chew on these, and your parents will be hopping mad. (But who could *stay* mad at such a *cute widdle wabbit*?)

Skunks

Skunks CAN be pets. If they are introduced to humans as babies (and are legal in your state), a skunk can be treated like an indoor cat that happens to hibernate in the winter! Few people know that skunks hate the smell from their musk glands as much as other animals do. That's why skunks only spray when they really have to. What we're trying to say is that **skunks think skunks stink.**

However, baby skunks take a little while to figure out their superpower. Litters of young skunks will sometimes have shoot-offs where everyone sprays everybody else, and then they all stink. (If you think that's weird, we guarantee that human boys would probably do the exact same thing if they could!)

For a skunk to be house-friendly, it needs to have its musk glands removed from near its butt. Like other pets, the skunk should also be neutered or spayed. Skunks should NOT just be fed cat food, like a lot of people think. Because they're omnivores, skunks need vegetables and fruit, along with meat. Finally, skunks are pretty lazy but since they're nocturnal, they sleep during the day, and then want to play in the evening.

Little Creatures

There are all sorts of really little animals that can be pets.

Praying Mantises. Praying mantises grow to be four inches long and are a fun addition to the backyard. It's easy to get praying mantis egg cases over the Internet or at pet shops, and they are legal bugs to have in every state! When the little mantises start to hatch in their jar, be sure to release them in your backyard or they will eat each other. Once in your yard, they will start to eat the bugs out there, and you will see them from time to time and be able to say "Hi!"

Crickets. The Chinese have kept crickets for pets throughout much of their history. They're considered good luck! (Remember the cricket in *Mulan*?) If you want to try catching one, go out on a summer's evening with a flashlight and a jar. Listen for chirping. Walk toward it, and when it stops, you should stop. Be patient, and sooner or later, he will start chirping again. (Only male crickets chirp.) When you're close enough, gently scoop him up.

Your cricket will need a small piece of moist sponge in the aquarium or jar you keep him in. (Crickets need moisture.) Crickets eat a lot of things, including ripe bananas, cereal, or bread moistened with milk, and little bugs. (They don't need drinking water.) If your new friend doesn't chirp inside, you probably got a female by accident. If your new friend constantly chirps and drives you nuts, just put him back where you found him!

Butterflies. Keeping a cocoon for a moth or butterfly indoors until it opens can also be pretty amazing to watch. You can either feed a caterpillar until he wraps himself up or find a cocoon and keep it inside a bug jar. (Make sure there are holes in the lid!) Once the moth or butterfly emerges from the cocoon, be careful not to touch its wings! This could ruin them forever. Let it get its wings extended all the way out and adjusted, and then release it into the wild!

Ladybugs. Finally, ladybugs are cool to have around, especially if you have a backyard or garden. You can even buy ladybugs at gardening and pet stores. They sleep at low temperatures, so you can store them in the fridge! Take them out and release them at dusk; watch them climb up your finger and then fly away.

In Japan, giant stag beetles are traditional pets. They can also be expensive! A beetle once sold for $30,000. Think all bugs are alike? Think again! "They have different personalities. When I hold my beetle, I have real affection for it," said one stag beetle owner.

Ladybug, ladybug fly away home! Your house is on fire and your children will burn!

I hate that saying!

Fun Animal Items

1. **Polly Wants a @#!$%# Cracker!** Many U.S. presidents kept pets in the White House, and this kept life interesting. For example, Andrew Jackson (president from 1829–1837) taught his pet parrot Pol (short for Polly) all sorts of *very* bad words. When Jackson died, the parrot was kept with Jackson's body to keep him company. Unfortunately, visitors paying their respects to the president were shocked at the parrot's language. Pol eventually had to be removed from the room.

2. **Bad Monkey!** In India, monkeys are generally allowed to do what they want. This permissive attitude has resulted in some monkeys becoming *criminals*! One very troublesome monkey was even sentenced to life in an official monkey prison.

3. **Amphibious Assault!** If you would like a frog the size of a small cat, get a goliath frog. These dainty little fellows from western Africa can weigh up to seven pounds. Be careful when you feed them—your whole hand can fit in their mouth!

4. **What's in the Back?** If you don't see unicorns in your local animal shelter or pet store, show one of the volunteers or workers this book and wink. This is the secret sign to let you go in the back, where "imaginary" animals like unicorns, dragons, and grindylows are kept.

5. **No Wildlife for Profit!** Prairie dogs are popular pets in Japan. But they often cannot be sold as pets in the United States because there are state laws against selling wildlife for profit.

SHOPPING AND ADVERTISING

"The quickest way to know a woman is to go shopping with her."
~Marcalene Cox

Think about money. Everyone knows that a $100 bill is worth a hundred times more than a $1 bill. But why? The two bills are the same size, shape, and color. It just so happens that one of them has a different number in the corner. That's the only difference!

Money is a game of make-believe. We all pretend that money is actually worth something. We put different numbers in the corners of pieces of paper to show how much they're worth. So what! We take our little pieces of paper (cash) or plastic (credit or debit cards) and act like they are actually worth something. But it's really just paper and plastic. The only value they have is in our minds.

Fun Ca$h Fact$!

$$ The first coin ever designed in the United States said "Mind Your Business" on it. Benjamin Franklin came up with the idea.

$$ The "$" sign originally had two vertical lines running through the **S**. The two vertical lines represented a **U** superimposed over the **S**, which stood for **U.S.**, the United States. Over time, the **U** lost its bottom and then lost one of its lines. The United States is the only country that used its own name on its money symbol. Today, the symbol means "money" all over the world.

$$ It costs about two cents to make, print, and cut a dollar bill. Guess how much it costs to print a $100 bill? About two cents!

$$ **Secret Information!** Look carefully in the top right corner of a $1 dollar bill. If you stare hard enough, you will see the little owl who lives up there.

But even though it's only make-believe, people devote a lot of time to money. Earning it, saving it, spending it, watching it, and worrying about it . . . many adults spend most of their time dealing with money! Have they forgotten it's not real? When adults get *too* caught up in money, this is what's called the *Rat Race*. (And the only ones who win that race are rats!)

Shopping

Girls love to shop! You're already good at it, but now it's time to get better.

Shop Smart

Girls usually spend most of their money on clothing, shoes, accessories, cosmetics, knick-knacks, and high-tech items (such as cell phones or iPods). So how can you be a smart shopper and make sure not to waste your money?

Ask Yourself These Questions:

1. Why do you want it? Shopping is not always logical. Sometimes you just want something *because* you want it. But can you figure out *why* you want it? Is it really cool, or is it just because everyone else has it?

2. If you want to buy something, can you make yourself wait a little? Try leaving the store, and then shop around to make sure there's not a better deal at another store. (This also will help you decide if you really want something.)

3. Does the item you want seem like it's at a fair price? Stores won't necessarily charge you a *fair* price. They will charge the amount people are *willing to pay*. This is called "charging what the market will bear." Name-brand items and "in" products usually cost more, because stores can get away with charging more.

Let's say that you want a new shirt. If you buy it new at a store, you are probably paying *twice* as much as the store paid the shirtmaker. And if you're buying jewelry, the store's markup is even worse! So is it a rip-off? (As long as you're wondering about this, you're a step ahead of most people.)

 They're Watching You! By charting where girls shop inside of stores, researchers have learned that girls spend most of their time on the *right* side of the stores they go into.

The Busiest Shopping Days of the Year! The two weekends before December 25 are the busiest shopping days of the year. The day after Thanksgiving is the *fifth* most popular.

You Don't Want to Hear This!

A survey of mall shoppers found that the most annoying thing a sales clerk can say is "That's not my department." Other most-hated phrases included "If it's not on the rack, we don't have it," "I'm on a break," "The computer is down," "Sorry, this is my first day," and "I don't work here."

But if you *really* want to save money . . .

Go Thrifting

Be smart about spending a little; after all, who said style has to be expensive?

You will need: A desire to save money and to have a good time.

Where can you buy a skirt, tank top, belt, blazer, and silk blouse for just $30? Try your local Salvation Army or Goodwill stores. If you want to be a smart consumer or just want to find a killer deal, your local thrift shop is the place to do it. Of course, there's a lot of stuff there that's "junky," but just think of it as a treasure hunt!

"Vintage" clothes definitely have character, and they set you apart from everyone else. Plus, there's nothing like bragging about the name-brand "find" you scored for $15!

When you go thrifting, you'll know you're not getting ripped off, and we bet you have a lot of fun. BTW, it's fine to *shop* cheap, but be careful about buying tube tops, small miniskirts, or short shorts. *Looking cheap* is never cool!

Thrift shops are great places to find Halloween costumes.

Clothes

If you find a pair of pants or a sweater (or whatever) in a style you really like and that looks good on you, buy more than one. Get it in different colors or patterns, because if it's a winner, it's a *winner*! Focus on clothes that highlight your strong points. Once you know what looks good on you *and* what you like, you're all set.

Be sure to check the "washing instructions" on the label of any clothes you're thinking about buying. (And to leave the tag on any clothes you buy until you're sure that they fit the way you want them to.) If an item needs dry cleaning, you might want to think twice about buying it. Dry cleaning is sort of a hassle and it can be expensive.

Hot Tip! If you're thinking about buying something, try to think of *three* pieces of clothing you already own that could go with it. If you can't think of three, you might want to pass on it.

If you feel like being a spazz, go into a clothing store's fitting room and sing out loudly, "I see London, I see France!"

Buy It on Sale!

If you've ever made a special trip to a store only to find the place closed, you know that *timing is important*. To have the right timing on some great sales, shop sometime between the middle of January through the start of February. This is when a lot of stores put leftover items from the holiday season up for grabs at good prices.

Shoes

This may seem like obvious advice, but make sure to get shoes that fit! About half of all women are wearing shoes that are TOO SMALL for them. (See pages 223–225 for more info.)

Try on shoes late in the day, because (believe it or not!) your feet widen as you walk around, so they actually get bigger. Also, the odds are that one of your feet is bigger than the other one, so have your feet carefully measured and then always try the shoes on *both* feet.

 News flash! Most men and boys don't *ever* look at anyone's feet, and they don't care how big a girl's shoes are.

If you are planning to actually *walk* much in your new shoes, the heels shouldn't be more than an inch high. And remember that shoes with heels should be almost as cushy and comfy as sports shoes. If they're not, don't buy them!

Cosmetics

Many companies that sell makeup price their products way too high, and they know it. This sounds crazy, but their sales are better when they *overprice* the makeup! Helena Rubenstein made millions of dollars in the makeup business, and she said, "Some women won't buy anything unless they can pay a lot."

In other words, the makeup is so expensive it somehow makes it seem worth it. *Reverse psychology!* How dumb is that?

High-Tech

You're the expert. Your parents may not even have *had* cell phones growing up, and if they had computers, it was something like an abacus with an electric plug. For them, a *portable music device* was a kazoo, not an iPod. Since you are probably more of an expert on electronic gadgets than most adults, use your wisdom wisely.

 Are Your Eyes Sensitive? Teenaged girls buy twice as many sunglasses as boys do. (Maybe this is because sunglasses make your eyes seem big, and they help you hide from the paparazzi.)

Wacky Product Warnings

It's good that companies include safety information with their products. But some companies are so worried about safety (and getting sued) that their product warnings can get a little ridiculous. A group called Michigan Lawsuit Abuse Watch has a contest to find the nation's "wackiest" directions. Read the following product warnings and ask yourself: Is the company incredibly stupid or do they think we are? All the warnings are taken from real products!

On a folding baby stroller: "Remove child before folding."

On a toilet brush: "Do not use for personal hygiene."

On a TV remote control: "Not dishwasher safe."

On a scooter: "This product moves when used."

On a CD player: "Warning—dangerous warning inside."

On a thermometer used to take a person's temperature: "Once used rectally, the thermometer should not be used orally."

On a wheelbarrow: "Not intended for highway use."

On a blender: "Never remove food or other items from the blades while the product is operating."

On a 9 x 3 inch plastic bag of air used for packing: "Do not use this product as a toy, pillow, or flotation device."

On a robotic massage chair: "Do not use massage chair without clothing . . . and, never force any body part into the backrest area while the rollers are moving."

On a snowblower: "Do not use snowthrower on roof."

On a dishwasher: "Do not allow children to play in the dishwasher."

On a three-pronged fishhook: "Harmful if swallowed."

On a bottle of drain cleaner: "If you do not understand, or cannot read, all directions, cautions, and warnings, do not use this product."

On a smoke detector: "Do not use the Silence Feature in emergency situations. It will not extinguish a fire."

On a can of pepper spray: "May irritate eyes."

Top Secret Shopping Information!

Only use the following advice if you *really, really, really* need something when you are out shopping with one or both of your parents. (This will probably work better with your dad.)

Here's the situation. You see something that you want. *A solar-powered sundress? I must have it!* You know if you just ASK for the dress, you will probably get "No" for an answer. Try hanging out near the item you want and start a conversation like this. (Try to look very wistful and pitiful while you speak.)

You: Dad, do you ever get sad thinking of all the lonely people?

Your Dad: Why are you worrying about that, honey?

You: I don't know. I just look around sometimes and think about how unfair life is.

Dad: Wow, my daughter sure is a thoughtful person.

You: Not really. I just wonder why some people have such sad lives. (*Look very sorrowful now.*)

Dad: Take it easy! You need to cheer up!

You: I guess so. (*You give a weak smile.*) Say, this solar-powered sundress is sort of cute.

Dad (reaching for his credit card): It's yours!

Obviously, this is not a strategy you should use a lot, because it is wrong. So just try it once a year! ☺

While we're on the topic, many girls (and boys) use *whining* on their parents to get them to buy "stuff." We hope you know whining is unworthy of you. It's so lame and babyish! However, if you calmly give evidence as to why you should have an item, you are not *whining*. You are making a *reasonable suggestion*.

Whining — Please, please, pleeeaasse?

Still Whining — I Really need it!

Reasonable Suggestion — Mom, having this laptop will make me a better student. I will be able to get the best education possible and fulfill my ambitions.

Advertising

"Imagine a mousetrap set up with a piece of cheese. The TV ads are the trap, the programs are the cheese, and you are the mouse."

~Shari Graydon

Ads are supposed to *persuade* a girl to spend her money. And advertisers are really smart. As a matter of fact, they *think* they are smarter than you! Even though advertisers know that girls don't have as much money as adults, they try extra hard to sell things to girls.

That's because girls do a lot of shopping. American girls will spend over $100 billion next year. And amazingly, 76 percent of teenaged girls go to the mall for about four hours a week. And online shopping is open 24/7. So the odds are high that a girl is almost always in a spot where she can buy something.

The advertisers do their research, and they know that most girls are impatient. If a girl *wants* something, she often just goes out and gets it, sometimes without waiting to see if she really needs it. This is called an *impulse buy*.

How to Shop Smart!

How to Avoid Impulse Buys

One good way to avoid impulse buys is to make a list at home of what you need and stick with it!

So basically, advertisers think girls are suckers. An ad executive who specializes in selling clothing to girls put it this way: "The key to selling our product is to make the teenaged girl feel that she will be a loser without it." 😕 So if an ad makes you believe that you won't be "pretty" or "cool" unless you have the product, the ad wins! The advertiser is hoping that you'll make a "clone buy," which is a purchase that you make to be like everyone else.

Here are two examples of "clone buy" ads: A Candie's shoe ad read, "She was the only girl in high school that didn't own Candie's . . . maybe that's why she never had a date." How horrible is that? Another ad for Sun-In hair products showed a picture of a pretty girl. The ad read, "Four out of five girls you hate ask for it by name. Stop hating them. Start being them." This ad manages to play on hatred, jealousy, and clone buying all at once!*

 Target Practice: Advertisers call girls "targets," as in, "We want our targets to talk about our brand without even knowing they're doing it."

So advertisers do *not* see you as the cool, unique person you are. They see you as a *target* they can trick out of some money. But if you buy what *you* want, and not what someone else says you should want, you're not a target or a sucker. You're a cool, unique person who uses her brain!

Test Your Ad Knowledge

How far do you think an advertiser will go to get into your purse? Let's see if you can judge which of the following ad strategies are real and which ones we just made up.

A. A popular clothing company gave free clothes to "popular" kids who the company thought were "trendsetters." The idea was that the less-popular kids would copy the trendsetters' style and buy the clothes.

B. Companies hire people to go online and write comments about how great a movie or soft drink is. Anyone reading the comments might assume it's a young person giving his opinion about a product, when it could be some strange person who's paid to pretend he's a teenager.

C. An ad agency paid college students to walk around for three hours in public with the logo of a company temporarily "tattooed" on their faces. (Another company sells ad space on the sides of cows.)

D. A business has been researching how to beam commercials directly into a sleeping person's dreams. The idea is that the dreams have ads in them, and when the person wakes up, she'll want to buy the product.

E. One advertiser set up movie websites that were designed to be easily hacked into. Hackers then "stole" footage from upcoming movies and e-mailed the "top secret" scenes to friends and family. By doing this, the hackers were giving free advertising for the movies without realizing it.

Look below to see how you did!†

---

* The company did choose to stop running the ad after a group called Dads and Daughters ran a campaign against it.

† You probably already figured it out . . . these are *all* real! (Except for D.)

Not Me! Even though ads work on everyone, most people don't think ads affect them. But many ad research experts think these might actually be the people ads affect the *most!*

Hit the Mute Button

If you're watching a program, hit the Mute button when commercials come on. This reduces noise pollution, since ads are often set at a higher volume level than programs. Muting ads also reduces brainwashing. And finally, by hitting Mute, anyone who's with you can now *talk* and *think*, which experts agree is good for us.

Of course, advertisers know about the Mute trick, which is why more and more ads are being made with messages that are told with *images*, not words. Oh well!

They Are So SNEAKY!

If you ever see a specific product in a movie or show, that's an *ad.* (For example, a character goes to the refrigerator and pulls out a can that obviously says Coca-Cola.) This is a sneaky kind of ad called *product placement.* Companies pay the television or movie studio to *place* their *product* into the story. (If you have a soft drink machine in your school, it's the same thing!) And we don't even realize we're watching an ad unless we're careful.

Another sneaky ad you may not notice is the *label slave* ad. Anyone who pays for clothes with visible logos is giving free advertising to that brand. And that's what a *label slave* is!

Telly Tax! Just to *own* a television in England, you have to pay a license fee of about $250.

When you see any ad, remember that there's *a reason for everything.* It's almost fun watching advertisers try to trick you. But to do this, you have to *stay alert.* A lot of people disengage their brains when they see ads. Have you ever asked someone what she's watching on television or the computer and she doesn't even know? *She's in an electronic coma!*

The average American girl spends four hours and twenty-five minutes each day watching television. (Japanese girls spend four more minutes a day watching TV.) And 30 percent of girls admit that they have dieted or dressed so that they could look more like a character they've seen online or on TV.

There's a reason for everything. Stroll through a supermarket, and you'll see there's a reason for the way it is laid out. For example, the bestselling items in supermarkets are milk, bread, and meat. Are these conveniently located in the front of the store? *Of course not!*

By making you walk all the way to the back of the store to get your milk, bread, or meat, the store owners are hoping that you'll see something else you want along the way. To make sure this happens, they might cleverly put the cereal aisle right in front of the milk section. See? As you walk toward the milk, you think, *Mmmmm, Cap'n Crunch.* And the kid's cereals with lots of sugar are usually on the second or third shelf up from the bottom, right at a little kid's eye level.

The same thing works in clothing stores. Women shop most frequently for underwear and socks. Because of this, many stores put these items at the back of the women's clothing area, so that you see all the latest fashions on the way.

Ad Types

Here are a few of the ad strategies that research shows work especially well on girls.

The Eye Candy Ad

Everyone likes looking at beautiful people. That's why they show up in so many ads: if you ever see a handsome man or pretty girl in an ad, they're eye candy to get you to pay attention.

That's why pretty women are used to sell products that have *nothing* to do with women. It is so stupid! Models (often wearing little clothing) are used to sell men's razors, beer, lawn mowers, you name it! Fashion models don't even usually *use* those products. There is a word for what these ads are: *sexist.*

The "You'll Be Sexy" Ad

One lame way to advertise is to pressure a girl to be pretty, or even "sexy." Companies often don't care how inappropriate their ads are, either. The message is if you buy our product everyone will be in love with you and you'll be the hottest chick (or guy) in town! Abercrombie & Fitch ran an ad campaign like this and sold T-shirts with mottos like "Who needs brains when you have these?" and "Blondes Are Adored, Brunettes Are Ignored." Yuck!

The "Everyone's Doing It!" Ad

Anytime you see an ad where three or more people are enjoying themselves with a product, the idea is that you'll want to go along with the crowd. That's because some people imitate what everyone else is doing without really thinking about it.

The Everywhere Ad

A bus with a huge ad on the side rolls by. You turn on your cell phone and get an ad. On the floor of a supermarket, on the door of the bathroom stall, flashing on a website, in an elevator, on your cell phone, or on a T-shirt, there are ads EVERYWHERE!

These ads are like a computer virus that companies are trying to get into your brain by having them everywhere. It's all about *repetition, repetition, repetition*. There might be a short slogan to help their virus stick with you: Just do it. Do the Dew. Taste the rainbow. Drivers wanted. Party Like a Rock Star. (Buy another copy of *The Big Book of Girl Stuff*!)

The Little Kid Ad

Have you ever seen your little sister see an ad and then *instantly* want the product? Studies show that 90 percent of preschoolers will ask their parents for products they see in advertisements. *Wow!* Advertisers have learned two things about little kids:

A. They don't understand that what's online and on TV isn't real.

B. They don't understand that ads aren't the same thing as a "regular" show.

So for a little kid, *an ad is just as real as reality*! Because of this, advertising for little kids is *illegal* in some countries. (But the United States isn't one of them.)

You're No Sucker!

But if you're not going to be one, you have to pay attention!

You will need: To be awake.

Now you know about ads and how they work. For the rest of your life, whenever you see an ad, ask yourself, "What kind of an ad is it? What strategies is it using? Is it trying to trick me?" By answering these questions, you will be nobody's fool.

Making a Difference

If you see an ad that you think is stupid or sexist or just wrong, don't buy the product. This is called "boycotting" a product. (Hey, why not "*girl*cotting"?) Even better, you can complain right to the company. The company has a website. Just go to it and find the "Contact Us" button. Explain what ad you're complaining about, and ask them for a reply. You may also want to complain to the website, TV station, or magazine where you saw the ad. Your opinion is very powerful and can get things changed!

WISE WORDS FROM WISE WOMEN

A good quotation can give us new perspectives, inspiration, or just make us laugh. Here are some of our favorites.

"Sometimes I think creativity is magic; it's not a matter of finding an idea, but allowing the idea to find you." ~*Maya Lin*

"Shoot for the moon, because if you miss, you'll hit the stars." ~*Cammi Granato*

"The most beautiful discovery true friends can make is that they can grow separately without growing apart." ~*Elizabeth Foley*

"I don't want to be stinky poo-poo girl, I want to be happy flower child." ~*Drew Barrymore*

"A good education is another name for happiness." ~*Ann Plato*

"I always wanted to be something, but now I see I should have been more specific." ~*Lily Tomlin*

"Think like a queen. A queen is not afraid to fail. Failure is another stepping-stone to greatness." ~*Oprah Winfrey*

"Dad, as intelligence goes up, happiness often goes down. In fact I made a graph . . . I make a lot of graphs . . ." ~*Lisa Simpson*

"If you judge people, you have no time to love them." ~*Mother Teresa*

"If at first you don't succeed, destroy all evidence that you ever tried." ~*Phoebe McKeeby*

"I always preferred having wings to having things." ~ **Pat Schroeder**

"Smoking kills. If you are killed, you have lost a very important part of your life." ~ **Brooke Shields**

"Advice is what we ask for when we already know the answer but wish we didn't." ~ **Erica Jong**

"Whenever you have to TRY to fit in, it's a sign you're trying to be with the wrong people." ~ **Kathy Buckley**

"What's the sitch?" ~ **Kim Possible**

"Someone once called me the ultimate cheerleader and I am because I believe that if we do things together, there is hope." ~ **Wilma Mankiller**

"No day is so bad it can't be fixed with a nap." ~ **Carrie Snow**

"The world is extremely interesting to a joyful soul." ~ **Alexandra Stoddard**

"Always believe in yourself. Feel free and never be afraid, because fear robs you of your powers and passions." ~ **Alexandra Nechita***

"The only time to eat diet food is while you're waiting for the steak to cook." ~ **Julia Child**

"In every girl is a goddess." ~ **Francesca Lia Block**

"My theory is that if you look confident, you can pull off anything—even if you have no clue what you're doing." ~ **Jessica Alba**

"The best and most beautiful things in the world cannot be seen or even touched. They must be felt with the heart." ~ **Helen Keller**

"I hope you will leave the world a better place than you found it." ~ **Jane Yolen**

---

* Alexandra made over a million dollars from her art by the time she was 15.

"Sugar. Spice. And everything nice. These were the ingredients chosen to create the perfect little girls. But Professor Utonium accidentally added an extra ingredient to the concoction . . . Chemical X. Thus the Powerpuff Girls were born." ~*from* **The Powerpuff Girls**

"'Dumb' is just not knowing. 'Ditzy' is having the courage to ask!" ~*Jessica Simpson*

"Go for it, never back down, and don't give in, because there's no greater satisfaction in life than using your gifts to help others and to contribute to your community and country." ~*Madeleine Albright*

"How wonderful it is that nobody need wait a single moment before starting to improve the world." ~*Anne Frank*

"On the path between the homes of friends, grass does not grow." ~*Norwegian proverb*

"The biggest sin is sitting on your ass." ~*Florynce Kennedy*

"It's all about you. Don't look to a guy to make you feel like you have a sense of value." ~*Sara Levinson*

"I feel my best when I am happy." ~*Winona Ryder*

"We will open the book. Its pages are blank. We are going to put words on them ourselves. The book is called Opportunity and its first chapter is New Year's Day." ~*Edith Lovejoy Pierce*

"I don't understand why Cupid represents Valentine's Day. When I think about romance, the last thing on my mind is a chubby toddler coming at me with a weapon." ~*Chutney McGillicutty*

ACKNOWLEDGMENTS

"Silent gratitude isn't much use to anyone."

~*Gladys Browyn Stern*

When I'm asked what book I'm proudest of, my answer is always *The Big Book of Girl Stuff*. *I had the most fun writing it, I learned the most while researching it, and I got to work with a huge team of the coolest people I know.* See, I may be gender handicapped (and rather dim), but when I started this project, I did something *smart*: I begged my five sisters to help me!

And because they're thoughtful and loving sisters (who don't like watching a grown man cry), they agreed. (Yay!) The King sisters are . . .

Gretchen (a.k.a. *Fotch*): Human resources manager and people person.

Kathleen (a.k.a. *Weenie*): Middle school teacher and fairy godmother.

Melinda (a.k.a. *Boom*): Lieutenant colonel and will-o'-the-wisp.

Sarah (a.k.a. *Eah*): Registered nurse and shrinking violet.

Mary (a.k.a. *El Twerpo*): Park ranger and resident type A personality.

These women provided *The Big Book of Girl Stuff* with important touches, like an enlightened outlook, a feminine perspective, and really bad jokes. In fact, their contributions went so well, the book's think tank was then expanded to dozens of young women, from middle school through college, who'd suffered through my classroom. I am so grateful to them for finding time to offer their collaboration and suggestions for this book.

The core group of the *Girl Stuff Brain Trust: Mariam Kanso, Allyson Scharpf, Miranda Schwabauer, Alex Fus, Rachael Mejia, Allison Moore, Megan McKittrick, Kylie Nomi, Kim Fouse, Sarah Wilson, Amanda Lapato, Rebecca Pankow, Sophie Moshofsky, Jessica Hooper, Kelcey Van Orman, Amy Schick, Kristina Chou, Shannon Twomey, Paige and Greta Lundy,* and *Rachel Hahn.*

And many thanks also to these esteemed contributors: *Raluca Moldovan, Danielle Towne, Tay Fravel, Anna Reilly, Cassandra Phelps, Sydney Rausch, Katie MacCaskill, Anna Miller, Shannon Brophy, Sahara Scott, Katelyn Wright, Linda Job, Layla Ingwerson, Gretchen Gehlbach, Seher Siddique, Sarah Alisawa, Kristina Trindle, Jenna Grabarek, Karissa Bargmann, Natalie Kisby, Lauren Middleton,* and *Meredith Kelley* (who was WAY more helpful than *Molly!*).

Finally, a special shout-out to: *Janet King, Pat King, Cindy King, Virginia Wassink, Carlye Krohn, Kathryn Fitch, Amy and Brody vanderSommen, Shannon Brophy, Bob Kevoian, Tom Griswold, Kristi Lee, Chick McGee, Dean Metcalf, Will Pfaffenberger, Kim Schwabauer, Branden McClain, Lauren Mead, Bethany Withycombe, Brittany Lindeman, Kelsi Harris, Hailey Larson, Claire Weaver, Annie Weaver, Kenzie Smith, Betsy Mepham, Laura Erkeneff, Marilyn Erkeneff, Daniel Fredgant, Ana Dupuis, Tyler Kelly, Genevieve Smith, Graham Harker, Georgia Harker, Lindsey and Lauren Zehner, Patty and Lee Wassink, Chan Lundy, Deb Hartman, Tammi Vincik, Karen Kroner Amstutz, Ron Martin, Kathy Logan, Carolyn Wood, Peggy Brandt, Anne Stevenson, Lynn Schukart, Nadine Chauncey, Rick Kristoff, Douglas Bayern, Janice Johnson, JoAnn Thomas, Madeleine Levin, Beth Levin, Linda Hall, Patti Larson, Tona Hattery, Leslie Redman, Debbie DuMez, Karen Hughes, Robin Squire, Debbie Groves, Marsha Goldwasser, Karen Youngs, Lisa Sacconaghi, Kristin Heintz, Kim Woodberry, Lisa Senter, Luke Twomey, Mike King, Lainie King, Greg Lauzon, Rochelle Muller, Pam Erlandson, Kira Porton, Christine Foye, Katie King,* and *M. Gleason.*

Also, our sincere thanks to the Multnomah County Library staff, especially *Tama Filipas, Peter Ford, Deborah Gitlitz, Marci Davis,* and *Alison Kastner.*

Much gratitude to *Suzanne Taylor* for coming up with this idea. Special credit to *Jennifer Adams, Alison Einerson, Christopher Robbins, Dawn DeVries Sokol,* and *Shanna Knowlton* for their hard work on this project.

Through the kindness of girls and women, this book evolved from a bad beginning into the resplendent mess that you hold in your hands. We hope you liked it!

—*Bart King*

BIBLIOGRAPHY

Adams, Natalie Guice, and Pamela J. Bettis. *Cheerleader: An American Icon.* New York: Palgrave Books, 2003.

Adelman, Kim. *The Ultimate Guide to Chick Flicks.* New York: Broadway Books, 2005.

Aidin, Beatrice. "Beluga Caviar? Only Your Hairdresser Knows." *New York Times,* November 10, 2005.

Albregts, Lisa, and Elizabeth Cape. *Best Friends.* Chicago: Chicago Review Press, 1998.

Almond, Steve. *Candyfreak: A Journey Through the Chocolate Underbelly of America.* Chapel Hill, NC: Algonquin Books of Chapel Hill, 2004.

Alun-Jones, Deborah, and John Ayton. *Charming: The History of Charm Jewelry.* London: Thames & Hudson, 2005.

Alvarez, Lizette. "Jens and Vita, but Molly? Danes Favor Common Names." *New York Times,* October 8, 2004.

———. "Washington: "The Ultimate Bad Hair Day." *New York Times,* April 22, 2005.

American Girl. www.americangirl.com.

American Society of Plastic Surgeons. 2013 Plastic Surgery Statistics. www.plasticsurgery.org/news/plastic-surgery-statistics/2013.html.

Amos, Deborah. "Pop Culture Drives Desire for Nose Jobs in Iraq." National Public Radio, October 10, 2005.

Associated Press. "Teenagers Have Reason to Feel Miserable." *San Francisco Chronicle,* January 20, 1993.

———. "American manners poll." USA Today, October 14, 2005. www.usatoday.com/news/nation/2005-10-14-rudeness-poll-method_x.htm.

Baer, Greg. *Life: The Odds (and How to Improve Them).* New York: Gotham Books, 2003.

Bakalar, Nicholas. "Ugly Children May Get Parental Short Shrift." *New York Times,* May 3, 2005.

———. "Why the Sleepless Nights?" *New York Times,* May 31, 2005.

———. "Bonds of Friendship, Not Family, May Add Years." *New York Times,* June 28, 2005.

———. "The Road to Obesity Begins at Your TV." *New York Times*, September 20, 2005.

Bany-Winters, Lisa. *On Stage: Theater Games and Activities for Kids*. Chicago: Chicago Review Press, 1997.

Baranauckas, Carla. "A Dairy Queen, Oops, Princess, in All Her Buttery Glory." *New York Times*, August 27, 2005.

Barbie Collector.com. www.barbiecollector.com.

Baumgarten, Mark. "Rainy Day Pranks." *Willamette Week*, June 23, 2004.

BBC News. "Anti-Barbie becomes Russian icon." April 14, 2004. http://news.bbc.co.uk/2/hi/europe/3625213.stm.

BBC Radio. "From Our Correspondents." December 3, 2005.

Beckerman, Ilene. *Makeovers at the Beauty Counter of Happiness*. Chapel Hill, NC: Algonquin Books of Chapel Hill, 2005.

Bell, Ruth. *Changing Bodies, Changing Lives*. 3rd ed. New York: Times Books, 1998.

Belluck, Pam. "What's the Name of That Lake? It's Hard to Say." *New York Times*, November 20, 2004.

———. "Toy's Message of Affection Draws Anger and Publicity." *New York Times*, January 22, 2005.

Belson, Ken, and Brian Bremner. *Hello Kitty*. Singapore: John Wiley & Sons (Asia), 2004.

Berkenkamp, Laurie. *Kid Disasters and How to Fix Them*. Norwich, VT: Nomad Press, 2002.

Beyer, Rick. *The Greatest Stories Never Told: 100 Tales from History to Astonish, Bewilder & Stupefy*. New York: HarperResource, 2003.

Blackstone, Margaret, and Elissa Haden Guest. *Girl Stuff: A Survival Guide to Growing Up*. San Diego: Gulliver Books, 2000.

Blakeslee, Sandra. "If You Have a 'Buy Button' in Your Brain, What Pushes It?" *New York Times*, October 19, 2004.

Bondeson, Jon. *A Cabinet of Medical Curiosities*. Ithaca, New York: Cornell University Press, 1997.

Bonnell, Jennifer. *D.I.Y. Girl*. New York: Puffin Books, 2003.

Borgenicht, Joe. *What Not to Name Your Baby*. New York: Simon Spotlight Entertainment, 2005.

"Born to Lead." *Cosmogirl*, July 2004.

Bosman, Julie. "What's Cool Online? Teenagers Render Verdict." *New York Times*, September 28, 2005.

Bibliography

Bowler, Peter. *The Superior Person's Second Book of Weird & Wondrous Words*. Boston: David R. Godine, Publisher, 1992.

——. *The Superior Person's Third Book of Well-Bred Words*. Boston: David R. Godine, Publisher, 2001.

Brody, Jane E. "The Widening of America, or How Size 4 Became a Size 0." *New York Times*, January 20, 2004.

Brown, Lyn Mikel. *Girlfighting: Betrayal and Rejection Among Girls*. New York: New York University Press, 2003.

Brown, Paul B. "No. Seriously. Save the Bananas." *New York Times*, August 13, 2005.

Bruce, Judith, with Barbara S. Mensch and Margaret E. Greene. *The Uncharted Passage: Girls' Adolescence in the Developing World*. New York: Population, 1998.

Burkhard, Bilger. "Sole Survivor." *The New Yorker*, February 14 & 21, 2005.

Burnett, Thane. "Tiny rooms filled with tiny murder victims are part of U.S. criminologists teaching method. So, who whacked Barbie?" *Toronto Sun*, October 24, 2005.

"Bust Up." Snopes.com. www.snopes.com/business/origins/bra.asp.

Butcher, Nancy. *The Strange Case of the Walking Corpse*. New York: Avery, 2004.

Cabot, Meg. *Princess Lessons*. New York: HarperCollins Publishers, 2003.

Cain, Chelsea. *The Hippie Handbook*. San Francisco: Chronicle Books, 2004.

The Care and Keeping of Friends. Middleton, WI: Pleasant Company Publications, 1996.

Carey, Benedict. "The Secret Lives of Just about Everybody." *New York Times*, January 11, 2004.

——. "Payback Time: Why Revenge Tastes So Sweet." *New York Times*, July 27, 2004.

——. "Deja Vu: If It All Seems Familiar, There May Be a Reason." *New York Times*, September 14, 2004.

——. "Have You Heard? Gossip Turns Out to Serve a Purpose." *New York Times*, August 16, 2005.

Charon, Susan, and Harry Charon. *The Book of Lists for Teens*. New York: Houghton Mifflin, 2002.

Chase's Calendar of Events, 2014. McGraw-Hill, 2013.

Cohen, Roger. "Loops and Flourishes of France's Job Market Applicants." *San Francisco Chronicle*, October 31, 1993.

Coontz, Stephanie. "Historically Incorrect Canoodling." *New York Times*, February 14, 2005.

Curtis, Bryan, editor. *The Explainer*. New York: Anchor Books, 2004.

Davis, Cortney. "Her Heart's in the Right Place. Or Is It?" *New York Times,* December 21, 2004.

Dee, Catherine, editor. *The Girls' Book of Wisdom*. New York: Megan Tinley Books, 1999.

——. *The Girls' Book of Friendship*. New York: Megan Tinley Books, 2001.

——. *The Girls' Book of Success*. New York: Megan Tinley Books, 2003.

Dent, Susie. *Larpers and Shroomers: The Language Report*. Oxford University Press, 2004.

DeVillers, Julia. *GirlWise*. New York: Three Rivers Press, 2002.

Disney Princess. http://princess.disney.com.

Dominguez, Alex. "Study: Breakfast helps girls stay slimmer." *Oregonian,* September 10, 2005.

Dowd, Maureen. "Men Just Want Their Mommy." *New York Times,* January 13, 2005.

Duenwald, Mary. "How Young Is Too Young to Have a Nose Job and Breast Implants?" *New York Times,* September 28, 2004.

Dunkling, Leslie Alan. *Our Secret Names*. London: Sidgwick & Jackson, 1981.

Dunnewind, Stephanie. "Teen recruits create word-of-mouth 'buzz' to hook peers on products." *Seattle Times,* November 20, 2004.

Dworkin, Andy. "Piercings in cartilage elevate risks of infection." *Oregonian,* February 25, 2004.

Eisenberg, Anne. "Hello Kitty, Hello Clone." *New York Times,* May 28, 2005.

Ellin, Abby. "Games Children Played." *New York Times,* January 16, 2005.

Erard, Mitchell. "Just Like, Er, Words, Not, Um, Throwaways." *New York Times,* January 3, 2004.

Ettus, Samantha, editor. *The Experts' Guide to 100 Things Everyone Should Know*. New York: Clarkson Potter Publishers, 2004.

"F as in Fat 2005: How Obesity Policies Are Failing in America." Trust for America's Health. http://healthyamericans.org/reports/obesity2005/.

Feldman, David. *Do Elephants Jump?* New York: HarperCollins Publishers, 2004.

Fenster, Bob. *Duh! The Stupid History of the Human Race*. Kansas City: Andrews McMeel Publishing, 2000.

Fisher, Len. *How to Dunk a Doughnut: The Science of Everyday Life*. New York: Arcade Publishing, 2002.

Forero, Juan. "A Bevy of Teeny Beauties, Minds Set on Being Queens." *New York Times,* April 15, 2005.

Fortini, Amanda. "The Escalating High-Heel Shoe." *New York Times Magazine,* December 12, 2004.

Fountain, Henry. "Tarzan, Cheetah, and the Contagious Yawn." *New York Times,* August 24, 2004.

——. "Nine Lives, but No Sweet Tooth." *New York Times,* July 26, 2005.

Fox, Lara, and Hilary Frankel. *Breaking the Code.* New York: New American Library, 2005.

Frean, Alexandra. "Barbarism begins with Barbie, the doll children love to hate." *New York Times,* December 19, 2005.

Fulghum, Hunter S. *Office Dirty Tricks.* Kansas City: Andrews McMeel Publishing, 2000.

——. *The MANual: The Guy's Guide to Being a Man's Man.* New York: Broadway Books, 2004.

Furman, Irv. *Amazing Irv's Handbook of Everyday Magic.* Philadelphia: Quirk Books, 2002.

Fuyuno, Ichiko, and Queena Sook Kim. "Dressing up like Barbie: Mattel hopes human fashions renew dolls' cachet." *Oregonian,* February 3, 2004.

Garfield, Patricia. *The Dream Book: A Young Person's Guide to Understanding Dreams.* Toronto: Tundra Books, 2002.

Geraghty, Laurel Naversen. "When It's Hair, You Can Be Too Thin." *New York Times,* September 22, 2005.

Gibb, Fiona, and Tucker Shaw. . . . *Any Advice?* New York: Alloy Books, 2000.

Gilman, Susan Jane. *Hypocrite in a Pouffy White Dress: Tales of Growing Up Groovy and Clueless.* New York: Warner Books, 2005.

Glaser, Gabrielle. "Embraceable Youth." *Oregonian,* January 21, 2004.

Glazer, Sarah. "Manga for Girls." *New York Times Book Review,* September 18, 2005.

Goodman, Susan. *The Truth About Poop.* New York: Viking, 2004.

Gordon, Linda Perlman, and Susan Morris Shaffer. *Why Girls Talk and What They're Really Saying.* New York: McGraw-Hill, 2005.

Grahn, Judy. *Blood, Bread, and Roses: How Menstruation Created the World.* Boston: Beacon Press, 1993.

Graydon, Shari. *Made You Look: How Advertising Works and Why You Should Know.* New York: Annick Press, 2003.

Grau, Andrée. *Dance.* New York: Doris Kindersley, 1998.

Green, Joey. *Potato Radio, Dizzy Dice, and More Wacky, Weird Experiments.* New York: Perigree Books, 2004.

Green, Karen, and Tristan Taormino, editors. *A Girl's Guide to Taking over the World: Writings from the Girl Zine Revolution.* New York: St. Martin's Griffin, 1997.

Griffin, Margot. *The Sleepover Book.* Tonawanda, NY: Kids Can Press, 2001.

Guinness World Records. www.guinnessworldrecords.com/index.asp.

Hancock, Noelle. "The Botox Babies." *New York Observer,* October 4, 2004.

The Handbag Book of Girly Emergencies. San Diego: Laurel Glen, 2001.

Harmon, Amy. "Internet Gives Teenage Bullies Weapons to Wound from Afar." *New York Times,* August 26, 2004.

——. "Reach Out and Touch No One." *New York Times,* April 14, 2005.

Harris, Judith Rich. *The Nurture Assumption: Why Children Turn Out the Way They Do.* New York: The Free Press, 1998.

Harrison, Ian. *The Book of Inventions.* Washington, DC: National Geographic, 2004.

Hartman, Holly. *Girlwonder.* New York: Houghton Mifflin, 2003.

Hayt, Elizabeth. "Kiss My Puffy Lips." *New York Times,* August 4, 2005.

Healy, Christopher. "A nation of little princesses." Salon.com, November 24, 2004. www.salon.com/mwt/feature/2004/11/24/princesses/.

Heaner, Martica. "Snooze Alarm Takes Its Toll on a Nation." *New York Times,* October 12, 2004.

Heergaard, Lauran. "25% of men don't wash after using toilet." *Oregonian,* September 22, 2005.

Heffernan, Virginia. "Epithet Morphs from Bad Girl to Weak Boy." *New York Times,* March 22, 2005.

Henig, Robin Marantz. "The Price of Perfection." *Civilization,* April 1996.

Herbert, R. K. "Sex-based differences in compliment behavior." *Language in Society,* Vol. 19, 1990.

Hill, Richard L. "Question guys' masculinity? Dose of macho likely answer." *Oregonian,* August 10, 2005.

Holder, R. W. *How Not to Say What You Mean: A Dictionary of Euphemisms.* Oxford University Press, 2002.

Holmes, J. "Paying Compliments: A Sex-Preferential Politeness Strategy." *Journal of Pragmatics,* Vol. 12, 1988.

Hopkins, Jerry. *Extreme Cuisine: The Weird & Wonderful Foods That People Eat.* Singapore: Periplus, 2004.

Bibliography

Hunt, Elizabeth, with Will Pearson and Mangesh Hattikudur, editors. *Condensed Knowledge*. New York: HarperResource, 2004.

Jacobs, Andrew. "The New Manly Tool? Eyebrow Tweezers." *New York Times*, December 31, 2004.

Jukes, Mavis. *Growing Up: It's a Girl Thing*. New York: Alfred A. Knopf, 1998.

Kahn, Eve. "Murder Downsized." *New York Times*, October 7, 2004.

Kantor, Jodi. "Love the Riches, Lose the Rags: Younger fans embrace Cinderella, updated as the Material Girl." *New York Times*, November 3, 2005.

Karr, Laura. *Pop It, Stir It, Fix It, Serve It*. New York: Hyperion, 2005.

Keva, Marie, and Super Clea. *Hey, Day!* New York: HarperTrophy, 2001.

King, Jan. *It's a Girl Thing*. Kansas City: Stark Books, 2000.

Kreahling, Lorraine. "In the Relentless Pursuit of Fashion, the Feet Pay the Price." *New York Times*, August 31, 2004.

Krull, Kathleen. *Lives of Extraordinary Women (and What the Neighbors Thought)*. New York: Harcourt, 2000.

Kuczynski, Alex. "You Paid How Much for That Haircut?" *New York Times*, November 21, 2004.

———. "Try Some Play-Doh Behind Your Ears." *New York Times*, July 14, 2005.

———. "A Dress-Up Doll for Retro Girls (Scram, Barbie)." *New York Times*, December 29, 2005.

La Ferla, Ruth. "Rock Star? Boring. Fashion Designer: Cool." *New York Times*, September 5, 2004.

———. "Teenagers Shop for Art of the Deal." *New York Times*, September 22, 2005.

———. "Dress Like Your Dad? He Rocks." *New York Times*, December 1, 2005.

Ladd, Cheryl. *Token Chick: A Women's Guide to Golfing with the Boys*. New York: Hyperion, 2005.

Laing, Jennifer. "A Long Way from Levi." *New York Times*, January 2, 2005.

le Jeune, Véronique, with Melissa Daly and Philippe Eliakim. *Feeling Freakish? How to Be Comfortable in Your Own Skin*. New York: Sunscreen Books, 2004.

Lednicer, Lisa Grace. "More young female drivers die." *Oregonian*, September 26, 2004.

Lee, Carol E. "It's Only May, and the Tanorexics Are Already Complaining." *New York Times*, May 13, 2005.

Lee, Jeffrey. *Catch a Fish, Throw a Ball, Fly a Kite*. New York: Three Rivers Press, 2004.

Levenson, Barry M. *Habeus Codfish: Reflections on Food and the Law.* Madison, WI: University of Wisconsin Press, 2001.

Levy, Joel. *Really Useful: The Origins of Everyday Things.* Ontario: Firefly Books, 2002.

Linn, Susan. *Consuming Kids: The Hostile Takeover of Childhood.* New York: The New Press, 2004.

Lithgow, John. *A Lithgow Palooza!* New York: Simon & Schuster, 2004.

Lock, Carrie. "Deception Detection: Can Science Spot a Lie?" *Muse,* April 2005.

Lord, M. G. *Forever Barbie: The Unauthorized Biography of a Real Doll.* New York: William Morrow, 1994.

Lovric, Michelle. *Women's Wicked Wisdom.* Chicago: Chicago Review Press, 2004.

Lyall, Sarah. "No Telly in the House? Expect an Official Warning." *New York Times,* December 28, 2004.

Maloney, Field. "Cannonball!" *The New Yorker,* August 30, 2004.

Marriott, Michel. "Amanda Says, 'You Don't Sound Like Mommy.'" *New York Times,* August 25, 2005.

Martin, Susan Taylor. "Coverup girl." *St. Petersburg Times,* January 12, 2004. www.sptimes. com/2004/01/12/Floridian/Coverup_girl.shtml.

Masatche, Harriet S., and Karen Unger. *Too Old for This, Too Young for That: Your Survival Guide for the Middle School Years.* Minneapolis, MN: Free Spirit Publishing, 2000.

Mason, Margaret. "Worth Her Weight in Gold." *New York Times,* February 10, 2004.

McClain, Dylan. "Record-Breaking Chess." *New York Times,* August 4, 2005.

McElherne, Linda Nason. *Jump Starters.* Minneapolis, MN: Free Spirit Publishing, 1999.

McFarling, Usha Lee. "Behavior's No Laughing Matter for Researchers Studying Brain." *Seattle Times,* November 24, 1998.

——. "Scientists locate part of brain responsible for our ability to react to humor." Knight Ridder/Tribune, Washington Bureau (DC), March 31, 1999.

McGrath, Ben. "Chew On." *The New Yorker,* February 9, 2004.

McInerny, Vivian. "Redheads: so fashionably hot, they're cool." *Oregonian,* July 17, 2005.

McNab, Nan. *Body Bizarre Body Beautiful.* New York: Simon & Schuster, 1999.

Medina, Jennifer. "New York Know-How: A Skirt above the Knees, Not Beyond the Pale." *New York Times,* September 3, 2004.

Bibliography

Michigan Lawsuit Abuse Watch. Past Winners of M-Law's Wacky Warning Label Contests. www.mlaw.org/wwl/pastwinners.html.

Milholland, Charlotte. *The Girl Pages*. New York: Hyperion, 1998.

Milner, Murray, Jr. *Freaks, Geeks, and Cool Kids: American Teenagers and the Culture of Consumption*. New York: Routledge, 2004.

Moka, and Melissa Daly. *Just Us Girls*. New York: Amulet Books, 2004.

Monson-Burton, Marianne, editor. *Girls Know Best 2*. Hillsboro, OR: Beyond Words Publishing, 1998.

——. *Girls Know Best 3*. Hillsboro, OR: Beyond Words Publishing, 1999.

Moore, Anne Elizabeth. *Hey, Kidz! Buy This Book*. Chicago: Soft Skull Press, 2004.

Morgenson, G. "The Feminization of Seventh Avenue." *Forbes*, May 11, 1992, Vol. 149:10.

Moynihan, Colin. "City of a Thousand Handshakes." *New York Times*, May 22, 2004.

Nagourney, Eric. "A Gender Gap in Dental Hygiene." *New York Times*, May 18, 2004.

National Organization for Rare Disorders. www.rarediseases.org.

Navarro, Mireya. "Store Mannequins Can Now Breathe Out." *New York Times*, November 14, 2004.

Neuberger, Karen, and Nadine Schiff. *The Secret Language of Girlfriends*. New York: Hyperion, 2005.

——. "Never talk on the telephone during a thunderstorm." *New York Times*, January 4, 2005.

——. "Babies tend to look like their fathers." *New York Times*, March 22, 2005.

——. "Never wake a sleepwalker." *New York Times*, September 13, 2005.

O'Brien, Richard. "Walk of Ages." *Via*, March/April 2005.

O'Neil, John. "E-Mail Doesn't Lie (That Much)." *New York Times*, March 2, 2004.

Onion, Amanda. "Ancient Women Used Dung, Grease as Makeup." August 4, 2003. http://abcnews.go.com/Technology/story?id=97572&page=1&singlePage=true.

Ornstein, Norman J., with Thomas E. Mann and Michael J. Malbin. *Vital Statistics on Congress, 2001–2002*. Washington, DC: AEI Press, 2002.

Osborne, Lawrence. "Inward Bound." *New York Times Magazine*, July 18, 2004.

Pease, Barbara, and Allan Pease. *Why Men Don't Have a Clue and Women Always Need More Shoes*. New York: Broadway Books, 2004.

Perlstein, Linda. *Not Much Just Chillin': The Hidden Lives of Middle Schoolers.* New York: Farrar, Straus and Giroux, 2003.

Petras, Kathryn, and Ross Petras. *Unusually Stupid Americans: A Compendium of All-American Stupidity.* New York: Villard Books, 2003.

Pipher, Mary. *Reviving Ophelia: Saving the Selves of Adolescent Girls.* New York: Ballantine Books, 1994.

Pitman, Joanna. *On Blondes.* New York: Bloomsbury, 2003.

Post, Elizabeth L., and Joan M. Coles. *Teen Etiquette.* New York: HarperCollins, 1995.

Prada, Paulo. "Felons All, but Free to Try Being Beauty Queen for a Day." *New York Times,* December 1, 2005.

Presidential Pet Museum. www.presidentialpetmuseum.com/whitehousepets-1.htm.

Ray, C. Claiborne. "Technicolor Dreams." *New York Times,* January 27, 2004.

——. "Growth at Your Fingertips." *New York Times,* November 23, 2004.

Rediker, Marcus. *Villains of all Nations: Atlantic Pirates in the Golden Age.* Boston: Beacon Press, 2004.

Reed, Ken. "Elitism in Youth Sports Yields Physical Fatness." *New York Times,* February 1, 2004.

Richtel, Matt. "All Thumbs, Without the Stigma." *New York Times,* August 12, 2004.

Riordan, Teresa. *Inventing Beauty.* New York: Broadway Books, 2004.

Roach, Marion. *The Roots of Desire.* New York: Bloomsbury, 2005.

Rocca, Mo. *All the Presidents' Pets: The Inside Story of One Reporter Who Refused to Roll Over.* New York: Crown Publishers, 2004.

Roehm, Michelle, editor. *Girls Know Best.* Hillsboro, OR: Beyond Words Publishing, 1997.

Rohter, Larry. "A Quest to Save a Tree, and Make the World Smell Sweet." *New York Times,* August 30, 2005.

Rubenstein, Alice, and Karen Zager. *The Inside Story on Teen Girls.* Washington DC: A.P.A. LifeTools, 2002.

Sacks, David. *Language Visible: Unraveling the Mystery of the Alphabet.* New York: Broadway Books, 2003.

Schott, Ben. *Schott's Food & Drink Miscellany.* New York: Bloomsbury, 2004.

Schroeder, Barabara, and Carrie Wiatt. *The Diet for Teenagers Only.* New York: Regan Books, 2005.

Bibliography

Seamans, Sally. *Crafts for Girls*. Middleton, WI: Pleasant Company Publications, 1995.

Severson, Kim. "So Much for Squeaky Clean Cookies." *New York Times*, March 9, 2005.

Shanker, Wendy. *The Fat Girl's Guide to Life*. New York: Bloomsbury, 2004.

Sherman, Alexa Joy, and Nicole Tocantins. *Happy Hook-Up*. Berkeley, CA: Ten Speed Press, 2004.

Sherman, Josepha, and T. K. F. Weisskopf. *Greasy Grimy Gopher Guts: The Subversive Literature of Childhood*. Little Rock, AR: August House, 1995.

Shiraz, Yasmin. *The Blueprint for My Girls in Love*. New York: Simon & Schuster, 2005.

Silby, Caroline, and Shelley Smith. *Games Girls Play: Understanding and Guiding Young Female Athletes*. New York: St. Martin's Press, 2000.

Simmons, Rachel. *Odd Girl Out*. New York: Harcourt, 2002.

———. *Odd Girl Speaks Out*. New York: Harcourt, 2004.

Singer, Natasha. "The Surgical Way to Have Lips a Trout Could Love." *New York Times*, August 4, 2005.

———. "Face It, Princess, Your Skin Is Probably Quite Common." *New York Times*, October 13, 2005.

Slatalla, Michelle. "Clean and Crisp Even When You Aren't." *New York Times*, May 19, 2005.

———. "Searching for Beads, Finding a Jewel." *New York Times*, September 22, 2005.

Small, Meredith F. "Dare to Bare." *New York Times*, October 11, 2005.

Smith, Dian G. *World's Greatest Practical Jokes*. New York: Sterling Publishing, 2004.

Smith, Elinor Goulding. *Horses, History & Havoc*. New York: World Publishing, 1969.

Smoll, Frank L. "Problems with Parents?" Athletic Search.com. www.athleticsearch.com/bonus8.html.

Snapple lid. "Real Fact #322."

Spitznass, Jill. "The names that rock the cradle." *Portland Tribune*, June 28, 2005.

Staff, Colors, and Oliviero Toscani. *Cacas: The Encyclopedia of Poo*. Taschen, 2000.

Standage, Tom. *A History of the World in 6 Glasses*. New York: Walker & Company, 2005.

Stanford, Phil. "Now here is a real holiday bonus." *Portland Tribune*, December 3, 2004.

Stein, Jeannine. "Kids can get a health kick out of soccer, study says." *Daily News*, November 1, 2004.

Stein, Sara. *Great Pets! An Extraordinary Guide to More Than 60 Usual and Unusual Family Pets.* North Adams, MA: Storey Kids, 2003.

Storm, Hannah, and Mark Jenkins. *Go Girl! Raising Healthy, Confident and Successful Girls through Sports.* Naperville, IL: Sourcebooks, 2002.

Swami Shivananda. "Tilak." *Understanding Hinduism.* www.hinduism.co.za/tilak.htm.

Sykes, Plum. *Bergdorf Blondes.* New York: Miramax Books, 2004.

Talbot, Margaret. "American Girl crazy!" Salon.com, May 10, 2005. www.salon.com/mwt/feature/2005/05/10/talbot/.

Tallmadge, Alice. "UO students cast a line on a nutty sport." *Oregonian,* May 16, 2004.

Tattersall, Nick. "Force-fed women fight the fat." Reuters, September 22, 2005.

Thomas, Karen. "Tyra Banks in 112 Carats Is Uplifting." USA Today.com, October 12, 2004. www.usatoday.com/life/lifestyle/2004-10-11-diamond-bra_x.htm.

Thompson, Ginger. "On Mexico's Mean Streets, the Sinners Have a Saint." *New York Times,* March 26, 2004.

Thompson, Kristi Collier. *The Girls' Guide to Dreams.* New York: Sterling Publishing, 2003.

Trebay, Guy. "The Clowning, Rump-Shaking, Wilding-Out Battle Dancers of South Central L.A." *New York Times Magazine,* June 19, 2005.

Trexler, Phil. "Inside Job Will Put Couple Inside." *Beacon Journal,* February 23, 2004.

Trumble, Angus. *A Brief History of the Smile.* New York: Basic Books, 2004.

Uncle John's Bathroom Reader for Kids Only! Ashland, OR: Bathroom Readers' Press, 2004.

U.S. Census Bureau, *Statistical Abstract of the United States: 2012–2013* (131st Edition). Washington, DC, 2013.

Van Gelder, Lawrence. "TV: Screen Time." *New York Times,* March 31, 2004.

——. "When You're Smiling . . ." *New York Times,* December 15, 2005.

Vilbig, Peter. "Advertising's Attack." *New York Times,* April 8, 2002.

Wade, Nicholas. "Your Body Is Younger Than You Think." *New York Times,* August 2, 2005.

Walker, Laura Jensen. *Girl Time: A Celebration of Chick Flicks, Bad Hair Days & Good Friends.* Grand Rapids, MI: Fleming H. Revel, 2004.

Walker, Rob. "Color Coding." *New York Times Magazine,* July 31, 2005.

Waters, Richard. *Phobias: Revealed and Explained.* New York: Barron's, 2004.

Bibliography

Watters, Carrie. "Gimme an M, Gimme an A, Gimme a D . . ." *Rockford Register Star*, November 13, 2004.

Weitz, Rose. *Rapunzel's Daughters: What Women's Hair Tells Us About Women's Lives*. New York: Farrar, Strauss & Giroux, 2005.

Wiatt, Carrie, and Barbara Schroeder. *The Diet: For Teenagers Only*. New York: Regan Books, 2005.

Widman, Adam. "'Human Flesh Alternative' Sells on the Web." *Stanford Daily*, May 25, 2005.

Wilkes, Angela. *Children's Quick & Easy Cookbook*. New York: DK Publishing, 1997.

Williams, Alex. "Cheerleading Demands the Field for Itself." *New York Times*, August 15, 2004.

——. "Can't Sleep? Change Towns, Not Sheets." *New York Times*, November 14, 2004.

Williams, Florence. "Toxic Breast Milk?" *New York Times Magazine*, January 9, 2005.

Williams, Lee. "Still crazy for 'Clueless.'" *Oregonian*, July 19, 2005.

Wilson, Eric. "Au Courant Camouflage." *New York Times*, February 13, 2005.

Wilson, Steve. "Grown-ups dare to defy gravity." *Portland Tribune*, August 23, 2005.

Wiseman, Rosalind. *Queen Bees & Wannabees*. New York: Three Rivers Press, 2002.

Wolf, Naomi. *The Beauty Myth: How Images of Beauty Are Used Against Women*. New York: Perennial, 2002.

Yalom, Marilyn. *A History of the Breast*. New York: Alfred A. Knopf, 1997.

——. *Birth of the Chess Queen: A History*. New York: HarperCollins Publishers, 2004.

Yearwood, Lori Teresa. "Long in the Saddle." *Oregonian*, January 28, 2005.

Yikes! A Smart Girl's Guide to Surviving Tricky, Sticky, Icky Situations. Middleton, WI: American Library, 2002.

Young, Louisa. *The Book of the Heart*. New York: Doubleday, 2003.

Yue, Charlotte, and David Yue. *Shoes: Their History in Words and Pictures*. Boston: Houghton Mifflin, 1997.

Zoepf, Katherine. "This Doll Has an Accessory Barbie Lacks: A Prayer Mat." *New York Times*, February 13, 2005.